For my mother

Neil Spencer is a journalist and broadcaster. He has edited several magazines, among them *New Musical Express, Arena, Straight No Chaser* and *20/20*, and written for many others. He has also co-written three well-received short films; *Paris Brixton, Suri & Trainers* and *Soul Patrol*. For the last seven years he has written for the *Observer* about popular music, culture and astrology.

TRUE AS THE STARS ABOVE

Adventures in Modern Astrology

*

Neil Spencer

ORION

An Orion paperback

First published in Great Britain in 2000
by Victor Gollancz
This paperback edition published in 2001
by Orion Books Ltd,
Orion House, 5 Upper St Martin's Lane,
London WC2H 9EA

A CIP catalogue record for this book is available
from the British Library.

ISBN 0 75284 382 6

Printed and bound in Great Britain by
The Guernsey Press Co. Ltd, Guernsey, C.I.

Frankie and Johnny were lovers
Lordy, how they did love
Swore they'd be true to each other
Just as true as the stars above

'Frankie and Johnny', American folk song

ACKNOWLEDGEMENTS

✳

Thanks to all the astrologers with whom I have conversed, either in person or in cyberspace, and for their answers to my bothersome queries and brain-picking questions. For the selfless sharing of their expertise and wisdom, I am particularly indebted to Laura Boomer, Nicholas Campion, Frank Clifford, John Etherington and Fiona Graham.

I would also like to thank Justine Picardie, who commissioned me to write about astrology for the *Observer's* *Life* magazine, and Andrew Purvis and David Vincent, who edited my column with a helpful mixture of enthusiasm and incredulity. Thanks, too, to Chris Salewicz, who first persuaded me to write about astrology; to Geoff Hill, who first showed how stellar tradition might apply to contemporary life; to Michal Levin for her insight; to Ian MacDonald and Jon Savage for their help; to my patient editor, Sara Holloway; to my agent, Lisa Darnell, to Maggie Hanbury, and to Philip Parr for his skilful critique.

Thanks and love to my wife, Meena Krishnamurthy, and to Morgan, Nadine and Jasmine, for putting up with an astrologer around the house.

CONTENTS

✳

INTRODUCTION

✳

In the late 1980s it emerged that the world's most powerful man, US President Ronald Reagan, and the world's most glamorous woman, Diana, Princess of Wales, had both been taking astrological advice. Their interest went way beyond the occasional consultation of the sort discreetly sought by many politicians and upper-class ladies. Reagan, as we shall see, organised the schedules of election debates and Cold War summits according to the forbidding demands of 'electional' astrology. Diana appears to have developed the public persona for which she remains celebrated after some inspirational advice from one or more of the three astrologers she employed and befriended, and whom she phoned constantly for help, succour and the lowdown on her estranged husband's horoscope.

It was as if we had undergone a time slip back three thousand years, to the age when the earliest astrologers plotted the planets' movements for the benefit of monarchs, rulers and nations (ordinary people didn't get their horoscopes cast until a few centuries later). Or to the royal courts of the sixteenth century, when monarchs summoned the court astrologer before marshalling their generals or marrying their daughters.

How did we get here? According to the stentorian tunes that have accompanied the march of scientific rationalism, astrology should by now be as extinct as the Tasmanian tiger, as discredited as the flat Earth theory. It should definitely not have been lording it over the destiny of the globe via a hot-line to the White House, or, for that matter, helping the future British Queen (as Diana then was) run her affairs.

Much to the chagrin of its opponents, astrology has arguably never been more popular. In the new millennium, its manifestations run from the brazen opportunism of phone-in forecasts to the labyrinthine pretensions of psychological astrology. While women's magazines promise to improve their readers' sex lives by analysing the position of Mars in their man's birth chart, financial and business corporations huddle covertly with their astrological advisers to anticipate the swings and cycles of the world's stock markets. At times the subject seems to be getting almost respectable (almost, but never quite). These days, only the most highfalutin papers and magazines dare dispense with a star-sign column, if they know what's good for their circulations. Successive surveys of Western societies declare that a large part of the population think there is 'something in' astrology, a proportion that is substantially higher in most parts of the developing world.

How and why has astrology survived? Its rationalist opponents usually attribute its survival to superstition, to the obstinate human need for reassurance and the comfort of religion, or to blind fatalism. Doubtless some geneticist will soon identify 'the astrology gene' in DNA to explain the fascination of the unruly subject for individuals.

For religious orthodoxy, astrology's survival is proof that the devil is never idle for long, that the pagan demons against which they have fought for millennia remain unvanquished. The Church's relationship with astrology is longer and more tortuous than that of science, but though the various branches of Christianity have often ignored the star-gazers and soothsayers, and occasionally collaborated with them, they have most often seen themselves in competition with astrology. These days the Church is too preoccupied with fighting the more threatening monster of secular science to pay much attention to horoscopic conjurors, but the Church of England and the Vatican periodically fire off a broadside to warn that those taking the starry road do so at risk of their immortal souls.

Astrologers themselves tend to believe their art's survival is proof enough of its validity – if there wasn't something in it, it wouldn't have endured. The astrological community nevertheless yearns for respect-ability, for its art to resume its long-lost place in academies and universities, for its practitioners not to be treated as charlatans and fruitcakes. This is one reason why over the last century astrology has periodically attempted to 'prove' itself by empirical methods to the satisfaction of materialist science. Usually these efforts have been to no avail, although, as we shall see, sceptical scientists have been badly wrong-footed by at least one such experiment, conducted to investigate the so-called 'Mars Effect' identified by French statistician Michel Gauquelin.

Even without statistical 'proof', there are plenty of other rationales for studying astrology: that it has played a major role in human history and human civilisation; that its symbolic language is eloquent and perceptive beyond the linguistic abominations inflicted by psychology and sociology; that this same language has held in thrall some of our greatest thinkers and poets; that astrology's symbolic system corresponds to what Carl Jung termed the 'archetypes' of the human psyche.

True as the Stars Above is an attempt to explore all these aspects of astrology. 'Aspects' as in facets, that is, rather than the 'aspects' of an astrological chart. This is not a 'How To' or 'Teach Yourself' book. There are already many of those, written by far more adept practitioners of the art than myself, for whom its technical demands have always been one of its least appealing characteristics. It is not difficult to learn to draw up a horoscopic chart, but as I discovered when I first became interested in astrology at age twenty, the calculations involved are tedious, which is one reason why my interest in the subject waned for many years.

I returned to astrology in earnest only in 1996, when an editor at the *Observer* newspaper asked me to write a weekly column, one whose tone was to be sympathetic but questioning, rather than credulous or sceptical. One thing I discovered was that the cyber-age had mercifully removed the sweat from astrological endeavour, if not the problems of deciphering its complex web of planetary and zodiacal ciphers: 'Moon in Aquarius', 'Venus in Cancer', 'Jupiter in the Fourth House' and so on. Here, too, there are numerous volumes – cheerily known to astrologers as 'cookbooks' – offering a detailed breakdown of astrological language and meaning.

This is not, then, a textbook, though I have tried to convey the flavour of astrological symbolism, and the rudiments of technique.

Rather it is a storybook, a series of tales from and about astrology, and an exploration of the part star-lore has played in Western cultural life. This seems to me substantially greater than its critics allow or even realise. Many of those fascinated by astrology (and other esoterica) have, understandably enough, kept their interests secret. For centuries astrologers were persecuted as sorcerers and charlatans, whether by Rome's Emperors, the Vatican or monarchs. For the impertinence of free thought, and for following the example of Aristotle and Ptolemy, they faced jail, ruin and even, like Renaissance star-gazer and magus Giordano Bruno, death.

The laws forbidding 'fortune-telling' that put the famous English astrologer Alan Leo in court during the First World War (an experience shared in America by Evangeline Adams) were quietly repealed in 1989, but the social stigma attached to astrology remains, as Ronnie and Nancy Reagan discovered. The Poet Laureate Ted Hughes – and who can be flagrant in their beliefs if not poets? – kept his interest in the stars concealed from an intellectual establishment he sensed would wield it as a cudgel against him. Even now, after his death, Hughes's 'dottier interests' are quietly sidelined.

One of astrology's most distinguished modern critics, the zoologist Richard Dawkins, recently berated several of his favourite poets – D.H. Lawrence, John Keats, William Blake, William Butler Yeats – for their lack of scientific sympathy or rigour. Fair enough. Yet Dawkins does not acknowledge the obverse point: that symbolic thought – magical thought, if you like – is what enabled these poets to create their timeless verse, that symbols are, in their way, just as 'real' (a favourite Dawkins adjective) as the constructs of hardhat science. Symbolism challenges consciousness and nourishes imagination, inviting us to uncover deeper levels of meaning in our own experience and in the *animus mundi*, the spirit of the world. Without Yeats's astrological interests, there would have been no 'Second Coming'.

In the last century, astrology's influence has seeped into not only but also into music, film, psychology and even science. Astronomers, most of them deeply hostile to astrology, are stuck with the names and associations of planets and constellations handed down from the pantheons of Greece and Rome. The myths of the ancients still stalk the heavens that science regularly announces it has 'conquered; Scorpio remains a byword for murder and treachery, the Moon goddess continues to enchant tunesmiths and feminists, and, as the recent best-seller insists, men are still from Mars, women from Venus.

Astrology itself is from Mercury. At least, it was to the tricky, paradoxical but illuminating force of the wing-footed god that star-gazing was assigned in ancient times, whereas modern astrologers have handed their art to Uranus, planet of liberation. The slippery, shape-shifting character of Mercury, however, makes a better fit for astrology down the centuries. Apart from its ability to survive, the most consistent character of astrology has been its adaptability. To some of its champions, it has been a celestial science; to others, a vehicle of spiritual enlightenment, perhaps even a key to the mind of God. Other practitioners treat it principally as a handy instrument of divination, useful for foretelling football scores, finding lost property or winning battles. It is still used in weather forecasting, gardening, medicine and match-making. Like the skies from which it is derived, astrology seems, in short, to oblige whatever fancies and expectations are projected on to it, even though, as we shall see in a later chapter, the planets are actually somewhat distant from where Western astrologers place them.

For its opponents, our current knowledge of the physical universe, and the still-unfurling discoveries of astro-physics, are sufficient proof that astrology is bunk. Modern astrologers, contrary to what is widely assumed, are quite aware of the problems inherent in their passion. As the distinguished American astrologer Robert Hand put it in a lecture a few years back: 'We have no idea what brings anything about in astrology. It's a deep, dark mystery. There is no efficient cause.' That view, of course, hasn't stopped the ongoing search for a mechanism to explain how astrology might work; it's a search which, as will be shown later, has led its practitioners from the Earth-centred cosmology of Ptolemy to the speculative realm of quantum physics.

The attempt to discover what astrologers think and believe, rather than what their opponents assume they do, is another reason for this book. Of the many astrologers I have met in recent years, what has repeatedly struck me is not their credulity or foolishness but their intellectual rigour and openness. For sure, one also finds myopia, pomposity and waspishness – but then as much is true of journalists, politicians, sales staff or industrial chemists.

One also finds disputes, of course, and astrology has its share of doctrinal controversies as bitter, and as apparently trivial to the outsider, as those between, say, the champions of modern and trad jazz, or between 'gradualists' and 'punctuationists' in evolutionary theory. The debate over the value of Sun sign astrology and the familiar daily forecasts of newspapers has led to one such feud. Are they a valid part of the astrologer's art, or, as one senior figure succinctly told me, 'a load of pud'?

This dispute is of particular importance since, to most people, Sun sign forecasts *are* astrology, which, as one often reads, divides all humanity into twelve arbitrary character types. In fact, star-lore poses a quite different scenario: that each of us has a unique horoscope (well, virtually unique). Since the solar system is always in motion, and the Earth is always spinning, the position of the cosmos from our point of view is always changing. Even people born at precisely the same time have different birth charts according to *where* they are born, since the view of the heavens in London at dawn is different from the view in Sydney.

Unlike some astrologers, I have never thought a birth chart can summarise a person, any more than the fact that they are born into a particular race, country, town or family. Even the allegedly unique horoscope of our birth can only be a sophisticated clue to our identity. The mystery of human incarnation – and mystery it remains – is bigger than astrology, just as it is bigger than genetics and evolutionary theory.

Although astrology has mutated over the centuries, and been used in many different ways, its central purpose remains unchanged: to establish a meaningful relationship between humanity and the universe, to uncover the cosmic order that philosophers and artists have sensed exists, and which they have attempted to describe. Whether such an order is there, whether the stars above are as 'true' as the unknown writer of 'Frankie and Johnny' supposed, remains as open to speculation as ever, but astrology's search for it seems in itself a noble and endlessly fascinating enterprise.

1

ANCIENT SKIES

THE ORIGINS OF ASTROLOGY

✳

'As Above, So Below.' A small phrase, but ideas don't come any bigger than this, astrology's central conceit. Astrology is essentially an attempt to connect heaven and earth, to link human affairs to the cosmos, to suggest that the awesome glitter of the universe, available to all on a clear night, is made of the same stuff, and subject to the same laws, as life on Planet Earth; that we and the sky are one.

This simple but profound notion has seduced humanity for millennia; at least since the monuments of the ancient world were constructed between three and five thousand years ago, and probably for far longer. The appeal of the night sky to early civilisations is easy to understand. The blaze of stars, the vast arc of the Milky Way, the movements of the planets (the name means 'the wanderers'), the cycles of the Moon, the periodic spectacles of eclipses, the occasional incursions of meteorite showers and comets; together these were a source of religious awe, calendrical measurement and mythological speculation. The sky was simultaneously the celestial realm of the gods and the principal object of scientific endeavour, as humanity tried to measure and predict the movements of Sun, Moon, planets and stars.

The validity of astrology in the twenty-first century depends to a great extent on the validity of the ancient worldview that spawned it, not least because beginnings are always important in astrology. Certainly astrology's resurgence over the last hundred years has been driven less by its periodically vaunted credentials to be itself 'a science' than by its symbolic and mythical associations in an age that has discovered the power and extent of the unconscious or subconscious mind, a realm which is accessed principally by the language of symbolism.

The ancient world sought symbolic meaning in everything. The terrestrial world was alive with animistic spirits, river nymphs, fire salamanders and other elemental forces, while myths and fables were spun around mountains, oceans, rocks, trees, animals and plants, as well as stars and planets. Nature was viewed not as a fluke of inert matter, but as possessed of a purposeful spirit that was responsive to human intent and action. Some of the ancient world's ideas now seem quaint or downright ignorant, but its apprehension of the interconnection and unity of nature has proved defiantly resistant to mechanistic science's attempts to displace it, and in the twentieth century was revived in the guise of 'Gaia theory' and in the further regions of quantum physics.

For the ancients, the connection between the celestial and earthly realms was paramount. The contours of the sky were sought out in the contours of the land and the patterns of constellations replicated in temples and graves, which were also aligned to individual stars and to the rising of Sun and Moon at the solstices. The practice appears repeatedly in ancient civilisations. The Egyptian Temple of Karnak is aligned to the heliacal rising of the star Sirius, which presaged the annual inundation of the Nile. The chamber tomb of Newgrange in Ireland and numerous others from Scotland to Brittany are arranged so that the rays of the midwinter Sun penetrate the darkness within. The Mayan pyramids of Mexico are dedicated to the twin luminaries of Sun and Moon. Christian churches are oriented with the altar to the east, the source of light. All are based on the same symbolic principal: that by bringing sky and earth into alignment, heavenly perfection can be realised in the terrestrial realm.

Astrology grew out of the same impulse to link the celestial and the mundane. The roots of astrology are a dense tangle, stretching down through centuries and across cultures, intertwined with an assortment of religions and philosophies. Astrology as we know it today is essentially a Greek construct, but it was the Babylonians, the most sophisticated astronomers of antiquity, who conceptualised the zodiac and who attempted to draw parallels between the movements of the planets and human affairs, specifically the affairs of the king, and hence the nation. The astronomical records of Babylon stretch back to 1700 BC, their earliest-known horoscopes to the fifth century BC.

By then, Babylonian star lore was spreading throughout the Middle East, to the Persians, Indians, Egyptians, Greeks and others. Its promulgation was accelerated by Alexander the Great's conquest of Babylon in 331 BC and his establishment of an empire in which Greek became the lingua franca. The Mediterranean port of Alexandria, where Ptolemy, Alexander's general (not to be confused with the astrologer Ptolemy), proclaimed himself King of Egypt, was the crucible where the various stellar traditions of the ancient world were melted down and transmuted into the forerunner of today's astrology.

In the centuries preceding and following the birth of Christ Alexandria was the intellectual capital of the Western world, thanks in part to the famous library established there by Ptolemy, which endured until the fourth century AD. Alexandria was the site of the confluence of numerous religions, mythologies and traditions, not least that of Egypt itself, which for the occupying Greeks, as for we moderns, carried a formidable aura of antiquity and magic. To the millennia-old traditions of Egypt, the Greeks brought an inquisitive rationalism, the magical constructs of Pythagorean mathematics, the cosmology and philosophy of Plato, Aristotle and others, and the astronomy of Babylon.

One result of this extraordinary confluence was astrology, which fused elements of the various cultures into a complex but versatile system, beguiling in its ability to describe the the shape and meaning of the night sky. The pantheons of the gods, and their abodes, the planets, became correlated; for example, Venus, the star of Ishtar for the Babylonians, became the star of the Greek Aphrodite. The division of the sky – or, rather, that part of it along which the Sun and the planets travel – into the twelve signs of the zodiac was also taken from the Babylonians, though the names of the constellations were sometimes changed. Aries, for example, which was 'The Hired Man' to Babylon, became known by its Egyptian title of 'The Sheep' or 'Ram'. Prominent stars were also incorporated into astrology's scheme; Spica, for example, was a star of good omen, Algol one of ill-fortune. By understanding the meaning of planets, constellations and stars, and by plotting the movements of the Sun, Moon and planets, astrologers seductively claimed to divine the future.

The development of the horoscope was crucial to such judgements. On one level the horoscope is simply a map of the skies for a particular time and place, but it is also a conceptual device enabling the astrologer to judge the relative power of the planets, and in which area of life their influence is likely to fall. The term 'horoscope' is derived from the Greek term *horos skopos* – 'hour pointer' – and shows the importance attached to another factor: whichever stars and planets were rising over the eastern horizon, the so-called Ascendant. These indicated the nature of what was 'coming into being'. In this, as in many other respects, modern astrology continues to follow the precepts of its ancient predecessor.

Also established, or at least formalised, during the centuries before Christ was the 'doctrine of correspondences', which has remained central to astrology throughout its history. In this magical view of the world all phenomena – be they animal, vegetable or mineral, beast, plant or stone – are assigned to a particular planet or constellation. The process is analogical rather than logical. Thus the golden Sun is said to 'rule' both golden plants like the sunflower and gold itself. To the silvery Moon, with its influence over the tides, belong aquatic creatures and silver. Mars, being considered fearsome, rules stinging plants like the nettle, savage animals and iron.

From early on, the doctrine of correspondences was also applied to the human body, with each sign 'ruling' part of the body. Aries, the first sign, is given the head, Taurus the throat, and so on, down to Pisces, the last, which is given the feet. This was one way in which astrology and medicine became intertwined; as early as the fifth century BC the legendary healer Hippocrates was cautioning that 'a physician without knowledge of astrology has no right to call himself a physician.'

The doctrine of correspondences became pervasive, and was honoured in the days of the week. When the Emperor Constantine established the seven-day week early in the fourth century, the sequence of days was arranged according to planetary lore. Sunday belonged to the Sun, Monday to the Moon, Tuesday to Mars (*mardi* in French), Wednesday to Mercury (*mercredi*), Thursday to Jupiter (*jeudi*, Jove's day), Friday to Venus (*vendredi*) and Saturday to Saturn.

Astrology shares the system of correspondence with another manifestation of ancient Alexandria: the body of magical and religious texts attributed to the generic authorship of Hermes Trismegistus ('thrice-greatest Hermes'), which were claimed to have been transmitted directly from the Greek and Egyptian gods of learning, respectively Hermes and Thoth. This body of lore – fragmented, often contradictory and collectively known as the Hermetica – has been highly influential through the centuries, and remains one of the touchstones of Western magical and esoteric thought. Astrology's favourite saying, 'As Above, So Below' – or, to quote the much repeated aphorism in its entirety, 'As above, so below, that the unity of the one may be perpetrated' – first appears in an Alexandrine tract of esoteric lore known as the Emerald Tablet.

Although astrology stands distinct from hermeticism, thanks in part to its astronomical content, it has remained entangled in the latter's embrace. Astrology has always been among the first ports of call for those embarking on an exploration of occult lore, for which it is a primary language; the planetary correspondences of metals, for instance, were central to Renaissance alchemy. The tension between astrology as a scientific construct, dedicated to the study and explanation of the cosmos, and astrology as an esoteric system, which can be used in acts of divination and magic, or to unlock the secrets of spirituality, runs throughout its history. St Augustine and Dante both complained that astrologers used necromancy rather than horoscopes to arrive at their predictions. Those modern astrologers who want their art to be seen as a dispassionate discipline or as an extension of psychological theory are embarrassed by its continuing association with fairground fortune-tellers and woolly Wiccans casting love spells.

Aside from astrology's claim to be able to foresee the future, which in the ancient world, as now, was a major part of its appeal, early astrology also claimed it could explain the characters of men, something never previously thought possible or worthwhile for lesser mortals than royalty. The advent of Greek astrology thus marks the emergence of the individual in human history, as distinct from the king or ruler, for even slaves could have horoscopes if they knew the time of their birth. Even if they didn't, they could still consult astrologers on particular questions by 'horary' (divinatory) methods. Astrology thus shared the democratic impulse that Greek culture had introduced into the world, and extended it to *hoi polloi*, the many. Astrology's twin role as learned adviser to royalty and rude friend of common folk has borne it along ever since.

From Alexandria, Greek astrology spread rapidly, not least to the emerging power of Rome, which, as in most things other than central heating, followed where Greece and Egypt had led. Astrology overran Rome at the start of its expansionist conquests and stayed as long as its empire lasted, whispering in the ears of its emperors and hanging around its amphitheatres offering cheap fortunes and the planetary odds on gladiatorial combats.

With the collapse of the Western Roman Empire early in the fifth century, astrology effectively disappeared from the Western world for several hundred years, along with the philosophies of Plato, Aristotle and other ancients. The hostility of the emergent Christian Church towards anything that smacked of paganism, and the fact that few people could read Greek texts, ensured astrology remained in exile until it was reimported from the Middle East early in the medieval era.

In the Eastern Roman Empire astrology and other ancient lore lived on, despite the destruction of the library at Alexandria and the attentions of the fiercely Christian Emperor Justinian, who closed the philosophical schools in Athens in 527. The learning of the ancient world was inherited by the Islamic empire established by the Arabs in the seventh and eighth centuries, where astrologers such as Masha'allah and Abu M'shar refined and expanded the astronomical and astrological tenets they inherited. That Masha'allah was a Jewish Egyptian living in Basra, and M'shar an Afghanistani who lived in Baghdad, indicates the cosmopolitan plurality of the Islamic empire, which included among its subjects Christians, Zoroastrians, Hindus, Jews and numerous sub-sects.

The diversity of the Islamic world helps account for astrology's escape from persecution there. Astrologers also presented their planetary studies as science rather than religion, and it was received as another exotic import from the West – just as the Greeks had previously taken it up as a secret from Babylon and the Romans as a revelation of the Greco-Egyptian mysteries. As Theodore Zeldin puts it: 'Wherever it went astrology remained foreign ... The future was

While winds blow and towers fall, a trio of Arabian astrologers measure the heavens. The need for accurate astrological data was a major spur to astronomical observation. (A Venetian woodcut from 1513.)

effectively put on the map as a foreign country, needing foreign eyes to explain it.'

Astrology returned to the West with the crusaders of the twelfth century as part of the rediscovered classical world, although its fortunes were mixed through the Middle Ages and the Renaissance. Arabic texts – either translations of classical authors or original works – were eagerly translated and consumed in the newly established universities of Europe. Aristotle, who had imagined the universe as a series of concentric spheres surrounding the Earth, around which the planets moved and beyond which lay the realms of the stars and the seat of God, became the cosmologist *par excellence*, his scheme adapted to the Christian hierarchies of seraphim and archangels. Claudius Ptolemy, a second-century AD Alexandrian, became the ultimate authority on astronomy and astrology, and his compendious textbooks, *The Almagest* and *Tetrabiblos*, essential parts of the academic curriculum. Ptolemy, about whom almost nothing is known, became one of history's most famous obscurities. For centuries he was hailed as a genius, though his originality is now disputed – we simply do not know how much of his work was borrowed and how much original – but his ideas were enormously influential, and the 'Back to Ptolemy' school of astrology remains in rude good health even now.

The medieval Church struggled to reach an accommodation with classicism and astrology. The battle against paganism had been won, but many of the classical teachings were clearly heretical and the fatalistic strand of astrology that had so alarmed the early Church still contradicted the doctrine of freewill. The solution was supplied by Thomas Aquinas, whose famous fudge on the issue of destiny and freewill – 'The stars incline but do not compel' – remains much quoted.

Regular edicts against astrology were nevertheless regularly issued from Rome, and devotees of hermetism persecuted. Here, too, little has changed. The Vatican's official line on astrology remains that astrologers are 'consorting with demons', while the Church of England's 1997 report on New Age heresies, *The Search for Faith*, expressed concern about astrology's popularity.

Astrology was, in short, too pervasive in the medieval mindset for the Church to suppress. The great Gothic cathedrals of the age often included zodiacal imagery – the magnificent stained-glass window at Rheims cathedral is but one example – alongside other esoteric symbolism and Pythagorean 'sacred geometry', all suggesting the 'secret gospel' of correspondences was covertly at work within the Church itself. The four evangelists became identified with the four 'fixed' signs of Taurus (St Luke), Leo (St Mark), Scorpio (St John) and Aquarius (St Matthew), whose symbols – respectively, Bull, Lion, Eagle and Man – feature in medieval Christian imagery. Moreover, at a time when every court in Christendom had an astrologer on hand to dispense advice, various popes and bishops were wont to seek discreet stellar advice of their own.

In the Renaissance the art and philosophy of the ancient world were rediscovered once more, and Arabic, Roman and Greek texts (particularly Plato) were championed by such luminaries as the Florentine scholars Pico della Mirandola and Marsilio Ficino. The magical thinking and polytheism of hermeticism flourished again, much to the alarm of the Church, and astrology remained an indispensable part of the metaphysical lexicon for the Renaissance magus. The elegant discourse on the planets written by Ficino, who taught the young Michelangelo, offers a dazzling insight into the Renaissance mind, and has recently been revived and discussed by Thomas Moore in the light of Jungian psychology.[1] The cryptic sixteenth-century prophecies of the French seer Nostradamus were in part astrologically based; his prediction for the year 1999, for example, when 'Mars rules happily', was evidently based on that year's astrological clash between Mars, Saturn and a total solar eclipse, fearful omens in Nostradamus's times. In England Dr John Dee, mage, mathematician, geographer and reportedly 'the wisest man in Europe', was employed by Elizabeth I, using astrology to choose her coronation date and acting as her espionage agent on his European travels, using the now familiar codename of 007.

Yet the fresh mood of confidence that coursed through Western culture from the fourteenth century chafed against the fatalism of medieval astrology, which saw man's life and fate as predetermined. Shortly before his death in 1495 Pico della Mirandola launched a scathing attack on astrology, in which he railed, among other things, against the zodiac's 'inane menagerie of animals', the idea that the planets are causes of events on earth, and astrologers' pretensions to know the future. He also pointed out that people who shared the same birth time did not share the same character or the same fate.

That many of Pico's objections were drawn from the writings of the second-century Roman philosopher Plotinus is a reminder that objections to astrology, imagined by many to have arrived with the rise of secular science, have always been with us. Cicero, writing in the first century BC, condemned astrology as empty superstition, and two hundred years later the poet Juvenal was mocking people who couldn't take a bath or a meal without first consulting their ephemeris. In a further echo of modern times Juvenal was particularly sarcastic about women's infatuation with astrology, complaining that they consulted astrologers to discover when their husbands were going to die. Even the astrologers' ultimate authority, Ptolemy, attacked his peers for their claims to know the future.

From whichever source they have come, attacks on astrology have never managed more than its short-term suppression. In the sixteenth century neither a renewed offensive by the Vatican, upset by the astrologers' penchant for predicting papal deaths, nor the hostility of Martin Luther, founder of the Protestant Reformation, succeeded in discrediting astrology. Indeed, Luther's lieutenant, Philipp Melanchthon, was himself a keen astrologer.

Far more damaging in the long term was the advent of the Sun-centred cosmos proposed by Nicolas Copernicus in 1543 and subsequently substantiated by Galileo and Johannes Kepler. Contrary to most scientific histories, none of this trio of astronomers was opposed to astrology *per se*, yet the death blow they delivered to the ancient view of the universe was to help propel astrology's slide from grace. (In chapter three, the relationship between science and astrology is explored in more detail.) Even shorn of its astronomical credentials, however, and ridiculed from the seventeenth century onwards by the triumphant forces of secular science, astrology's vision of a heaven and earth unified by symbolism ensured its survival until its renewal at the end of the nineteenth century. It is to that symbolism, then, that we should first turn.

2

MYTH AND IMAGINATION

A BRIEF GUIDE TO ASTROLOGY

*

THE ZODIAC

To understand the role that astrology has played in the history of ideas and culture – the kind of stories explored later in this book – a grasp of its rudiments is useful. Astrology's symbolic lexicon is mostly straightforward, and endlessly stimulating to explore, and the ensuing chapter is intended as a guide to the symbolism and basic techniques in use; although, as we shall see, disputes surround even the meanings of signs and planets.

Although for most people astrology begins and ends with the twelve signs of the zodiac, in practice astrologers have always taken more notice of planets than signs. The planets represent active energies, whereas the signs merely (a very large merely, granted) show how those energies are being expressed. 'Planets are verbs, signs are adverbs,' as Robert Hand succinctly concludes in *Horoscope Symbols*.

The zodiac – the word is Greek, meaning 'circle of animals' – is the band of stars that marks the 'ecliptic', the Sun's annual passage through the sky. Because all the planets of the solar system orbit the Sun on much the same plane, with none more than a few degrees higher or lower than the others (known as declination), the stars of the zodiac provide the backdrop to them all. The various constellations of the zodiac are not so obliging as to parcel themselves up into exact 30-degree divisions; some, like Pisces, sprawl across their boundaries, while others, like Cancer, are comparatively skinny. Astrology's division of the sky into twelve is thus rooted in cosmological reality, but remains essentially symbolic.

As the planets pass through these 30-degree divisions of the sky, they are said to be 'in' the sign concerned. Since the Sun represents our essential identity, the sign it occupies is especially important and gives rise to the familiar assertions of 'I'm a Gemini', 'I'm a Pisces' and so on.

The energies represented by the other planets are also modified by whichever sign they occupy. The combination of Mercury, representing mental powers, in the dreamy sign of Pisces is described as impressionable and poetic but impractical. Mercury in airy Aquarius becomes intellectual. Jupiter, representing growth, indicates resourcefulness when in earthy Capricorn; generosity and ambition when in fiery Leo. There are numerous astrological 'cookbooks' detailing the meanings of each placement.

The zodiac is the most orderly part of the astrological system, with each sign assigned a 'ruling' planet, one of the four elements of earth, water, fire and air, and one of the three qualities of cardinal, fixed and mutable. The character of each sign is derived from a combination of its symbol (the Lion is brave, the Bull stubborn), its planet, its element and its quality. The system can be easily seen in diagrammatic form (see Figure 1).

The nature of the four elements is straightforward enough. Fire is linked to such qualities as impulsiveness and inspiration and is future-oriented; it is frequently, though not very helpfully, talked of as 'spirit'. Earth is simply 'down to earth'; it is about pragmatism and physicality and the here and now, about 'matter' rather than abstraction. Air is linked to abstract thought, to mental powers and the world of ideas. Water is emotional, sensitive, intuitive and is linked to the past.

The three 'virtues' or 'qualities' are less familiar but equally uncomplicated. They are best explained as an energy flow: cardinal signs initiate actions and ideas, fixed signs give them stability and endurance, while mutable signs complete and distribute them.

Put this threefold division together with the four elements and you have a symmetrical pattern that yields a cardinal, fixed and mutable version of each element. The four cardinal signs are fiery Aries, watery Cancer, airy Libra and earthy Capricorn. The fixed signs are earthy Taurus, fiery Leo, watery Scorpio and airy Aquarius. The mutable signs

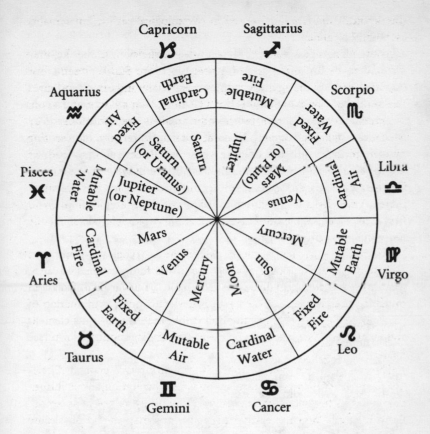

Figure 1: The division of the zodiac by the four elements and three qualities, together with the planetary rulerships of the signs.

are airy Gemini, earthy Virgo, fiery Sagittarius and watery Pisces. The cardinal signs stand at the start of each season – Aries bringing a surge of energy for spring and so on – while the season comes to a height under a fixed sign and mutates into the next season under a mutable one.

The zodiac's present classification by element and quality seems to be largely the work of Ptolemy in the first century AD. Beforehand, the signs featuring animals were allotted to earth, those with human signs to air and those with watery creatures to water, with fire not included (Leo, being ruled by the Sun, might have been the exception). Ptolemy, a great systems man, insisted on symmetry.

Periodically there are allegations, usually from astro-sceptics, that there are really thirteen signs in the zodiac, the constellation of Orphiucus most often being claimed as the missing sign. The Royal Astronomical Society launched just such an attack on the astrological zodiac in January 1995. An alternative argument is that there used to be only eleven, the sign of Libra being a relatively recent interpolation. The latter claim is partly true, since before Libra became the Scales, the constellation was described as 'The Claws of the Scorpion', but it was still counted as a separate zodiacal sign, to make a round dozen.

The zodiac reflects the significance accorded to the number twelve in the ancient world. Examples of twelve's sacred associations are legion; both Zeus and Odin, for example, presided over a twelve-strong pantheon, Christ had twelve disciples, there were twelve tribes of Judah, twelve tribes in Plato's idealised Republic and twelve gates to the New Jerusalem described by St John the Divine. The reason for the exaltation of twelve is uncertain; it may simply be based on the fact there were twelve lunar months in a year, but the number is certainly practical, being divisible by 2, 3, 4 and 6. Simple expedience may likewise account for the division of the heavens into 360 degrees (i.e. 6 × 6 or 12 × 3), a number that corresponds closely to the year's 365 days.

Furthermore, the Pythagoreans thought that numbers carried implicit meaning. Twelve was evidently important because it was the product of 3 × 4, just as 7 was important because it was the sum of 3 + 4. Accordingly, there are numerous examples of the sacred seven in ancient thought: seven colours of the rainbow, seven chakras in the body, seven metals in alchemy and, of course, seven astrological planets in the sky.

The zodiac can be seen as a projection of such numerical and symbolic principles on to the sky, a cosmically inspired mandala. Such a view helps Western astrology out of one of its biggest bugbears, the issue of the Tropical versus the Sidereal zodiac. Because of the phenomenon known as the precession of the equinoxes – which is caused by a wobble in the Earth's axis – the zodiac slips slowly backwards in the sky, by a degree every seventy-two years, making a complete backward revolution every 26,000 years. The phenomenon is discussed more fully in Chapter 7.

At the time Ptolemy wrote his textbooks, the spring equinox, on 21 March, fell at 0 degrees Aries. Thanks to precession, it now falls at around 6 degrees Pisces, yet Western astrology has continued to measure the zodiac from 0 degrees Aries. As a result, none of the planets is actually where Western astrology claims it is, but 24 degrees further backwards in the sky. So while astrology describes Venus at, say, 10 degrees Libra, its physical location is halfway through the constellation of Virgo. Indian astrology, on the other hand, still uses the real-life positions of the planets for its deliberations: this is the Sidereal zodiac, as opposed to Western astrology's Tropical zodiac.

Astrology's critics regularly claim that astrologers are so astronomically lax that they are oblivious to the fact that their planets are in the wrong place. They are not, but the issue is an embarrassment. Various arguments are thrust forward in defence of the Tropical zodiac, principally that at latitudes where the seasons have such a strong influence it makes sense to bring our experience of the year in line with the identity of the twelve signs: energetic Aries signalling the surge of spring, Capricorn falling in bleak midwinter and so on. Most astrologers simply cite their own experience as evidence that the Tropical zodiac works. Nevertheless, in the mid-twentieth century several notable star-gazers, led by Ireland's Cyril Fagan, broke ranks and took up the Sidereal zodiac, but the movement had a limited impact. Almost all Western astrologers use the Tropical zodiac, while those that are sceptical of it have turned to Vedic astrology.

The figures conjured up by the shape of the constellations varied between the ancient cultures that bled into astrology – Babylon's archer became Greece's centaur – and their meanings are likewise accretions gathered over centuries. The zodiac has continued to mutate in the modern era, with twentieth-century developments parcelled out among the ancient constellations: aviation to Aquarius and Sagittarius, for example. New ways of dividing the zodiac also owe little to tradition. The twelve signs are increasingly considered as six interlocking pairs, twinning signs that face each other on the zodiacal wheel: Aries and Libra, Cancer and Capricorn, and so on. Each pair of signs is claimed to manifest much the same principle – Taurus physical stability, Scorpio emotional stability – and to carry an echo of its opposite number. By this token, peace-loving Librans have a confrontational Arien warrior in them and the sober face of Virgo conceals a freewheeling Piscean.

Splitting the zodiac into two halves is another development, with the second six signs considered as socially oriented versions of the self-centred first six. Hence Leo, a sign concerned with childlike self-assertion, turns into Aquarius, a sign concerned with society's collective values. Cancer, the sign of the family, turns into Capricorn, the sign of an ordered society. Today's psychological astrologers also warn that our opposite sign is a shadow to be accommodated, so a Leo who doesn't acknowledge the demands of society at large (Aquarius's concern) stays a selfish brat.

The zodiac is, in short, endlessly flexible, with a structure that can be correlated with human character and physical appearance, natural phenomena or human constructs. In its universality lies its strength.

ARIES
Cardinal fire, ruled by Mars

For astrology, life begins at the spring equinox, when nature bursts back into activity and Aries kick-starts the zodiacal cycle. Its position as the first sign of the zodiac permeates the character of Aries. Fiery, and ruled by energetic Mars, everything about Aries is urgent, making those born under the Ram pioneers, eager to lead from the front and impatient with faint hearts and foot-draggers. Its Mars ruler also makes Aries the sign of combat and militarism.

In the 'heavenly body' Aries rules the head, and the sign is always portrayed as headstrong, a battering ram leading the charge. Some astrologers even describe the sign as slightly crazy – Vincent Van Gogh repeatedly shows up in lists of famous Ariens, as does troubled Goon Spike Milligan, both of them Aries Suns. In appearance Aries is judged to indicate wiriness, with the broad brow and long, narrow chin of its emblematic beast.

Aries's glyph, most obviously a pair of ram's horns, can also be seen as a young shoot pushing blindly above ground. Fresh and vigorous, this is also the sign of childhood, the first part of life, making Ariens either charmingly childlike or infuriatingly childish. Aries' self-centredness means the sign is indifferent, even oblivious, to the judgement of others.

Emotions, other than enthusiasm and anger (neither of which is sustained for long) are not Aries' forte. Its masculine qualities would seem to make Aries an uneasy Sun sign for women, but female Rams are reckoned able to hold their own with men in physical prowess and derring-do, and are likely to number as many men as women among their friends.

TAURUS
Fixed earth, ruled by Venus

The Bull is the zodiac's most intractable creature, and Taurus comes yoked to a reputation for stubborn consistency that accords with both its symbol and the qualities of fixed earth. This is the most earthy of all signs, arriving when spring is in full, glorious bloom, making Taurus the sign of agriculture, farmer and gardener. Thomas Hardy, a Sun Taurus, described the archetypal Taurean in the character of Gabriel Oakes, in Far From the Madding Crowd.

The feminine charms of Taurus's ruling planet, Venus, jar with the image of a snorting, muscular bull, but accord with Taurus' lush, fertile qualities. Venus makes Taureans lovers of beauty and sensuality, which, allied with their earthy nature, casts them as collectors of objets d'art, with an affinity for luxury. Taurus is also the sign of ownership, possessions, and of economics; Karl Marx, creator of dialectical materialism, had Sun and Moon in Taurus. Banks and financial institutions likewise belong to Taurus.

Perfectly happy when dragging their plough along a straight furrow, those born under the Bull are said to become confused by the need to change tack, turn around, and go back the other way. Consistency, in other words, easily hardens into dogmatism. On the other hand, the bull is an angst-free zone; where other signs worry, he or she simply gets on with the job in hand.

Taurus rules the throat, which in physical appearance is accentuated as a bull neck or the long, graceful neck of Venus. Either way, Taurus is considered an adept orator.

GEMINI
Mutable air, ruled by Mercury

The shift from laborious Taurus to flitting Gemini is abrupt, a transition from the material outlook of earth to the heady concerns of air, from the obstinacy of a fixed sign to the inconstancy of a mutable one. Given that Gemini is ruled by Mercury, quicksilver planet of communication, the customary picture of Gemini is as restless, rootless and intellectual.

The symbol of the Twins – the constellation includes the twin stars Castor and Pollux – suggests constant movement from one point of view to another. Gemini's duality is always emphasised. Gemini's subjects can be contradictory, blowing hot and cold in the same breath, unable to resolve their warring impulses, a conflict articulated by Bob Dylan (Sun, Mercury and Venus in Gemini) as 'I fought with my twin, that enemy within, till both of us fell by the way'. Locked in perpetual embrace, both twins need to be accommodated.

At best Geminis are depicted as knowledge-seekers, educators, orators, wits, literati (the sign governs writing) and journalists. Endlessly curious, Gemini likes to be first with the news. Although not particularly emotional, Gemini is thought humanist in outlook (it is represented by people rather than beasts).

Conversely, Gemini is painted as a fickle-minded chatterbox: 'a meere frantick fellow, constant in nothing but idle words and bragging,' as William Lilley dimissed the sign three centuries ago. Worse, Gemini is easily perverted to criminal ends, becoming thief, perjurer or con-man; the zodiac's own Artful Dodger. The opposing twin of the untrustworthy Gemini is Sherlock Holmes, the intellectual sleuth created by Conan Doyle (Sun in Gemini), able to absorb a dozen details at a glance and a master of disguise; both Mercurial talents.

Fashion is put under Gemini's rule, as are juggling, card games, board games, word games and all such mental frivolity. The sign rules the hands and arms, and Gemini is thought a fidget. Naturally young at heart, Geminis are said to retain their youthful looks.

CANCER
Cardinal water, ruled by the Moon

The zodiac's first water sign is also cardinal, making Cancer emotional but dynamic. With the Moon goddess herself as its ruler, this is the female sign *par excellence*, for which the Crab is an unflattering but relevant symbol.

Cancer's realms are the primordial oceans where life began, the planet's womb; they and the Moon that controls their tides represent the great mother, our origins. It follows that ancestry, the family and the past are all Cancerian concerns. As the sign of the mother – the womb and breasts come under its rulership – Cancer is at best a nurturing force, responsive to others' needs and loyal to a fault.

Cancer's emotional, sensitive nature comes protected by the Crab's tough, outer shell. Yet Cancer is unable to be merely a shrinking violet – as a cardinal sign it is active, making it a sign of somewhat pushy self-interest. Moodiness, aggression (those claws carry a sharp nip) and self-obsession are among Cancer's negative traits, along with the tendency to nurse grudges and brood about the past. Marcel Proust, introverted author of *Remembrance of Things Past*, was born with Sun in Cancer. By reputation, home is where Cancer's heart is lodged, and winkling its subjects from their familiar shell is tough work. Tender it may be, but the Crab is also tenacious.

As the sign of the mother, Cancer is reckoned an easier sign for a woman than a man, in contrast to Cancer's opposite: patriarchal Capricorn. Cancerian women are habitually portrayed as matriarchs who know how to get their way and who aren't above emotional manipulation and blackmail. This mother can also smother. By contrast, Cancer men find it difficult to express their emotional, lunar self. Though they soften up at home, the outside world's experience of them is more likely to be a tough shell and sharp pincers.

Cancer's maternal association also helps make it the sign of nutrition. The stomach falls under Cancer's rulership and sensitivity to food (particularly seafood) is cited as one of the Crab's weak points.

LEO
Fixed fire, ruled by the Sun

Coming at the summer's blazing peak, Leo is the Sun's own sign, and its function is the exaltation of the self. Its element, fixed fire, indicates the Sun in all its glory; Leo is radiant and full of largesse, a spirit that burns with regal pride. Royal lines from Egypt's pharaohs to the House of Windsor have laid claim to the symbolism of Sun and Lion, and Leo's subjects are natural-born monarchs, kings and queens to themselves, if not to others. If you're the Sun, the world revolves around you.

Leos are therefore accused of arrogance and of having ideas above their station, but, like royalty, lap up flattery. Ruling the heart, Leo also boasts a reputation as big-hearted and courageous, for which one can also read foolhardy, intractable and unable to learn from mistakes. What others see as self-aggrandisement, however, is self-dramatisation for Leo; above all, the sign celebrates individuality and the idea that 'every man or woman is a star'. Creative and playful, Leo, like Aries, has strong associations with those natural extroverts, children.

As with the other fire signs, deception does not come easily to Leo, but claims that Leo 'lacks malice' are fanciful, as testified by the impressive roster of flamboyant nationalist autocrats born with Sun in Leo, among them Louis XIV (the Sun King himself), Napoleon, Haile Selassie ('the Lion of Judah'), Mussolini and Fidel Castro.

The sign's rampant leonine symbolism also claims its subjects resemble their symbol, being shaggy of mane, slim of hip, and with a feline gait; rock royals Mick Jagger and Robert Plant (both with Sun and three other planets in Leo) fit the profile cannily.

VIRGO
Mutable earth, ruled by Mercury

Virgo's subjects are usually described as practical hard-workers and fussy perfectionists, as abstemious, prudish, obsessive and, inevitably, virginal. Such descriptions stem not just from its symbol, a chaste maiden, but from the combination of its element, mutable earth, and ruling planet, Mercury. This is one of the most contradictory mixtures in the zodiac. How can earth be Mercurial? The usual answer is that Virgos apply their able intellects to practical matters; hence, Virgo the list-compiler and clerk, the precision craftsman, computer programmer and messenger, forever on missions hither and thither. Virgo, making its busy way through the world, also becomes the sign of the conformist.

A deeper understanding of Virgo's function comes from its symbol, a maiden bearing a sheaf of corn. The allusions to harvest time and Ceres the corn goddess are obvious. Less evident is that Virgo's purpose is to glean the wheat from the chaff, to reach the unsullied germ of things – the issue is not cleanliness or virginity but purity. Virgo's rulership of the intestines in the zodiacal body amplifies the idea of the sign as discriminator, breaking down what we ingest into the nutritious and the expendable; truly a critical function.

The critic is another Virgo guise, again derived from the idea of discrimination and detail. If Mercury's other sign, Gemini, loves ideas for their own sake, Virgo puts them to the test. The first dictionary was compiled by the critic Samuel Johnson, born with Sun in Virgo.

The Virgoan quest for perfection can include perfect health – diet is a particular concern – and art. Literary astrologer Paul Wright suggests Virgo arbitrates between civilisation and savagery, order and disorder, themes dominant in such Virgoan authors as D.H. Lawrence (*The Rainbow*), William Golding (*Lord of the Flies*), James Fenimore Cooper (*Last of the Mohicans*) and Leo Tolstoy (*War and Peace*). Both Tolstoy and Lawrence preached work and simplicity.

LIBRA
Cardinal air, ruled by Venus

As an air sign ruled by fair Venus, Libra is traditionally about harmony, grace and romance. Its symbol, the Scales, lends further credence to Libra as the sign of peace and balance, as well as of décor, dress and appearance. Yet Libra's Scales are rarely in equilibrium; the smallest imbalance sends them swinging wildly. Libra's air is cardinal and dynamic, making it a sign of extremism, with its subjects prone to sudden enthusiasms and see-sawing moods.

Other people are crucial to Libra's mission. As the seventh sign, it marks the divide between the first six personal signs and the second, socially oriented half-dozen. Libra needs to share its experience with others, and is all too aware of their opinions. Ruled by the goddess of love, Libra is the great romantic, in love with love, forever pursuing the ideal partnership.

Its sensitivity to others' opinions makes Libra the sign of the diplomat, but this can become a desire for 'peace at any price' and an evasion of issues where frankness would be a better policy. The sign's inability to make up its mind as it weighs up the pros and cons of issues is often remarked on. Yet Libra's diffidence can be over-stressed. Perhaps in an echo of its opposite sign of Aries, the sign is not scared of confrontation, as evidenced by a roll-call of such Libran Suns as Margaret Thatcher, Jerry Lee Lewis, John Lennon – a fighter who preached 'Give Peace a Chance' – and Mahatma Gandhi, another 'peace warrior'.

As an air sign Libra at its best is thought idealistic, able to balance 'the scales of justice', but there is no guarantee those ideals will be shared, as shown by the example of Heinrich Himmler, a Libran Sun who knew the value of a well-cut uniform. Although the sign of peace, Libra is also the sign of strategy – chess comes under its rule – making it a good sign for a general.

Physically, Libra rules the kidneys, which help balance the body's bloodstream, while Librans are by tradition regular of form and feature, and often good-looking.

SCORPIO
Fixed water, ruled by Mars

Sex, death, war, intrigue – for sheer drama, no other sign can compete with Scorpio, whose qualities have made it a byword for malice and double-dealing. Scorpio's reputation for vengefulness stems from its rulership by Mars, which ancient astrology deemed a malefic influence. Still, as a water sign, Scorpio is fundamentally emotional, though the concept of 'fixed water' is an unhappy one; Scorpio's affinities are not with the fertile seas of Cancer and Pisces but with stagnant pools, brackish marshes and the murky oceanic depths where strange fish swim and which humans cannot fathom.

Add to this the scorpion's deadly sting, and the sign's rulership of the genitals, and you have the scheming, venal Scorpio of legend, an archetype personified by the celebrated sexpot and First World War spy Mata Hari, who was Sun in Scorpio. Scorpio's poisonous betrayal has a long history; in the sixteenth century Pope Paul III was assured by his private astrologer that Martin Luther would go to hell because he was born under the sign.

Modern astrology has toned down Scorpio's villainy and made intensity its key theme. By this token, Scorpio subjects feels more keenly, love more passionately and cannot help but wound more deeply. It's as if the sign lives at a heightened emotional pitch such as most people only experience during wartime (and Mars makes Scorpio a natural warrior).

Scorpio's association with death and sex (*le petit mort*) is these days linked to a desire for transcendence and resurrection, for while Scorpio is prone to self-destruct by its own sting, it is also the sign of transformation and rebirth, with the phoenix among its symbols. The assignation of Pluto, Lord of the Underworld, as its new or joint ruler has amplified the idea that the sign is about transmutation, but made Scorpio no less doom-laden.

There are compensations for those born during the 'season of mists and mellow fruitfulness' celebrated by Keats, a Scorpio Sun who followed one of his sign's traditional occupations, surgeon. Scorpio's perspicacious vision is meant to see beyond the surface of things to deeper truths – Scorpios are often described as having a profound gaze.

SAGITTARIUS
Mutable fire, ruled by Jupiter

Half-horse, half-human, the bow-wielding Centaur allows Sagittarius to be beast or beauty, lusty or high-minded, feet on the ground or head in the stars. Or all at the same time.

Classical and medieval astrologers set great store by the sign's rulership by Jupiter, largest and luckiest of the planets. Sagittarius is therefore portrayed, obviously enough, as jovial (from the Latin *jovialis*, 'of Jupiter'). Jupiter's associations with good fortune and good sportsmanship, along with the natural ardour and optimism of a fire sign, resulted in a stereotype of Sagittarius as a ruddy-faced squire, happy with hounds and hunting or buying in his round at the local tavern.

It's an image at odds with Sagittarius's alternative reputation as noble and religious: the sign of the idealist, visionary, philosopher and teacher. Jupiter's expansiveness, however, works on all levels, making Sagittarius a seeker of new horizons, whether geographical or mental; the Centaur gallops far and aims high. Its demand for personal freedom and self-expression can make the Centaur a social misfit or an intrepid explorer.

The sense of space, the 'big picture', informs the work of many Sagittarian artists: the thunderous joys of Beethoven (Sun and Moon in Sagittarius), the celestial wars of John Milton (Sun and Ascendant), the dark jungles of Joseph Conrad (Sun) or the sci-fi excursions of Jimi Hendrix (Sun and Ascendant) and Steven Spielberg (Sun and Mercury).

The sign's symbolism inevitably ties it to all things equine. Sagittarius rules the thighs, handy for horse-riding, while the Centaur's bestial instincts are sometimes claimed to make the sign lustful, as well as clumsy.

Worst of all is Sagittarius astride its high moral horse, lambasting lesser mortals. In this case the 'bow of burning gold' and 'arrows of desire' evoked by the visionary William Blake (Sun and Jupiter in Sagittarius) become weapons of the intolerant fundamentalist. The sign is notoriously blunt when passing judgement, and even the archer's easy-going Jovian jests can carry a wounding barb; though, like the other fire signs, Sagittarius is unlikely to be duplicitous.

CAPRICORN
Cardinal earth, ruled by Saturn

Capricorn comes with a reputation as materialist, ambitious and ruthless, a character derived chiefly from its ruling planet, Saturn, which signifies cold calculation. When applied to a sign whose element is cardinal earth, the result is unyielding realism. Capricorn is less interested in the high moral principles of Sagittarius than in practical methods. The symbol of the Mountain Goat shows the way Capricorn works: in a steady, sure-footed ascent to the top.

Unexpectedly, Capricorn has an association with humour, since ironic, observational humour is a necessary escape valve from the tension of self-control – the bawdy Roman festival of Saturnalia was held at the winter solstice. The Capricorn Goat is also more than a mountain climber: it's the mythical sea-goat, possessed of a fishy tail, suggesting that its subjects can be profound and mysterious, and a reminder that Capricorn has a stake in its opposite sign, sensitive Cancer.

While Cancer represents the mother, Capricorn represents the father, a role that can be expressed positively or otherwise. Capricorn's purpose in life is said to be caring for others, to become truly benevolent. This is just how those 'great fathers' Stalin and Mao (both Capricorn Suns) liked to present themselves, while acting out the 'bad father' and repressing and purging their disobedient children, that is, anyone who threatened their power.

Control is a Capricorn forte. FBI supremo J. Edgar Hoover, control freak incarnate, had Sun and Ascendant in Capricorn. Oddly enough, Hoover's most hated adversary, Martin Luther King, was another Capricorn, one who arguably manifested the sign's socially responsible 'good father'. While the tenth sign takes easily to conformism and has problems 'letting go', its ability to shape and build are vital. The skeleton and the skin are governed by Capricorn; bones create the structure for the body, while skin contains us.

Thanks to Saturn's association with time, things are said to become easier for Capricorns as they grow older. The sign is associated with a difficult childhood, blighted by authority figures, with its subjects overly serious for their age. Yet while other signs struggle with adult responsibilities, the mature Capricorn often lightens up and becomes the 'old goat' of folk wisdom.

AQUARIUS
Fixed air, ruled by Saturn/Uranus

Represented by the Water Bearer, Aquarius is often mistaken for a water sign. The opposite is true. Aquarius's element is air, and the sign's affinity is not with emotion but with the abstract realm of ideas. If anything, Aquarius is rather removed from the rest of humanity.

The concept of fixed air is problematical, there being no obvious image to correspond to it, unless it's the stultifying atmosphere of office and lecture room. Aquarius's airy ideals are nevertheless broader than those of Gemini or Libra; as the penultimate sign, it is concerned with social issues, and where its opposite number, Leo, rejoices in a sense of self, Aquarius relates that self in the context of the collective. The Water Bearer is the sign of the crusading reformer and zealous radical; Abraham Lincoln and Franklin Roosevelt were both Aquarius Suns.

Traditionally, Aquarius is ruled, like Capricorn, by Saturn, which gives both signs self-discipline, orderliness and a desire to investigate the structure of the world, be it material or organisational. Aquarius's rulership of blood circulation ties in, just, to its concerns with social currents.

Uranus was added as Aquarius's co-ruler in the nineteenth century, bringing a different flavour to the sign, tying it to the age of electricity, technological invention and revolution. The sign's glyph of two wavy lines, originally representing water, also resembles the airwaves. Aviation was later appended to Aquarius's impressive list of concerns – the pioneering pilot Charles Lindberg and French aviator and author Antoine de Saint-Exupéry both had Aquarian Suns. The new science of psychology was also given to Aquarius, presumably because of its attributes of cool detachment and humanitarian concerns.

Underpinning Aquarius's disparate interests is the symbolism of the Water Bearer, who pours forth succour for all humanity, regardless of creed, caste or sex, this being one reason for the idealised Age of Aquarius. Yet, like all fixed signs, Aquarius is stubborn rather than easy-going. Intolerance is part of the shadow cast by this social reformer, while individual relationships are, again perversely, not easy for the great humanitarian, who tends to be a little too detached for human contact.

PISCES
Mutable water, ruled by Jupiter/Neptune

The twelfth and last sign of the zodiac, Pisces is also the most all-embracing and formless, with a reputation for sensitivity and other-worldliness. This comes from its element, mutable water. Whether sea, river or spring, Pisces's quick waters seek out the easiest channel for their course, taking on any shape offered. Likewise, Pisceans swim with the current, adapting easily to new situations. If anything, Pisces' subjects suffer from an excess of wateriness, making them sentimental and tearful.

Piscean impressionability links the sign to the arts and mysticism. The flowing forms of music and dance, in particular, belong to Pisces' fluid domain, with the brilliance of ballet dancers Nureyev and the unhinged Nijinsky (both Pisces Suns) being popular examples. Furthering its dance credentials, Pisces governs the feet in the 'heavenly body', giving its subjects unusually graceful or, conversely, flat feet.

Traditionally ruled by cheery Jupiter, Pisces was assigned nebulous Neptune in the nineteenth century, adding to its reputation for dissolution and drunkenness. Pisces's sensitivity extends to psychic abilities and to empathy with others. The sign is associated with madness, with the isolation of the hermit and the monk, and with selfless service via healing and hospitals. Sympathy with the animal kingdom is often cited. Inevitably, fishermen and sailors also find their literal way into Pisces's domain.

Its very adaptability makes defining Pisces problematical. Fish, after all, come in many shapes and sizes, from tiddler to shark, and can be difficult to catch. Pisces's slipperiness has its advantages, allowing its subjects to take on whatever character they like, to be all things to everyone – acting is a traditional Pisces occupation. Slippery escapologist Houdini had Sun in Pisces.

Some see the twin fishes as the real clue to Pisces's identity. Joined at the mouth, they face in opposite directions, indicating a choice between swimming with the current or against the flow; battling upstream leads to real achievement, heading downstream is the quick route to ruin. The miserable, drug-related deaths of pop innovators Brian Jones and Kurt Cobain (both Pisces Suns) carry more than a trace of Piscean dissolution.

POSTSCRIPT: 'I'M ON THE CUSP!'
(Oh no you're not!)

You hear it whenever someone is dumb or desperate enough to ask, 'What sign are you then?' 'I'm on the cusp,' comes back the reply. 'I was born on the 20th, so I'm a bit Sagittarius and a bit Capricorn.'

It's a cute response, combining a nugget of astro-jargon, a sensible refusal to have your character classified by some chump who happens to have read *Star Signs For Swinging Lovers*, and the co-option of two signs where most people are stuck with the one.

It's also meaningless as far as many astrologers are concerned. While some star-gazers go along with the notion that signs bleed into each other, with their characteristics blurring at the edges, most take the contrary view. The Sun, they argue, is either at 29 degrees, 29 minutes and 59 seconds of Pisces or at 0 degrees 0 minutes of Aries. There is no halfway house. Astrology is, in part, a cosmic clock, and, like Cinderella at the ball, until the clock strikes twelve you're a princess and not a kitchen drudge – or a watery dreamer, not a fireball. As any child knows, when the chimes finish sounding, your ballgown and coach revert to rags and pumpkin not by degrees but instantaneously. Whammo, you're an Aries!

In fact, most astrologers argue that the Sun, or any other planet, is at its strongest in the first degree or so of a sign, meaning that far from having their sun sign's characteristics tempered, those born at its beginning are likely to be extra-typical.

The confusion of those born around change-over time is understandable. The Sun sign dates given by newspaper and magazine horoscopes vary considerably, and if your birthday is August 23, you can be a Leo in one paper and a Virgo in the next. What's more, either could be right, since the exact time the Sun changes sign varies slightly from year to year: 8.30 in the evening one year, 2.30 in the morning the next. The only way to be sure in such cases is to consult an ephemeris.

Those who bask in the ambiguity of being, say, half-Crab, half-Lion, need not feel thwarted. There are so many variables on a birth chart it's always possible to find get-out clauses. You may turn out to have a Leo Sun, but a moon in Cancer. And since the inner planets, Mercury and Venus, never stray far from the Sun's position to our earth-bound eyes, it's common to find them in a sign adjacent to the Sun in a birth chart. You may not be able to stay on the cusp, but you can stay on the fence.

THE PLANETS

OVERVIEW

The planets, rather than the signs of the zodiac, are at the heart of astrology's system, and are considered to be energetic forces whose characters accord with their mythological namesakes, and often with their physical behaviour. Mercury's swift orbit, for example, fits its role as the planet of communications.

For the Babylonians, the planets were the abodes of the gods, rather than gods themselves, though the distinction is a fine one. The Greeks originally gave guardianship of each planet to a Titan and Titaness – Tethys and Oceanus guarded Venus, for instance – but later took up the Babylonian model, substituting similar deities from their own pantheon; Babylon's Marduk became Greece's Zeus, and was later to become Rome's Jupiter.

Whether Greek astrologers saw the planets as literal gods who intervened directly in human life, or as characters whose 'rays' caused things to happen, remains unclear. Doubtless some did, as did astrologers of later ages, yet Platonic thought, with its concept of perfected 'forms', was capable of conceiving planetary functions as abstract or internal processes rather than literal ones. Renaissance neo-Platonists such as Marsilio Ficino certainly understood the astrological planets as a psycho-spiritual system. Modern astrology, under the influence of Jungian psychology, sees the planets as representing archetypal forces that exist both in the individual psyche and in the *animus mundi*, the soul of the world.

Although the heliocentric solar system revealed by Copernicus and Galileo destroyed the Earth-centred cosmos of Aristotle and the medieval age, it did not affect astrology's orderly planetary system. The discovery of Uranus in 1781, on the other hand, sundered the pleasing symmetry of the seven astrological 'planets'. What did this newcomer, invisible without a telescope, signify? To which sign, if any, did it belong? It took many years for the dwindling band of astrologers to decide. In 1825 the English painter and astrologer John Varley watched his house burn down with aplomb, since the conflagration proved the incendiary nature of Uranus, which was active in his horoscope that day.

Most astrologers were happy to observe the action of the new planets Uranus and Neptune (discovered definitively 1846), and later Pluto (discovered 1930), from a less personal perspective, noting especially the cultural and political events that accompanied their discovery. Uranus, being discovered in the era of the American and French revolutions, for example, was quickly linked to demands for liberty.

The very nature of a planet's discovery has also been reckoned to echo its astrological principle. That Uranus overturned the old cosmic order proves its iconoclastic character. That Neptune was first spotted in 1795 by a French astronomer who refused to believe his eyes echoes its elusive meaning. That Pluto stayed resolutely invisible to those who knew it was there was entirely in accord with its underworld associations. It is also claimed by some that planets only become visible when humanity is able to respond to the energies they signify. On this basis, a handful of astrologers maintain that the currently invisible planet of Vulcan, which allegedly orbits the Sun on an inside track from that of Mercury (which, together with the Sun's glare, shields it from sight), will become apparent once humanity 'evolves' sufficiently to use its energies.

Nor is Vulcan the only hypothetical planet in use by astrology. The so-called Hamburg School, established early in the twentieth century by German astrologer Alfred Witte, claimed that no less than eight trans-Neptunian planets were at work: namely, Cupido, Hades, Zeus, Cronos,

Apollon, Admetos, Vulkanus and Poseidon. Then there is Lilith, Planet Earth's 'Dark Moon', first heralded by the nineteenth-century English astrologer Sepharial and since then enthusiastically endorsed by some (mostly American) astrologers as 'a primal, impersonal, creative instinct'.

Another imagined planet is Transpluto, which has been posited since the 1930s, and which since 1972 has had its own emphemeris (table of positions). As its name suggests, Transpluto supposedly exists in the furthest reaches of the solar system. Astronomers suspect something is causing the wobble in Neptune's orbit, and may even have found it in the form of TL66, a tiny planetoid of a mere 330 miles diameter, which was discovered in 1998. Lying beyond the collection of thirty-odd 'ice dwarf' asteroids called the Kuiper Belt, TL66's highly eccentric orbit around the Sun takes some 800 years to complete. Among the aliases bandied about for Transpluto are Bacchus, the Roman god of wine, and Persephone, the goddess of spring abducted by Pluto and taken to the underworld. Californian astrologer Maya Del Mar was in no doubt what this distant speck signifies: 'Transpluto represents the energy of resurrection ... change on a vast level, real rebirth.'

For some, though by no means all, astrologers, the names acquired by the outer planets (and the asteroids) are major clues to their identities. No matter, then, that Clyde Tombaugh, discoverer of Pluto, rejected the more popular names of Minerva or Cronus because Pluto started with the initials of Percy Lowell, the astronomer whose work he was following.

Traditionalists do not like what they see as the fanciful interpretations placed on the outer planets, and snort indignantly that Pluto has appropriated Saturn's dark powers of murder and oppression. Saturn, the dread of medieval star-gazers is now 'your personal trainer', according to one gee-wiz astro-Californian. Modern astrology's adoption of the planetoid Chiron, which was discovered in 1977, and the four major asteroids of Ceres, Pallas Athene, Vesta and Juno, which were discovered in the early 1800s, is even more contemptible. Any old hunk or orbiting rock, it seems, is up for co-option. Yet, on the basis of 'As Above, So Below', astrology has little choice but to find a home, however humble, for the assorted bodies that never bothered Ptolemy.

THE SUN: EVERYBODY IS A STAR

The Sun and Moon have long been considered an astrological duo. Appearing almost equal in size from Planet Earth, the two so-called 'luminaries' or 'lights' made a heavenly pair: God and Goddess, King and Queen, Father and Mother, the Sun ruling by day, the Moon by night.

Ancient astrology did not hand the Sun the importance it commands in modern times, treating the Ascendant and Moon as of equal or more importance, but in modern times Sun signs rule, and the Sun is the first factor considered in a horoscope. Moderns often make the analogy that as the Sun is the centre of the solar system, the hub around which the rest of the planets turn, so it represents our basic identity, our sense of self, the central organising principle of our psyche.

The Sun's might and power have always been revered, and the list of solar myths is extensive. There are solar deities like Egypt's Ra and Greece's Helios and Apollo, while the Sun also represents the questing hero: Jason, Hercules, Parsival and others, many of them dragon-slayers and other light-bringers.

The Sun's astrological associations are legion. It represents royalty and all things regal. Proud and stately animals such as the lion – the Sun's own sign is Leo – and most things golden and yellow are assigned to the Sun's rulership, including gold itself. The Sun is also linked to the myth of the Divine Child, and to youth in general, these being filled with sunny vitality. As emblem of our inner self, it is linked to creativity and the arts, as well as to physical vigour.

Modern female astrologers are not especially happy about having all things bright and beautiful attirbuted to this male archetype, with the 'feminine' represented by the altogether trickier Moon, a body reliant on the Sun for its light. In recent times this has necessitated some readjustments, such as recognising the cultures in which the Sun is a female deity and the Moon male, and scripting in the queen alongside the usual 'kingly' virtues.

The Sun is not immune to other influences in a horoscope; poorly aspected, it is sometimes considered a mark of physical frailty or of a weak will. Even a well-positioned, well-aspected Sun can bring problems, indicating a rampant ego and an inclination to regal airs and graces that may not be merited. In general, though, the Sun is unambiguous; it shines for all.

THE MOON: LUNA TUNES

At a quarter of the size of our own dear terra – far bigger in proportion than the moon of any other planet – the Moon's gravitational influence on Earth is enormous, enough to lift the oceans by one ten-thousandth of their mass and help cause the tides. Since most Earth is water-based, including humans (we are for the most part liquid), it would be remarkable if we were not in some way held under lunar sway. Folklore has long maintained a connection between lunar cycles and weather patterns, plant life, menstruation, lunacy (a link reflected in the word itself) and the wanderings of ghouls, vampires and werewolves.

The astrological Moon comes draped in centuries of mythology. Babylon and Egypt gave the Moon to the male gods Sin and Thoth, respectively, but Greece made the Moon feminine, worshipping her variously as Artemis, Selene and Hecate, while for Rome she became Diana, who was, like Artemis, a huntress. The Moon goddess could be comely virgin, pregnant mother or ancient crone – 'the triple goddess', according to Robert Graves and modern pagans, though the boundaries of the various classical Moon goddesses are blurred.

In astrology the Moon is powerful and matriarchal, ruling gestation, motherhood and infancy. The Moon's link with water, the element of emotion, is obvious, and gives her sway over such creatures as the crab, the symbol for her sign, Cancer. The Moon represents instinct, intuition and feelings – the anima in the psyches of both men and women, as opposed to the conscious will represented by the Sun. The Moon in a birth chart also indicates the mother; poorly aspected it might suggest a cold or remote mother; if touched by the eccentric force of Uranus a kooky mum.

The Moon also represents digestion and eating habits; a birth-chart Moon in critical Virgo suggests a fussy eater, in sensual Taurus a comfort eater. It can be a symbol of the public, so that a prominent Moon in a birth chart would show someone who enjoys being in the limelight.

The monthly passage of the Moon around the zodiac means it

changes sign every two and a half days and is the busiest of all celestial bodies. Its continual, shifting contact with the other planets makes it influential in daily affairs and a key tool for prediction. New and full Moons mark the start and climax of phases in the life of Planet Earth; whatever's begun at the new Moon (when the Sun and Moon are in conjunction) reaches fruition at the full Moon (when the Moon is in opposition to the Sun).

The intersection of the Moon's orbit around Earth with the Sun is responsible for solar and lunar eclipses. In the first the Moon blocks out the Sun; in the second Earth casts a shadow across the Moon. Eclipses remain major signifiers in astrology, suggesting dramatic developments in the lives of individuals or nations.

The points where the Moon's orbit crosses the Sun's apparent path, the ecliptic, are known as the lunar nodes and are marked in astrological charts. Traditionally referred to as the Dragon's Head (the northern node) and the Dragon's tail (southern node), these eclipse points were important in ancient astrology, which saw them as points of good fortune (north node) and ill fortune (south node). Moderns tend to ignore them, though the influence of Indian astrology – which treats the nodes as the 'shadow planets' of Rahu and Ketu – has added karmic connotations to them, making the north node the point where a soul's destiny lies, and the south node its past lives.

MERCURY: TRICK OR TREAT

The symbolic meaning of the planet Mercury is easily grasped, not least because the Roman messenger of the gods still flits through the modern world – his name is borrowed by companies from the telecommunications giant to local garages, and his winged heels and helmet now deliver bouquets for Interflora. The metal Mercury, once known as quicksilver, is uniquely mobile, while the planet's elusiveness in the sky – Copernicus rued on his deathbed that he'd never managed to spot it – likewise chimes with its slippery character. Mercury, with an orbit of eighty-eight days, appears from Planet Earth to scurry alternately before and after the Sun, going backwards in the sky for three weeks every few months.

Mobility and message-carrying, however, are but two facets of the astrological Mercury, which represents the intellect in all its forms. Rational thought, ideas, learning, language, ingenuity and quick wits all fall under his aegis. The forerunners of the Roman Mercury – the Greek Hermes and the Egyptian Thoth – were likewise gods of learning and language.

Mercury's position in individual horoscopes is therefore held to show one's mental cast. Mercury in secretive Scorpio makes you a natural conspiracy theorist; Mercury in dreamy Pisces an imaginative but impractical thinker; Mercury in Capricorn down to earth; and so on.

The volatility of the planet is reflected in the signs Mercury rules: Gemini and Virgo. Gemini, an air sign, is quick with ideas; a natural, sparky communicator. Virgo, an earth sign, gives Mercury practical ends; messages to run, analyses to make, dictionaries to compile (as in the case of Samuel Johnson).

Mercury's affinity with language makes it the planet of the writer, and journalism in particular – quickfire dispatches from the front line are Mercurial specialities, as are all forms of wordplay and double entendre. Mercury/Hermes is not merely superficial, however; he can offer insight and illumination. He was credited as the originator of music – Hermes played a tortoiseshell lyre – and of medicine. One of his symbols in the caduceus, the winged wand around which twin snakes curl towards a Sun disc, which remains the sign of the doctor and healer. Mercury is also the traditional ruler of astrology – chart-gazers were wont to call themselves Mercurii – a role he has lost to Uranus.

Mercury is, however, reckoned an amoral force, whose intellectual powers come uncoloured by ethical considerations (which are the province of judgemental Jupiter). The myth of Hermes has him stealing Apollo's cattle, and he was long both the guardian of the roads and a highwayman, protector and thief. Naturally, his silver-tongued craftiness makes Mercury the communicator the planet of the con-man. 'Mercury can make you a genius, he can also make you a crook,' summed up poet and astrologer Louis MacNeice in 1963.

The wily, duplicitous and sometimes zany side of Mercury is best seen in his role as trickster, a figure which haunts many of the world's cultures, often in the form of animal characters like Brer Rabbit

(America) or Anansi the Spider (Afro-Caribbean). Contemporary Jungian astrologer Alice Howell links Mercury with the kiddy cartoon world of Bugs Bunny and Mickey Mouse – Mercury also governs childhood – as well as with more ancient tricksters like the Fool and the Harlequin. Most clowns are Mercurial, she argues, though 'the sad ones are Neptunian'.

In the twenty-first-century world, where Mercury's wings whirr ever faster across the planet on traceries of optic fibre and silicone chip, the messenger of the gods would seem to be running amok. Yet, for some commentators, the real function of Mercury has been lost; he has become another corporate drudge, a conveyor of 'information' rather than inspiration. As psychologist Thomas Moore puts it: 'This is an age unhappy with Mercurial insights. We want conclusions and facts, not openings into neverending mysteries.'

Mercury Retrograde

Three times a year the god of communications stops in his tracks and retreats through the zodiac for three weeks, signalling a period when telephone calls don't connect, appointments are broken, letters go astray, business deals go belly up and the bus to work doesn't arrive on time. In short, wing-heeled Mercury is hobbled.

Of course, Mercury no more moves backwards than does Planet Earth, its retreat being an illusion generated by the different speeds of our orbits. All planets, other than the Sun and Moon, appear to go backwards sometimes – indeed, planets from Jupiter outwards spend between 30 and 40 per cent of their time retrograde – but Mercury's sway over travel and discourse makes its retro spells (20 per cent of its time) particularly significant.

What retrograde planets signify is an unresolved issue. The ancients saw retrogression as a sinister portent. The moderns have tended to downplay the phenomenon, positing that retrograde planets in a birth chart are merely muted in the expression of their qualities, or dismissing them as an irrelevancy. Others argue that periods when several planets are retreating show that human affairs will proceed slowly. All astrologers agree, however, that a stationary planet – the day or so when it pauses before moving backwards or resuming its forward path – intensifies its action.

A retrograde Mercury always sends astrological alarm bells clanging. It's the time when Murphy's Law swings into action; everything that can go wrong will, as Mercury the trickster strews banana skins before us. This is not the time to forge boldly ahead, least of all if Mercury is occupying your Sun sign. Decisions made during retrograde Mercury will need remaking once the planet has turned around and returned to the point where you made them, at which time fresh information will emerge. Since Mercury spends three weeks retreating, this can mean anything up to a six-week stretch before affairs truly start moving forwards. Modern astrology therefore regards retrograde Mercury as an ideal time for revision, reorganisation and reassessment. If you must make that journey or sign that contract, double-check everything.

VENUS: ROMANCE PLUS FINANCE

Throughout astrology's history the soft, greenish star of the solar system's second planet has been the goddess of love and beauty; Ishtar to the Babylonians, Aphrodite to the Greeks, Venus to the Romans. Even twentieth-century astronomers were wont to romanticise Venus, imagining that her lustre concealed a fertile world of mists and tropical jungles, primal seas and prehistoric creatures. The space explorations of the 1960s and 1970s revealed the opposite: Venus is an arid, scorchingly hot planet whose cloud cover is principally sulphuric acid.

Thank heaven, then, for her symbolism. Astrologically, Venus remains a fecund, female force, the planet of love, sensuality, beauty and harmony. Venus is about relating, both to others and to the world around us, which is why those born under the Venusian signs of Taurus and Libra are said to have a strong aesthetic sense, while Librans are burdened with an almost pathological need for other people, forever seeking lovers and partners.

Glamorous and seductive, the feminine power of Venus is distinct from the nurturing, motherly power of the Moon. Botticelli's 'Birth of Venus' is the most celebrated representation of the goddess – and one painted under the influence of Marsilio Ficino, hermeticist and astrologer – but she shape-shifts with the zeitgeist: Monroe (a blighted Gemini) and Bardot (Libra lite) are both Venusian creatures. Madonna (a mix of calculating Virgo and show-off Leo) might be considered a Venus wannabe, though she arguably packs too much Martian muscle truly to embody the Venus principle.

Venus's love of beauty and pleasure shades easily into laziness and hedonism. This particular goddess, it sometimes seems, is happiest when draped in the latest fashions, lolling around on satin cushions and nibbling marshmallows; a kind of divine, mindless Spice Girl. She is certainly a sensualist, and prone to fantasies. At her most negative, Venus becomes the calculating minx, ruthless gold-digger and heartless harpie.

Her other guises include the artistic muse, wielding intelligence, refinement and aesthetics to transmute experience into art, music and dance. She is also a great strategist. Libra, one of her signs, concerns not only peace and harmony but open enmity, and Libra's famed diplomacy can be seen as guileful manoeuvring. In divinatory astrology Venus can also signify victory, whether in love or war, and is an omen of money. Such signifiers don't appeal to all, though Venus's good looks and love of luxury evidently can't endure amid penury; the planet does, after all, rule earthy Taurus.

Venus, like the Moon, hasn't been viewed in the same way by every culture. The Mayans embodied Venus as the warring Quetzalcoatl, most powerful of their gods, and avidly followed the planet's 584-day cycle from morning to evening star and back again.

In the birth chart a powerfully sited Venus can indicate artist, hedonist, glamour queen or all three. Venus's position is reckoned to reveal our amorous side. In a woman's chart the planet signifies what she projects romantically and sexually. Venus in Scorpio might show sexual intensity, in Virgo emotional shyness, in Pisces emotional impressionability, and so on. In a man's chart Venus is scrutinised for what kind of woman attracts him; Venus in Virgo shows a man drawn to self-contained women, in Leo a sucker for show-offs, while Venus in Taurus would presumably show a man prepared to embrace Venus's shopaholic, chocaholic tendencies; a long way from Botticelli's radiant goddess.

MARS: ATHLETE OR THUG?

Our nearest planetary neighbour, Mars excites modern Earth-dwellers. We are forever imagining life on the red planet: astronomer Percy Lowell, science-fiction scribes H.G. Wells, Edgar Rice Burroughs and Ray Bradbury, and space cadet David Bowie are all part of the 'Life on Mars' clan. Even space probes like Pathfinder haven't dispelled the idea that there's something there; the enigmatic 'face' peering up from the surface and 1997's flap over a Martian meteorite alleged to contain traces of micro-organisms are recent examples of an ongoing obsession.

For astrologers, Mars holds both life and death. Thanks to Rome's tramping legions and Holst's *Planets*, even astro-sceptics know that Mars is the bringer of war, red of hue and bloodthirsty of intent. Medieval star-gazers deemed Mars 'the lesser malefic' (with Saturn as 'major malefic') and alongside war ascribed accidents, crime, lechery and fever to its influence. Savage beasts like the wolf and the mastiff fell under Mars' aegis, as did stinging, spiky plants like the nettle and thorn. Mars' metal, iron, made prime weaponry.

It stood to reason that if you were born with Mars prominent in your horoscope you would at best become a general and at worst a violent criminal – occupations to which those born under Martian Aries or Scorpio were particularly disposed. Mars' negative connotations started early, with the Greeks, who characterised him as the unwanted and unloved only child of Zeus and Hera, and a lover of battle for its own sake. Despite his unattractiveness, he was still able to attract Aphrodite, who gave birth to their daughter, Harmony. Mars and Venus, in other words, are complementary principles: lust and love, sex and sensuality. Rome, in contrast to Greece, exalted Mars.

Modern astrology has tamed Mars, turning him from warlord into muscleman. Like his familiar phallic glyph of an arrow poking from a circle, the Roman god of war has become 'the masculine principle', the polar opposite to feminine Venus. Now characterised as simply mucho macho, the once fearsome deity finds himself patronised as an ugly party animal, whose fierce energy is best harnessed as a healthy sex drive or for physical activity. Martial qualities, in short, need to be reined in. Uncontrolled, aggressive rather than defensive militarism takes over. Mars has been linked to the myth of Hercules, a heroic figure but prone to killing and wounding the wrong person. Given the military's capacity for inane brutality and the ghastly mistakes concealed by such terms as 'friendly fire', this seems a useful corrective to Rome's adulatory view of the red planet.

Seeking to understand the military mind and its love of war, Jungian psychologist James Hillman suggests there's 'a Venusian experience within Mars'. He identifies the heightened sensations of battle and the ritualistic pomp of uniforms, weapons, polish, plumes and brass bands as part of Mars' energising appeal. Hillman also makes a distinction between martial bravery and the all-consuming meltdown of nuclear war, reckoning that 'Apocalypse is not part of the myths of Mars. Mars asks for battle, not for wipe-out, not even for victory.'

Mars' energetic, combative qualities are linked to sport. The statistical experiments of Michel Gauquelin found a striking correlation between the position of Mars in the birth charts of several hundred sports champions. Mars, it seems, is as much jock as warmonger.

The ancestral Mars has not been completely subdued, however. A prominent Mars in a birth chart still indicates a short-tempered hot-head – prone to what sports psychologists call 'the red mist' – and the planet still indicates accidents, disasters and conflagrations.

JUPITER: PUMP UP THE VOLUME

Size matters – Jupiter insists on it. The astrological meaning of the solar system's largest planet is evident from its vastness; Jupiter spells abundance, growth and expansion. There is certainly a lot of Jupiter – the humble blue sphere of Planet Earth is a mere 1,300th its size, even though Jupiter hasn't a square foot of solid ground to its credit, being a giant ball of tempestuous, poison gases. Its size makes Jupiter easily visible in the sky, which may be why the Greeks named the giant planet after Zeus, king of the gods, to be succeeded by Rome's celestial ruler, Jupiter, or Jove.

Unlike Zeus, Jupiter is not the supreme authority in the astrological pantheon, though both were thunder gods and lightning throwers, a side of the deity lost in astrological translation. Astrological Jupiter has several faces. He is the 'jovial' host with a table groaning with food and drink, the booming voice on the board of directors, the fish with the biggest ideas in the think tank. He's the back-slapping good sport on the pitch, the lucky punter at the racetrack, the name of the booming unit trust.

Paradoxically, the 'money planet' has high moral principles, meaning his subjects include the philosopher and the priest, people whose lofty view on life goes beyond materialism. Jupiter has high ideals and expects others to live up to them.

Jupiter's urge to expand can also be geographical; it rules both Sagittarius, the sign of the explorer, and Pisces, sign of the boundless oceans. This is the planet of long-distance travel: much to the delight of twentieth-century astrologers, the space probe dispatched to investigate Jupiter and its moons was named Voyager. Though only four of Jupiter's many moons (fifteen and counting) could conceivably have been visible to pre-telescope star-gazers, their number resonates with Zeus' siring of innumerable children and Jupiter's alleged creativity.

Where is the downside to all this Jovian cheer and well-being? There isn't much of one. Jupiter's main vices are greed, gluttony and excess. Obesity is one symptom of Jupiter's tendency to overload, along with religious fanaticism and an overinflated idea of one's importance. Financially, rampant inflation and devil-may-care spending are also manifestations of the money planet running wild.

Astrology looks to Saturn, planet of restriction, to curb and balance the inflationary effect of Jupiter. The two planets make a complementary couple – the arch 'benefic' and 'malefic' – and for financial astrologers the pair indicate boom and bust in economic terms. The Jupiter/Saturn conjunction every twenty years, when the two planets reach the same spot in the heavens, has long been reckoned an important pulse of human history.

For individuals, Jupiter's 11.83-year orbit around the Sun is linked to our personal good fortune, whether wealth, health or happiness. Find the planet's position in your birth chart, goes the notion, and there you'll find your greatest opportunity. A Jupiter return – the moment when the planet returns to its position at birth, roughly every twelve years – is especially auspicious, bringing lottery tickets, hearty laughter and an invitation to join the golf club. Just go easy on the calories.

SATURN: PRESSURE DROP

The bleak midwinter, with grey mists rolling over a barren, frostbitten land, is the perfect time to contemplate Saturn, slow-moving planet of time, limitation and old age, and ruler of the two winter signs of Capricorn and Aquarius. In complete contrast to its physical composition, which is mostly light gases, the astrological Saturn is dense and heavy, associated with such qualities as control, inhibition, seclusion, convention, austerity and sobriety – and that's its good side. Saturn also spells selfishness, cruelty, melancholia and death.

Little wonder that Saturn was 'the greater malefic' to the ancient and medieval worlds, for whom it was the most distant planet. Since the planet was so slow-moving, with an orbit of twenty-nine and a half years, it was naturally associated with old age. In its taciturn restriction Saturn is the complement and antithesis of its freewheeling, beneficent neighbour Jupiter; the pessimist to Jupiter's optimist.

For the Greeks, Saturn was Kronos, a despot who consumed his own children to avoid being overthrown by them. Fooled by his wife Rhea into swallowing a stone wrapped in swaddling clothes instead of his son, Kronos was eventually overthrown by that son – Zeus – who subsequently imprisoned his father.

As the slowest-moving planet, Kronos was the creator of time, whose place on the edge of the (then-known) cosmos made the planet simultaneously guardian and jailer. Just as time is needed to build, and eventually destroys all things, so Saturn is deemed both builder and destroyer. By analogy, in the human body Saturn governs the skeleton (our basic structure) and skin (our outer limit). Since the discovery of the outer planets, Saturn is also thought of as marking the limits of personal consciousness; the realm beyond belongs to the collective unconscious postulated by Jung. In the physical world Saturn's kingdom includes the earthy realms of mining, real estate and agriculture, the last being a slightly incongruous left-over from Saturn's early incarnation as a Roman fertility god. Saturn's other correspondences are similarly earthy and weighty: its metal is lead, its colours black and grey, its plants holly, hemlock and nightshade. In his novel *The Colossus of Maroussi*, Henry Miller offers a dread list of Saturnian associations: 'tripe, dead grey matter, loathsome diseases, test-tubes, laboratory specimens, catarrh, rheum, melancholy shades, sterility, anaemia'.

For traditional astrology, a badly aspected Saturn in a horoscope spelled war and pestilence (particularly if Mars was involved), and in an individual's horoscope indicated a cold, calculating individual. Joseph Stalin and Mao Zedong (both Capricorn) are commonly brandished as super-Saturnians: ruthless and relentless individuals who posed as benevolent patriarchs of the nations they transformed. Marlon Brando's personification of Mario Puzo's Godfather is imposingly Saturnine: stoical, casually ruthless when necessary, yet protective to those prepared to work for and honour him.

Modern astrology, for which no planet is all bad, has diluted the dread of Saturn, partly by psychologising its function. Saturn is there to teach us the need for discipline and responsibility; it shows our limits and the way to transcend them, while offering us self-mastery. Medieval star-gazers called Saturn 'the dark Sun' and for today's astro-Jungians the planet represents 'the shadow self', the dark side of our selves that we must confront and accept in order to evolve.

At the same time, many of Saturn's scariest duties have been handed to Pluto, Lord of the Underworld, making a duo whose interaction is particularly terrifying; a cue for a major war, perhaps. With its impartial exactitude, Saturn is also identified with the world of science.

Since Saturn has the ability to blight any situation, its place in any chart is a major issue, especially its slow but remorseless progress around the birth chart, a cycle to which we now turn.

Saturn and Other Returns

The conventional birthday greeting 'Many happy returns of the day!' holds a kernel of astrological wisdom. 'The day' has returned because the Sun is once more at the point in the zodiac where it was when an individual was born. It's planet Earth that has really returned, of course, after making another loop around the Sun, but from Earth it's the Sun that's done the moving.

Birthdays mark what astrology calls a 'Solar Return'. All planets eventually return to their starting place in the birth chart. The Moon arrives back there every month. Mercury and Venus take around a year,

Mars two years, Jupiter twelve years and Saturn around twenty-nine years. The outer planets are much slower; Uranus needs 84 years, Neptune 164 and Pluto 248. Obviously, no one except for one of those phenomenally long-lived Old Testament prophets sees a Neptune or Pluto return.

For astrology, all planetary returns carry meaning, though those of the fast-moving inner planets are reckoned too lightweight and transient to signify much beyond a buoyant mood or a special day. By contrast, the cycles of expansive Jupiter and restrictive Saturn indicate major life-stages and events, as does the cycle of freedom-loving Uranus.

The resonance of planetary cycles starts with infancy, a time when life is experienced through a lunar haze. Since the Moon returns each month to the place it was when we were born, we experience twelve or thirteen 'lunar returns' before we enjoy the first 'happy return' of the Sun on our first birthday. As we grow, other planetary principles exert themselves. Mars, representing independence, anger and physical activity, first arrives back at its birth position at the age of two, when children experience their separateness from their parents and the customary response to all parental discourse is a howled 'No'.

The stages of childhood can be further calibrated to the passage of the major planets around our horoscopes. Rose Elliot (astrologer as well as cookery writer) suggests, for example, that the expansive principle of Jupiter is felt at five or six, when the planet is halfway around its twelve-year cycle and starting school widens our horizons. Saturn's quarter and half cycles at seven and fourteen are key stages in physical and social maturation (the arrival of our second teeth at seven chimes particularly well with Saturn, ruler of bones). Entwining the cycles of the various planets, thirteen/fourteen emerges as the age when we are bombarded by significant planetary aspects. In particular Saturn's demands to 'grow up' clash with the promptings of Uranus, planet of rebellion, which is then a sixth of the way around its eighty-four-year cycle.

The most celebrated of all planetary cycles is the Saturn return, so celebrated that in the 1990s the phrase shifted from esoteric astro-jargon to mainstream soundbite; British drum 'n' bass maestro Goldie named his 1998 album *Saturnz Return*.

A Saturn return is simply a Saturn birthday, and first falls somewhere between the ages of twenty-eight and thirty, its precise timing being dependent on the planet's periodic retrograde motion. In any case its effect is reckoned to be spread over a year or more. Saturn's return marks a point of reckoning, a crucial stage in our personal evolution. Since Saturn is the planet of limitation, responsibility and earned success, its return represents a time when boundaries are broken and outworn structures abandoned. Astrologer Marc Robertson, in *Crisis Ages in Adult Life*, complains that 'Society doesn't prepare its children for the fact that real adulthood comes between 28 and 30 – comes with a seething inner crisis that causes careers to crumble, marriages to fail, and individuals to face the most serious identity crisis of their early years.' As Goldie puts it, 'When Saturn returns, there is no escape.'

The Saturn return is beloved of astrologers because it so rarely fails as a signifier. Astrology books and magazines come plentifully supplied with examples of celebrity Saturn returns and their traumas. That Princess Diana's decision to go public with her marital tribulations coincided with her Saturn return in 1991, at age thirty, was much remarked on. Elizabeth Taylor's romance with Richard Burton commenced with her Saturn return in 1962, and led to her divorce from Eddie Fisher two years later.

The Saturn return celebrated by Goldie on his dyslexically titled second album provides a detailed example. Better known for the abrasion and invention of his drum loops than his celestial knowledge, Goldie seems an unlikely astrological devotee, but seems to have picked up some tips from his ex-girlfriend Björk (a double Scorpio who named a particularly ferocious track 'Pluto'). For Goldie (born 19 September 1965), Saturn arrived back at the same degree it occupied at his birth (12 degrees Pisces) shortly before his thirtieth birthday in June 1994, when he signed to a major record label. Saturn retreated for a few months before returning to 12 degrees Pisces just after his first hit, 'Inner City Life', sealed his reputation as a musical innovator. Intriguingly, what followed was not only fame and fortune, but a period when he made his reconciliation with his parents, locating the father he had never known and writing a sixty-minute orchestral epic dedicated to his mother.

Saturn's second return arrives around the age of sixty, which again calls for a major revision of life goals; 'it marks our passage to being an elder,' remarks Erin Sullivan in *Saturn in Transit*. 'Depending on one's attitude to maturity, citizenship and maturity,' she writes, 'this can be a liberating time, or, like the first Saturn return, a time of ossification and psychological death.'

Few people experience a third Saturn birthday around age ninety, but astrologers use the half and quarter cycles of Saturn to tick off other significant ages – 7, 14, 21, 35 and so on – at which times Saturn is making stressful aspects to its original position and, therefore, bringing the life course into sharp and often uncomfortable focus.

Of the three slow-moving outer planets, only Uranus, whose orbit takes eighty-four years, can return to its starting place in our birth charts, though its quarter and half cycles are thought significant. Since the Uranian influence is considered disruptive, 21, 42 and 63 become unsettling ages. The traditional mid-life crisis in one's forties coincides with a nexus of planetary cycles; Jupiter's bountiful influence, which peaks every twelve years, is waning. Saturn is halfway through its second cycle, Uranus halfway through its course and Neptune, which takes 164 years to orbit the Sun, is a quarter of the way around. From an astrological perspective it's small wonder that this is the age when people question what life is all about.

URANUS: WHAT'S IN A NAME?

The lamest jokes about astrology always involve Uranus, whose unfortunate name is a gift to schoolboy punsters. It could, arguably, have been worse. When the English astronomer William Herschel discovered the planet in 1781 he wanted to call it Georgium Sidus in honour of his patron and king, George III. Instead, the new planet became known as both Herschel and Uranus, the idea being that since Saturn was the father of Jupiter, the next planet along should be Saturn's father, Ouranus, husband of the earth goddess Gaia. But what did it mean and how could it be accommodated into the time-honoured scheme?

Beyond considering the planet a malefic influence, nineteenth-century star-gazers had no real answers. The modern era, using the formula that a planet governs whatever cultural and scientific developments accompany its discovery, has made Uranus the planet of rebellion, technology and cultural innovation, associating its arrival with the American and French revolutions, the Industrial Revolution, the discovery of electricity and the advent of applied science. The planet has also been granted the uneasy co-rulership of Aquarius, along with Saturn.

On a personal level, Uranus' electrically charged energy is reckoned to denote individualists, outsiders, reformers and intellectual brilliance; people who break the political or cultural mould. Karl Marx, Franklin Roosevelt, Sigmund Freud, Percy and Mary Shelley, Marie Curie and Bob Dylan are among those cited as having powerful Uranian currents running through their horoscopes, indicating their sparky, revolutionary qualities.

Uranus is certainly an astronomical maverick, alone in rotating horizontally, with its north pole pointing towards the distant Sun for half its year and towards outer space for the other half. Day and night are therefore each forty-two years long – half of the time Uranus takes to orbit the Sun, and to complete its passage round the zodiac. The eighty-four-year Uranus cycle is reckoned potent by astrologers, who cite the ages twenty-one, forty-two and sixty-three as meaningful staging posts in life.

The planet's correspondences and rulerships include electricity, television (its glyph, derived from H for Herschel, looks uncannily like an early TV aerial), the metal uranium, radioactivity, aviation and rocketry, and all manner of electronic gadgetry. Since the colour spectrum had already been allocated by the time the outer planets were discovered, Uranus is linked to shimmering, electric hues, specifically the cobalt blue of an electrical flash. The planet has also been handed the rulership of astrology itself, much to the disgust of the traditionalists, who still hold Mercury to be the star-gazer's planet. The switch may be due to the similarity of Uranus' name with that of Urania, the Greek muse of astronomy and astrology. A powerfully aspected Uranus is flourished as a powerful totem by astrologers.

Since Uranus was discovered around the time of the declaration of human rights by the revolutionary administrations of America and France – the first time that these had been enshrined in any constitution – Uranus can be humanist in impulse, though its disruptive qualities evidently extend as easily to bloodshed. The planet has maintained its revolutionary associations over the years; it's given a pivotal role in the October Revolution of 1917 and in the upsurge of youthful rebellion and Third World independence movements of the 1960s, and is the prime planetary suspect in any rattling of the status quo.

Modern astrology's major problem with Uranus is that the Greek myths surrounding the planet's namesake are at complete odds with its symbolic meaning. Ouranos was not a revolutionary or a maverick but an old sky tyrant who was castrated and overthrown by his rebellious son Kronos (the Roman Saturn), who, as we have seen, is himself no barricade-storming romantic. Contemporary astrology may treat Uranus as the great liberator, but Greek myth insists the opposite.

The solution has come from Richard Tarnas, a Californian professor of philosophy and psychology, whose own electric insight was simple but illuminating: astronomy got the wrong name. For Tarnas, Uranus' flashing, humanist impulses plainly belong to the myth of Prometheus, the Titan who taught humanity the arts of navigation, astrology, mathematics and architecture and who, as a rebellious firebrand, stole fire from Mount Olympus to give to humanity.

For this outrage Zeus condemned Prometheus to perpetual torment, chaining him to a rock where his liver was daily torn out by an eagle, only for the organ to regrow each night. Prometheus was only relieved from everlasting agony when the Centaur Chiron agreed to take his place. Chiron, until then an immortal, then died.

In his book *Prometheus the Awakener* Tarnas eloquently links the Promethean myth to the qualities astrology ascribes to Uranus, analyses the Uranus contacts in the charts of eminent individuals, and links the breakthrough work of such people as Freud, Darwin and Newton to the planet's cycle. Serendipitously, Shelley wrote his epic call for freedom, *Prometheus Unbound,* under Uranus's influence.

It is clearly time for astrology to break at least one if its tenuous links with astronomy, and rename Uranus as the pun-free Prometheus, an act of liberation entirely in accord with the planet's supposed principles. This, after all, is meant to be the planet of astrology, and who wants to work for an old sky tyrant?

NEPTUNE: LOST IN THE MIST

Neptune is confusing. That, indeed, is a major part of its function, according to modern astrology. Discovered by Johan Galle on 23 September 1846, Neptune lies 2.8 billion miles from the Sun, which it takes 165 years to orbit.

Neptune's meaning baffled astrology for the best part of fifty years before it was decided that astronomy's name for the eighth planet was no accident, and that the Roman sea god must represent aqueous themes such as impressionability, dissolution and formlessness. The boundless oceans of time and space were his, along with the misty realms of mystic experience, and the hazy states induced by drugs and alcohol. Eventually Neptune was also given the watery sign of Pisces, where he joined Jupiter in uneasy co-rulership, with the trident for his planetary hieroglyph.

The Victorian era duly supplied a host of Neptunian associations. In the same year that Neptune was discovered ether was first used in surgery. It was the age of gas lighting and foggy streets, of alcohol binges at the local gin palace, of consumptive Romantic poets yearning for transcendence and downing copious quantities of laudanum to achieve it. The rise of spiritualism and the occult revival, with their promises to go 'beyond the veil', fit the picture nicely. While Neptune is the planet of 'going beyond' and returning to the 'oneness' of the divine, it is also the planet of delusion and escapism, of being lost in a druggy haze or being duped that a medium's table-rappings really are a message from the other side.

Nothing is more Neptunian in nature than the medium of photography, which arrived in 1839, just before Neptune's discovery, and which, appropriately enough, is derived from chemical processes. (The word 'photography' was coined by Sir John Herschel, son of the astronomer William. Sir John, cannily, was a Pisces.) Photography shows real life in a way that painting never could, but is still prone to trickery and ambivalence. Cinema belongs *par excellence* to Neptune; we're there, in the court of Cleopatra, on the American prairie or in outer space, yet in reality we're in a darkened auditorium. It's simultaneously the ultimate illusion, an act of mass escapism and a source of entrancing glamour. On a more mundane level Neptune's correspondences include the colour sea-green, the metal platinum and such narcotic plants as the poppy.

Like the other outer planets and the assorted flotsam of asteroids, Neptune has increasingly come into fashion. In 1996 Liz Greene devoted a weighty, 480-page tome to the planet, subtitled 'The Quest for Redemption'. Neptune, she suggests, represents the urge to lose one's identity by merging with 'the redeemer archetype', be it god, guru or film star. The collective delirium that attends religious figures and pop stars is thus classic Neptunian behaviour: 'a state of ecstatic dissolution which, for many Neptunians, is the only possible resolution of the weariness of mortal existence'.

Neptune's placement in a birth chart can indicate the mystic, the artist or the drunkard (or all three). In the endless analysis of Princess Diana's birth chart, Neptune increasingly became seen as the main signifier for her mixture of martyrdom, glamour, compassion and ability to become a focus for the collective; a suitably confusing bundle for the most baffling planet.

PLUTO: MIGHTY ATOM

Tiniest and most distant of the planets, Pluto is nevertheless granted awesome powers by modern astrology. Indeed, the reverence and dread in which the planet is held is not easy to understand. Pluto is so slow-moving, taking 248 years to trundle around the zodiac, that entire generations are born with it in a particular sign, which was one reason why, for many years, astrologers were wont to discard its significance in the individual birth chart. Its almost perfectly elliptical orbit, which takes it inside Neptune's at times, means the time Pluto spends in each sign varies considerably; it take thirty years to trek through Taurus while scuttling through Scorpio in a dozen.

Pluto has been trouble from the start. Percival Lowell, the astronomer who posited the existence of 'Planet X' to explain the irregularities in Neptune's orbit, died before locating his planetary grail. It was Clyde Tombaugh, a raw twenty-three-year-old self-taught astronomer hired by the Lowell Observatory, who found the planet in 1930, more by the sheer thoroughness of the search, it seems, than by astronomical inspiration.

But what had he found? Pluto's very status as a planet has recently been called into question. It seems to be more like a glorified asteroid, or a burned-out comet trapped in the Sun's orbit. In 1978 it was found that Pluto was in reality two tightly connected worlds, with the planet locked in dumb-bell-like orbit with its moon, Charon (named after the ferryman who rowed souls across the Styx to the underworld). Moreover, its minuteness – Pluto is roughly one five-hundredth the size of the Earth – could not possibly exert the necessary gravitational pull to affect Neptune.

Whatever Pluto is, astrologers were quick to adopt it. By 1932 the German astrologer Fritz Brunhübner had identified Pluto with demagoguery and the masses, and by 1934 had declared Pluto as 'the cosmic aspect originating the Third Reich'. A decade later, with the unleashing of atomic warfare on Hiroshima and Nagasaki, Pluto became identified with the atomic age. Both events fitted obligingly into the mythology of Hades. What was Nazism if not a subterranean hell of torment and horror raised to the surface? Within the invisible underworld of atomic physics, as we know, lurks the terrifying power of nuclear weapons, while the deadliest of the radioactive elements is plutonium.

Much of Pluto's mystique comes via its mythological associations. Pluto to the Romans, Hades to the Greeks, the god of the underworld presided over the subterranean kingdom of the dead, wore a helmet that rendered him invisible when he visited the mortal world, and was best known for his abduction and rape of Persephone. Pluto is therefore associated with the underworld, with the realms of the invisible, the infernal, the dead and the damned. The planet is both destroyer and transformer, a Western equivalent of Kali, the Indian goddess of destruction.

These days Pluto is more written about than ever. For the esoterically minded US astrologer Jeffrey Wolf Greene, for example, the planet is the supreme symbol of 'the soul's journey'.

Some astrologers grant Pluto a function only on a collective level; its influence, they say, shows up not in individuals but in generations. The 'me generation' of baby-boomers, for example, were born with Pluto in the show-off sign of Leo (1939–56). Pluto's infrequent change of sign is also thought to signify major shifts in world events; it's pointed out that

Pluto's stay in sex-oriented Scorpio (1983–95) coincided with the onset of the AIDS epidemic.

Encounters between Pluto and other planets are usually seen as difficult at best, and at worst apocalyptic. In the birth chart a strongly placed Pluto might signify a powerful personality, a psychopath, the immense wealth of a plutocrat, or a spy. Whatever the crime, when someone barks, 'Round up the usual suspects,' Pluto's at the top of the list.

CHIRON AND THE ASTEROIDS

The discovery of another planet in 1977 threw down a further challenge to astrology. Not much of a challenge, however, since Chiron isn't much of a planet – at a mere 125 miles across, according to David Levy (of Shoemaker–Levy Comet fame), it's uncertain whether Chiron is a trapped comet, an asteroid or a 'planetoid'. Whatever it is, Chiron lies between Saturn and Uranus, has an elliptical fifty-year orbit, and was discovered by Charles Kowal, an American astronomer who also has the discovery of two moons of Jupiter and some eighty supernovae to his credit. Chiron, however, remains Kowal's unwitting gift to astrology.

Since a planet governs human activities synchronous with its discovery, what might Chiron rule? Punk rock, perhaps? There were few other obvious contenders. Fortunately, the new arrival came with a mythological name – astrologers would surely not have granted Chiron the same respect if Kowal had called it Loretta, after his daughter, the name he awarded another of his asteroid finds.

Astro-mythologists had their lead. In Greek myth Chiron was the Centaur king, half-brother to Zeus and chief sage in the art of healing, yet even Chiron's mastery of herbs could not cure the wound he received from one of Hercules' poison arrows. The Centaur was condemned to incessant agony, relieved only when he gave up his immortality in return for Zeus breaking the shackles that bound Prometheus.

The figure of the wounded healer (common to several mythologies) and the themes of compassion, suffering and sacrifice became central to Chiron's astrological meaning. For astrologers like Melanie Reinhart,

Chiron indicates a propensity for healing, or susceptibility to illness, while they claim the planetoid's discovery coincided with the acceptance of such 'fringe' remedies as homeopathy and acupuncture.

Others are less preoccupied with Chiron's wounds. British astrologer Dennis Elwell thinks the planet's discovery presages a super-hero consciousness. In the 'Age of Chiron', declares Elwell grandly, 'the perfectibility of the human being' will become a major theme, with astrology used to that end.[2]

More contentious than Chiron's meaning is the role of the four major asteroids of Ceres, Pallas Athene, Juno and Vesta, which are increasingly a subject of commentary among US astrologers. The asteroid belt – a collection of several thousand whirling boulders and rocks – lies between Mars and Jupiter, at the point where a planet should be sited, according to the numerical formula posited by eighteenth-century astronomer Johann Titius and known as Bode's Law, after its champion Johann Bode. The obvious conclusion is that the asteroids are the relics of a planet destroyed in a cosmic cataclysm, or which, Atlantis-like, destroyed itself.

The discovery of the major asteroids at the dawn of the nineteenth century did not at first disturb astrology's equilibrium. For one thing the quartet of Ceres (discovered 1801), Pallas Athene, Juno and Vesta (discovered 1807) was considered too small to take seriously – Ceres, the largest, is a mere 450 miles across. In any case, no one found the time or inclination to compile the necessary ephemeris to show their positions.

The publication of the first asteroid ephemeris in the early 1970s changed things dramatically, not least because its author, US astrologer Eleanor Bach, linked the largest four asteroids to the rise of feminism. Modern women, declared Bach, were not just lovers (Venus) and mothers (Moon): 'What about our resourcefulness, productivity, ingenuity and efficiency, our nurturing concern for life, our capacity for dedication, our humanity?' she demanded.

Named after powerful classical deities – Pallas Athene was Zeus's daughter, the other three his sisters – the previously ignored planettes quickly found themselves adopted as feminism's cosmic champions. For astrologer Demetra George, author of *Asteroid Goddesses*, they represented the 're-emerging Feminine' and marked 'the birth pangs of

How different schools of astrology see the problematical planetoid Chiron. (Cartoon by Paul Newman, from his book *You're Not a Person – Just a Birth Chart*.)

the Aquarian Age'. Specifically, George links Ceres to 'parental bonding', Vesta to 'personal commitment', Juno to 'intimate relationships' and Pallas Athene to 'our ability to formulate and attain our goals'. The immortal goddesses have clearly undertaken a crash course in West Coast psycho-babble.

The tussle for the meaning and importance of the asteroids is in its early days. Interpreting the career of Hillary Clinton, US astrologer Michael Wolfstar notes the nearness of Pallas Athene in her chart to that of the Moon in the USA's national chart, 'making here the perfect vehicle to publicly portray this goddess archetype'. For Wolfstar, Pallas Athene 'does not represent or advocate a feminist agenda. She supports her husband, but also believes in her own strength as a political equal.'[3]

Why stop with this female asteroid quartet, though? Since some 5,000 asteroids have names, they too can be co-opted into the great cosmic scheme, despite being named after astronomers' pet dogs or variously honouring the likes of Van Gogh, Duke Ellington, Toyota and Swissair. When dissecting the marriage and divorce of the Prince and Princess of Wales, for example, astrologers used such asteroids as Diana (number 78), Charlois (1510), Camilla (107) and Elisabetha (412). Perhaps space rocks such as the asteroids Shane, Lee and Amy really are harbingers of the Aquarian age, which is, after all, meant to be about the common human.

CHARTS, ASCENDANTS, PREDICTION

Serious astrology starts with the chart. This is where the symbolic language of astrology is applied to describe people, events, a question or anything else for which one cares to cast a chart, be it a country, a corporation, a question or a cat.

An unnecessary mystique clings to charts, spun mainly from their being written in unfamiliar glyphs rather than words. The glyphs are simply shorthand, and are easily learned. Charts also come encrusted with sinister associations derived from medieval magicians, bearded prophets and Dennis Wheatley diabolists. Alternatively, the chart, with its degree marks, numbers and geometric configurations, is presented as cosmic mathematics, comprehensible only to the higher mind of the trained astrologer. This conceit has been pushed by astrology itself.

The reality is that an astrological chart is no more than a map of the solar system as seen from a particular point on Planet Earth. It is as sinister as a road atlas and no more difficult to decipher. The upper half of the chart's circle is the sky, its horizontal line the horizon, with east to the left, west to the right. If the chart is set for dawn, there is the Sun rising in the east; if for noon, the Sun is high in the sky; if for dusk, the Sun is setting in the west; if for midnight, the Sun is invisible below the Earth.

The other planets are shown in the same way. From the Earth, the planets appear to move in a counter-clockwise direction around the wheel of the zodiac, all but the Sun and Moon slipping backwards (retrograde) from time to time, thanks to the relative speed of their orbit against Planet Earth's. At the same time, because the Earth is turning, the wheel of sky and zodiac revolves in a clockwise direction, making one revolution per day.

The chart therefore notes the position of the planets in two distinct ways: where they are in relation to the stars of the zodiac – that is, which sign they occupy – and whether they are rising in the sky, setting towards the west or invisible below the Earth.

The sign rising on the eastern horizon – the Ascendant – and the sign directly overhead – the so-called Midheaven or MC (after the Latin, *medium coeli*) – are considered vital to a chart's meaning. Their respective horizontal and vertical axes make a cross that has at its centre the place for which the chart is cast. If it's a birth chart, that centre is the person being born, placed at the centre of the universe.

The four points of the cross are known as the angles. Opposite the Ascendant is the Descendant. Opposite the MC is the IC (*imum coieli*). Any planets found near these four points are regarded as particularly important.

The Ascendant, in particular, is reckoned critical, though exactly what it signifies is often hazily defined. Tradition holds that the Ascendant shows 'what is coming into being', the defining signature of a chart. Today's astrology holds out various meanings for the Ascendant in a birth chart; it is 'the viewpoint towards life' (Liz Greene 1977), our 'way of manipulating the environment' (Martin Seymour-

Smith 1981), 'the future' (Alexander Ruperti[4]), 'the person one feels oneself to be' (Ronald Harvey), or it 'shows us as we really are' (Derek and Julia Parker). The easiest thing initially is to think of the Ascendant as an outreach of the chart, its antenna.

The MC/IC axis is more straightforward, the MC showing how we aim to make our mark on the outside world, our ambitions, and the IC our roots, our past and our family.

The other major factors in charts are aspects and houses. Aspects are the angles between planets, and show whether the energies represented by the planets are in harmony or conflict. Houses divide the wheel of the chart into twelve pizza-style segments, which are numbered from the Ascendant in a counter-clockwise direction. The houses represent the earthly focus of planetary energy. A planet in the sixth house, for example, would concern itself with matters relating to work, or health, while in the ninth house with travel or religion.

The classic formula for the three main elements of the chart thus goes like this: the planets represent different 'energies', the signs describe how those energies express themselves, and the houses show where they are expressing themselves. For example, a person with Venus, planet of romance, in the royal sign of Leo, and the ninth house of exploration, would theoretically incline to extrovert relationships that offer challenging experiences. One result: a trophy boyfriend who drives the subject overland to Bangkok. Alternative result: a girlfriend with a blonde mane who introduces the subject to Tibetan Buddhism. The symbolism is adaptable.

With ten planets, twelve signs, twelve houses and four angles in play, not to mention the multiple, highly ambiguous possibilities of aspects between planets, the chart can swiftly become a complex and baffling affair. Add in the mysterious lunar nodes (eclipse points), asteroids, minor planets and other considerations such as house cusps (the starting points of the houses) and mid-points (the halfway spot between planets), and you have a cryptogram requiring endless study to decipher.

It is beyond the scope of this book to provide a full exposition of interpreting a chart. In any case there are entire volumes given over to doing so and to each of the particular techniques involved. Numerous textbooks detail the meaning of every planetary position by sign, by

Sylvia Plath
27 October 1932
14.10 (EST), Boston, Massachusetts, 42N30, 71W37
Koch Houses, True Node

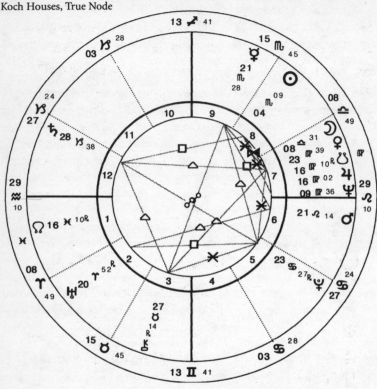

Source: Lois Rodden, Profiles of Women, data from Plath's mother

A typical representation of a birth chart, in this case that of the poet Sylvia Plath. Glyphs are used as shorthand for planets and signs (see illustration opposite), and the numbers show the degrees of the zodiac at which they are placed. For clarity's sake, the four major asteroids, which are increasingly used in charts, are omitted here.

A chart is a map of the heavens as seen from a particular place on the earth. The outer circle of the chart shows the zodiac. The visible sky is the upper half of the circle. The horizontal axis represents the horizon. The all-important Ascendant – the degree of the zodiac rising over the eastern horizon – is shown on the left-hand side of

SIGNS

♈	Aries	♎	Libra
♉	Taurus	♏	Scorpio
♊	Gemini	♐	Sagittarius
♋	Cancer	♑	Capricorn
♌	Leo	♒	Aquarius
♍	Virgo	♓	Pisces

ASPECTS

♂	Conjunctions
♂	Oppositions
△	Trines
□	Squares
⊻	Semi Sextiles
✳	Sextiles

PLANETS

☉	Sun	☽	Moon	☿	Mercury
♀	Venus	♂	Mars	♃	Jupiter
♄	Saturn	♅	Uranus	♆	Neptune
♇	Pluto	☊	North Node	☋	South Node
⚷	Chiron	⚴	Pallas	⚵	Juno
⚳	Ceres	⚶	Vesta		

(continued)
the chart. Plath's Ascendant is 29 degrees of Aquarius; if she had been born a few minutes later it would have become Pisces (which was the preference of her husband Ted Hughes). The Midheaven – the point of the sky directly above, and another important point in a chart – is shown by the vertical axis.

The twelve numbered segments of the chart are the 'Houses', which indicate different areas of life, whereas the planets show 'energies' and the signs how those energies are expressed.

house and by aspect. These so-called 'cookbooks' serve an admirable reference purpose, yet few offer any useful shortcuts to decoding a chart. Still fewer textbooks tell you how astrologers approach a chart in reality, rather than in the astrological theory that they preach.

Initially, at least, chart analysis tends to be abrupt, concentrating on the main features. The three totem pieces of information used by astrologers are the positions of the Sun, Moon and Ascendant. This trio often suffices for a thumbnail description of the chart. Prominent planets come next. Any planets on the angles are automatically potent. Planets that have precise or several aspects to others, especially the Sun and Moon, are also rendered important. Planets that are in the sign they rule become more powerful. The 'chart ruler' – the planet that rules the Ascending sign – is traditionally the subject of special scrutiny. The overall pattern of the chart is considered according to whether any one sign or set of signs (by element or quality) is accentuated. Some astrologers also classify charts according to whether planets are bunched or spread around the chart.

Aspects highlight significant relationships between planets, and are measured by geometrical angle. If two planets are in aspect, the energies they represent interact and spark off each other. Some aspects are considered easy, others difficult. The five main aspects are:

- Conjunction. This shows planets a few degrees apart and represents a fusion of energies.
- Opposition. The planets are opposite each other, 180 degrees apart, and their energies are clashing.
- Trine. The planets are 120 degrees apart, and are relating harmoniously, amplifying each other.
- Square. The planets are 90 degrees apart and in tension.
- Sextile. The planets are 60 degrees apart and assisting each other.

There are several other aspects in use, at 30, 45, 72 and 150 degrees, which are allowed more or less importance according to individual astrologers. Aspects do not need to be exact – planets 87 or 93 degrees apart are still considered square to each other – but cannot deviate by more than a few degrees. The degree of slack (the 'orb') allowed varies between astrologers and between planets. Aspects to the Moon, for example, are usually allowed a wider 'orb' than are those of other planets.

Disputes over astrological techniques are widespread and often bitterly contested. Few things in astrology cause as much argument as the meaning of the houses and how their division is calculated. In traditional astrology the houses are enormously important, whereas some moderns dispense with them altogether. There are several systems in use to calculate how much of the zodiac each house is allotted; dividing the zodiac equally produces houses with 30 degrees each, but the most commonly used systems, such as that formulated by the seventeenth-century Italian astrologer Placidus, result in houses of unequal size. Since the house 'cusp' – its starting point – is important in some predictive techniques, different systems of house division can produce different predictions.

The most common meanings ascribed to the houses coincide loosely with the meanings of the twelve signs and are:

- First House – The personality, well-being.
- Second House – Money and possessions.
- Third House – Mind, environment, siblings.
- Fourth House – Home, family, parents, the past.
- Fifth House – Creativity, children, pleasure.
- Sixth House – Work and health.
- Seventh House – Partnerships, marriage, open enemies.
- Eighth House – Sex, death, occultism, other people's money.
- Ninth House – Travel, education, religion, the law.
- Tenth House – Career, social status.
- Eleventh House – Society, politics, networking.
- Twelfth House – Seclusion, secrets, mysticism.

A chart suggests to an astrologer the nature of the issue under investigation, most commonly the character of an individual, which in the twentieth century became increasingly expressed in psychological terms. This is 'natal' astrology. A chart can also be 'elected', to provide an ideal time for starting an enterprise or undertaking a journey. An astrologer looking for an auspicious moment to open a bookshop, for example, would try to ensure that Mercury, which rules writing and books, was well placed, perhaps at the top of the chart.

A chart cast to divine the answer to a question – 'horary' astrology – has its own set of rules to produce an answer. For example, the Roman astrologer Dorotheus, writing in the first century AD, devotes considerable attention to uncovering thieves and retrieving lost property by horary methods; if the Moon was in Gemini, declared Dorotheus, then what was stolen was money, while the sign of Capricorn would signify a thief who was male and thin-legged 'with a face that resembles a goat's in the dark'.

Using horary methods to predict the winner of a contest – a pitched battle, a horse race, a football match – has always seduced astrologers. The methods employed by the thirteenth-century Italian astrologer Guido Bonatti to determine victory in castle besiegment have been used by the Australian astrologer Bernadette Brady to ascertain the outcome of cricket Test matches, and even the studiously scientific twentieth-century English astrologer John Addey had a fondness for gambling on horse races using astrological methods.

The most common methods used in predictive astrology, however, are 'transits' and 'progressions'. Transits are the current positions of the planets in relation to a chart. If, for example, Jupiter is moving across ('transiting') the Sun in a person's birth chart, good fortune is expected. If Saturn is opposite someone's Sun, the prediction is overwork, boredom and loneliness. Uranus transits signal unexpected events, Neptune transits confusion and Pluto transits the destruction of old patterns.

New Moons falling on planets in a chart are very important, suggesting a major new cycle (Tony Blair had just such a new Moon the week after he became British Prime Minister). Eclipses, either solar or lunar, falling on planets in a chart suggest decisive breaks with the past.

'Progressions' are similar to transits, but use symbolic, rather than real, planetary positions. Common methods include advancing the planets by 1 degree for every year of someone's life, or advancing planets by one day's movement for a year of life. There are several other methods – solar arc, tertiary, primary directions.

Most astrology books are about techniques, and some can be daunting. While a textbook or two is indispensable, it is not difficult to understand how astrologers approach charts in practice from the articles in magazines and journals, which often feature contemporary issues and people, reflect the wide variety of approaches in use and the occasionally acrimonious disputes between astrologers.

3

CONJURING GRAVITY

GALILEO, NEWTON AND THE HIDDEN
HISTORY OF ASTROLOGY

✳

'The pursuit of reason creates monsters.'

Goya

On the last day of 1995 Professor Richard Dawkins, celebrated zoologist and popular science writer, launched a blistering tirade against astrology in the pages of the English newspaper the *Independent on Sunday*. The attack, subsequently recycled as part of Dawkins's 1998 book *Unweaving the Rainbow*, was notable for its length and ferocity. Astrology, declared Dawkins, was not just a wrong-headed anachronism for whose claims there was not a smidgen of evidence, but a wicked fraud, 'an aesthetic affront' whose 'pre-Copernican dabblings demean and cheapen astronomy'. Astrologers, whom Dawkins 'detests', deserve more than just the ire of their opponents – they should be prosecuted for fraud. 'We should learn to see the debauching of science for profit as a crime,' rasped Dawkins, transformed from beacon of reason to chief of Thought Police.

Dawkins's thunderous broadside typifies astrology's problems with – and for – science, or at least that part of it that can be bothered to register more than indifference to what it sees as an irrelevant relic from the past. In the last quarter of the twentieth century, the conflict between believers and sceptics, familiar from the ancient world, burst out with increasing rancour. In 1975, 186 eminent scientists, including nineteen Nobel Prize-winners, put their names to the document 'Objections to Astrology', which was masterminded by the Dutch astronomer Bart Bok and published in the *Humanist* magazine. The document had several points to make: that astrology is an empty survival from ancient times with 'no scientific foundation for its tenets'; it is a system 'based on magic and superstition' followed by 'people who like to believe in a destiny predetermined by astral forces beyond their control'; moreover, newspapers and book publishers who disseminate astrology were contributing 'to the growth of irrationalism and obscurantism' perpetuated by 'astrological charlatans'.

The attack was wide of the mark; most Western astrologers believe not in 'predetermined destiny' but in freewill and self-determination, have little interest in magic and are no more guilty of charlatanism than car salesmen or corporate research scientists. Yet, on one level, the hostility is understandable. The curve of scientific progress over the last 200 years is so breathtakingly steep, its accomplishments so impressive, that the history of human thought prior to the Enlightenment is seen as a mere prelude to the main event. For the rationalists, the advent of modern medicine, our understanding of the physical make-up of the universe, and the ongoing breakthroughs of technology validate science, which has swept away millennia of ignorance and superstition and liberated humanity.

So goes the story anyway, for scientism can only carry off its self-congratulatory conceits by denial of science's own past. In particular modern astronomy's contempt for its mystically minded ancestor has required an acrobatic rewrite of history, in which the ideas of its pioneers have been bowdlerised and suppressed. Until the late seventeenth century, of course, almost all astronomers were also astrologers – the demand for accurate data on planetary movements for astrological charts spurred on much astronomical endeavour – but this fact is invariably glossed over, or explained away as an unfortunate necessity. The astronomical pioneers Tycho Brahe and Johannes Kepler, both of whom were keen astrologers, have their interests airbrushed from view, or are presented as unwilling prisoners of a superstitious past, forced to turn their hands to horoscopes to appease their patron, Austria's Rudolf II.

In reality, Kepler was obsessed with metaphysics, and believed the universe was organised according to the principles of Pythagorean mathematics. Kepler's first book, *The Mysterious Cosmos*, linked the orbits of the five planets with the five perfect geometric solids identified by Plato, which he likened to the musical scale in the manner of Pythagoras' 'Music of the Spheres'. A later book, *The Harmony of the World*, extended his ideas on the links between number, music, astrology and hermetism. Kepler wrote several treatises on astrology, which he wished to reform, revealing an approach strikingly akin to that of modern astrologers, disliking predictions and favouring character analysis and the astrology of families, which, he declared, often shared similar horoscopes. He even introduced a new planetary aspect into astrology (the 72-degree 'quintile') and famously declared, in his pamphlet *Third Party Intervening*, that astrology's opponents 'shouldn't throw out the baby with the bathwater'. This side of Kepler goes unremarked on in the astronomical history books. Even Galileo, borne aloft as the first man of modern astronomy for his championing of the heliocentric universe against the Vatican's zealotry, had a lifelong interest in astrology, repeatedly casting his own chart to ascertain his correct birth time ('rectification') by comparing the events of life to his chart. Galileo also drew up horoscopes for various wealthy clients, including the Grand Duke of Tuscany, and for his daughters, whose stars were found fit only for their lifelong incarceration in a nunnery.

Galileo, Brahe, Kepler and others like them were thus students not only of planetary movements and the structure of the heavens, but of the human significance of what they observed. Modern astronomy has rent the consciousness of its founders in two, accommodating what meets with its approval and discarding the rest as misguided superstition, which is rather like declaring that Michelangelo was a great painter, but that his interest in religion was misplaced.

Such furtive dishonesty runs through much of science's account of its history, and extends even to the life of its most potent figurehead, Sir Isaac Newton, mention of whose genius brings even Richard Dawkins to supplicating knee. 'One of the greatest minds that ever lived,' declaims modern astrology's most outspoken opponent of his hero.

Newton was undoubtedly a mathematical and scientific genius, but he was also a closet alchemist, deeply ensconced in what today's scientific establishment considers occult gobbledygook. Alchemy was in some respects the precursor of modern chemistry, its declared aim being to find 'the philosopher's stone' which allowed the transmutation of base metals into gold. Yet alchemy was also an esoteric spiritual practice, aimed at the transmutation of the soul into unsullied spirit.

Like the mad relation locked in the east wing of the family mansion, Newton's fascination with alchemy was for many years carefully obfuscated by his biographers, or presented as the great rationalist's quirky hobby. For a while Newton himself led almost a double life: the public rationalist and the private mystic. It was not until the economist John Maynard Keynes acquired a collection of Newton's papers at auction in 1936 that the truth started to emerge. After reading the papers, Keynes declared that far from being the first rationalist, Newton was 'the last of the magicians'. It emerged that Sir Isaac was obsessed with alchemy; his outpourings on the subject extend to over a million words and greatly outstrip his more conventional scientific writings. What's more, Newton spent many of his later years trying to decipher biblical chronology using the dimensions of the Temple of Solomon as his key, a task worthy of any Bible-decoding best-seller of the 1990s.

The conclusion of biographer Michael White in his recent *Isaac Newton: The Last Sorcerer* – that 'the influence of Newton's researches in alchemy was the key to his world-changing discoveries in science' – should discomfort both the champions of scientism and those whose image of Newton remains the inflexible arch-rationalist depicted in William Blake's celebrated painting: the Newton 'whose terrors hang like iron scourges over Albion'.

Since alchemy, like astrology, is based on the hermetic theory of correspondences and antipathies – a concept that seems to have inspired Newton's idea of gravity as a mysterious force acting at a distance – it's natural to wonder whether Newton the astronomical genius was an astrologer on the side; as much has long been alleged by astrological apocryphy. There is a much-cited story that Newton met a disparaging remark about his astrological interests from his colleague Edmond Halley with the response, 'I, sir, have studied the subject. You have not.' Alas, this splendid one-liner seems to have no basis in fact. On the contrary, Newton probably disapproved of astrology; as a devout follower of the Church of England he would have considered it degenerate and idolatrous.

Newton was not the only scientific pioneer seduced by the forbidden fruit of esoteric thought. Robert Boyle, one of the founding fathers of modern chemistry and a founder of the Royal Society in 1660, was almost as fascinated by alchemy as was Newton, and wrote two treatises on the 'Hidden Qualities' and 'Effluviums' of air, in which he admitted zodiacal influences worthy of consideration – otherwise 'we know planets only to know them', he concluded with an insight commendable to today's sceptics. Such was the opprobrium attached to astrology that Boyle forbad his speculations be made public before his death.

Sir Christopher Wren, greatest of all English architects and another Royal Society founder, was another who believed that astrology should be scientifically reformed rather than abandoned.

Nevertheless, Newtonian science quickly relegated astrology to the status of laughing stock. In England the hostility shown by polite society in general, and science in particular, derived from more than the dictates of reason. Astrology was heavily tainted by its identification with the radicals, revolutionaries and religious freethinkers who had fought against the crown during the English Civil War of 1642–9.

In the tumultuous years leading up to the Civil War and continuing until the restoration of the monarchy in 1660, the air was full of prophecy and predictions. The collapse of censorship in 1641 had resulted in an unprecedented upsurge of newspapers, polemical pamphlets and predictive almanacs, in which politics, religion and skywatching combined intoxicatingly. Most championed the republican cause, and proved astonishingly popular, selling in numbers exceeded only by the Bible itself. It was a time of millennial fever, when anticipation of the establishment of God's kingdom on Earth was entangled with the more realisable need to do away with earthly kings like Charles I, a pompous ruler even by the standards of the English monarchy, and one who duly lost his head.

High among Parliament's propagandists was the astrologer William Lilly, self-styled 'England's Junior Merlin', whose almanac was selling 30,000 copies a year by the end of the 1640s; no small figure in a country of perhaps 3 million, most of whom were illiterate. Lilly was a remarkable figure, whose fame was widespread and whose friends included the herbalist Nicholas Culpeper and Gerard Winstanley, leader of the revolutionary group the Diggers. Lilly's astrology continues to inspire cultish devotion even today. Aside from his almanac, in 1647 Lilly wrote the first English astrology book, *Christian*

Astrology, so-called as a disclaimer against those for whom casting horoscopes was akin to witchcraft. At his Corner House on the Strand Lilly was consulted by gentry and commoners alike, dispensing astrological advice on a sliding scale of charges according to the social class of his clientele. He became famous for the accuracy of his predictions, among them the outcome of several Civil War battles. His abilities landed him in trouble, and jail, on more than one occasion. After the outbreak of the Great Plague and the Great Fire of London in, respectively, 1665 and 1666, Lilly was hauled before a Parliamentary committee who suspected him of having started the conflagration to fulfil a prophecy he had made back in 1651; he was exonerated.[1]

There were astrologers on the royalist side, notably Lilly's rival John Gadbury, but the art of prophecy was identified principally with the republican cause, and with the radical religious sects that had proliferated during the heady years of Civil War and Commonwealth: the Quakers, Ranters, Levellers, Muggletonians, Familists, Rosicrucians and Diggers. For the dourer Puritans of Cromwell's England, some of these groups were heretical, their theology tainted by hermetic notions derived from ancients like Paracelsus, or from the Protestant mystic Jakob Boehme, 'the astrologer's philosopher'.

With their wild speculations about the meaning of comets and eclipses, and their deliberations on the nativities of royalty, excitable republican mystics had stoked the fires of millennial expectation throughout the interregnum. The solar eclipse of 29 March 1652 was so widely expected to herald disaster that, according to a contemporary report, 'hardly any would work, none would stir out their houses'.[2]

The restoration of the monarchy in 1660 required the discrediting and suppression of the religious and cultural ideas upon which social upheaval had fed. Under the new regime, astrologers found themselves censored, and they, their printers and publishers all became liable to imprisonment; the astrologer Peter Heydon was twice imprisoned, in 1663 and 1667, for the impertinence of calculating the king's horoscope. The printers of 1662's *Book of Wonders*, with its catalogue of imminent and apocalyptic celestial events, were likewise jailed, and their presses destroyed.

So began the self-appointed Age of Enlightenment. The founding of the Royal Society in the year of the restoration helped ensure that politics, philosophy, religion and art all partook of the same ideas of sober order and dutiful rank. In Christianity High Anglicanism was restored as the state religion and the mystical Protestant sects discouraged. In literature the tempestuous free verse of Milton gave way to the measured Augustan couplets of Dryden and Pope. In science materialist empiricism reigned, the universe conceived as an intricate pattern of tiny building blocks. The new science did not at first remove divine purpose from the universe; the religious Newton, like many of his fellows and successors, believed that science was simply uncovering God's laws. But God Himself became a kind of scientist – 'the Great Architect', as the Freemasons dubbed Him – with the solar system presented as a gigantic clock wound by His hand. As Richard Tarnas (1991) put it, 'The world was now neutral, opaque, and material, and therefore no dialogue with nature was possible – whether through magic, mysticism, or divinely certified authority.'

Certainly not through astrology, which after nearly two millennia finally became an irrelevance to philosophers, scientists and astronomers. Such was its disappearance in Europe that, according to historian James Holden, 'By 1800, outside of England, it would have been difficult to find anyone who understood astrology enough to be able to cast a horoscope and interpret it.' That the situation was different in Britain was due mainly to the ongoing tradition of almanacs, which continued to be popular among the lower classes, particularly in the countryside. The rise of the most famous almanac, Old Moore's, was phenomenal, its circulation rising from 25,000 in 1738 to a peak of 560,000 in 1839. The almanacs typically mixed a calendar packed with agricultural fairs, tide times, weather forecasts, royal birthdays and historical trivia with phases and signs of the Moon, eclipses, the Sun's passage through the zodiac, and predictions of politics, wars, horse races, floods and other 'wisdom gossip'd from the stars', as the peasant poet John Clare put it in 1825.

Another survival from the seventeenth century, and likewise frowned on by the educated and religious establishment, was the tradition of 'the cunning man' or 'cunning woman': a local dispensing herbal cures, folk remedies and astrological advice, much in the manner of Culpeper, whose *Herbal* remains in use today.

Yet folk wisdom was no match for the march of science. The ongoing discoveries of astronomy throughout the eighteenth and nineteenth centuries – the new planets of Uranus and Neptune, asteroids, galaxies, nebulae and a seemingly infinite number of stars – accorded to Newton's universal laws, but did not require the divine intent discerned by him. When the French astronomer Laplace published his *Celestial Mechanics* in 1799, Napoleon upbraided him for not mentioning the Creator. 'Sir,' replied Laplace, 'I had no need for any such hypothesis.'

The ancient and medieval conception of the planets as direct causes of earthly action was effectively destroyed by post-Copernican astronomy. Once Galileo's telescope had shown the sheer distances involved in space, and once Newton had posited gravity as the force that kept the solar system in orderly motion, astrology's ideas of direct influence from the planets and stars started to wane.

The hammer blow that split apart science and theology, seemingly irrevocably, came not from above, however, but from below, with the publication of Darwin's *On the Origin of Species* in 1859. Backed up by the fledgling sciences of geology and archaeology, Darwin's thesis on natural selection trashed the biblical history of the world; the Earth's history was shown to be measurable in millions of years rather than the six thousand upheld by clerical orthodoxy. More profoundly, Darwin's hypothesis removed humanity from the pinnacle of a divinely ordered creation, suggesting instead that our existence is the result of an ultimately purposeless struggle for survival via random mutation and metamorphosis. God, it seemed, was neither in heaven nor on Earth.

The impact of Darwinism on the educated and semi-educated public was far greater than the discoveries of astronomy. Without a telescope, the sky looked the same as ever (not that much of it was visible to the inhabitants of the booming industrial cities), whereas the notion that humanity is descended from apes, as Darwin's primary message became conceived, caused outrage and confusion, as well as the observation of more than one Victorian cartoonist that Darwin's looks were remarkably simian.

Darwin himself was outwardly apologetic about the implications of his theory for conventional religion. One reason why he kept *On the Origin of Species* under wraps for years was his reluctance to upset his deeply religious wife. Darwin was nevertheless preoccupied with debunking the psychics and spiritualists who were increasingly a feature of Victorian society. Similarly intent were his disciples, the biologist Thomas Huxley (self-styled 'Darwin's Bulldog'), Edwin Lankester (later to become director of the Natural History Museum, where he was hoaxed by the 'Missing Link') and Darwin's son George. Such was their preoccupation that Huxley, Lankester and Darwin Junior took to attending seances in order to disprove the claims of mediums, and succeeded in bringing the celebrity American medium Henry Slade to trial in 1876. When Slade was found guilty of fraud and sentenced to three months' hard labour, Darwin reacted with delight and contributed to the prosecution's costs. Slade was released on appeal but became an alcoholic on his return to New York.

Huxley's modern counterpart Richard Dawkins is similarly incensed by any assertion of spirituality that deviates from fundamentalist atheism. The offence of astrology for today's science is not just to defy the Newtonian universe but to describe and explain human personality in terms other than genetics, to use the symbolic language that spoke naturally to Kepler and even Newton to try to understand the psyche ('soul') for which Darwin found no place.

The shape astrology assumed from the late nineteenth century onwards was in part a defiance of Darwinism. It insisted on the reality of 'spirit' or 'soul', for whose existence biology and physics could find no proof and no need. Yet astrology also came to imitate Darwin, reasoning that if the world of matter could evolve, so could the world of spirit. 'Spiritual evolution', a concept unknown to the likes of Claudius Ptolemy, Thomas Aquinas, Marsilio Ficino and William Lilly, is now a commonplace of modern astrology, as of New Age thought in general. Its origin, like the idea of the 'New Age' itself, lies with the founder of theosophy, Madame Blavatsky, who despite a distinct lack of interest in astrology, nevertheless became one of its most influential figures.

4

RE-INVENTING ASTROLOGY

ALAN LEO, C.G. JUNG AND PLANETARY PSYCHOLOGY

*

Modern astrology came into the world in July 1895 in the shape of a magazine of the same name. *Modern Astrology* – the title signalled a deliberate break with the past – was published and edited by Alan Leo, the alias of William Allen, a travelling sweet salesman from London whose devotion to the stars extended to changing his name by deed poll to accord with his Sun sign.

Modern Astrology was not Leo's first venture into publishing. Five years previously he had started *The Astrologer's Magazine* in partnership with another astrologer, F.W. Lacey, but while the magazine had been a success of sorts, it had made little money, failing to attract the kind of mass readership still enjoyed by *Old Moore's Almanac* and its more upmarket and astrologically inclined rivals, *Raphael's Prohetic Almanac* and *Zadkiel's Almanac*.

Leo's dream was that his new magazine would popularise and modernise 'the ancient art', and although *Modern Astrology* never rivalled the almanacs' readership, Leo himself was to prove enormously successful in both respects. Born a Victorian (in 1860), Leo remains, for better or worse, the most influential astrologer of the modern era. Whenever someone asks, 'What's your sign?', sends off for a mail-order horoscope or shops for a pocket manual to the zodiac, they are paying unwitting tribute to Leo. Indirectly, they are also paying homage to the abiding passion in his life, theosophy, in whose terms much of his astrology came to be couched.

Today, theosophy is consigned to the footnotes of history, but in the

Leo's pride: together with his many books and pocket guides, Alan Leo's magazine helped re-popularise astrology in the Edwardian era. A century on, Leo, real name William Allen, remains an influential figure.

late nineteenth century it was ubiquitous, along with the name of its creator, Madame Blavatsky, who founded the Theosophical Society in 1875, and whose two mammoth tomes, *Isis Unveiled* (1877) and *The Secret Doctrine* (1888) provided its doctrinal core. Blavatsky's message was that the world's religions were underpinned by the same divine wisdom, which had been passed down from the ancients, and whose validity remained, even in the godless world that had been created by secular science. The ancient spiritual truths, hidden to escape persecution by the Western Church, were now re-emerging, along with the secrets of the East.

Into her pot-pourri of Western esoterica, Hinduism and Buddhism, Blavatsky mixed contemporary flavours. The legend of Atlantis, which had recently resurfaced in a book by the eccentric American politician Ignatius Donnelly, found its way into *The Secret Doctrine*, while Blavatsky's contempt for 'materialist science' (as opposed to her 'spiritual science') extended in particular to Darwin's evolutionary theories, which she counterposed with her own concept of humanity's 'spiritual evolution'. Blavatsky kept a stuffed baboon prominently displayed in her rooms to make the point clear. To add spice to her spiritual goulash, theosophy's imposing, pot-smoking matriarch (she had acquired a taste for hashish in the Near East) declared she was in touch with 'secret masters' who communicated to her astrally and via 'materialised' letters delivered through the ether from the masters' mountain fastness in Tibet.

A Russian adventuress of aristocratic stock, Blavatsky's considerable charisma was an essential ingredient in theosophy's appeal, though whether she was the age's most gifted seer or its most spectacularly successful charlatan depends on whose account one believes. In any case, theosophy seemed like spiritual manna to those sick from a diet of scientific atheism and empty religious orthodoxy. Its proto-New Age message proved instantly and enormously popular to an international following that included upper-class ladies, serious scholars and semi-educated self-improvers, with theosophical 'lodges' (a term borrowed from Freemasonry) established around the world, wielding particular influence in Britain, France, Germany and India.

Many of Blavatsky's teachings were to feed into modern astrology, and into the New Age movement in general. For example, at a time when the British Raj was at its height, the idea that Hindu and Buddhist philosophy had something worthwhile to impart to the West – a commonplace today – stemmed in large part from her patronage. Theosophy was well received in southern India and Sri Lanka, and the society's headquarters were established in Madras.

More fancifully, one is occasionally informed that astrology was imported into Chaldea or Egypt from Atlantis, a nugget of information unknown even to Plato, who started the myth of Atlantis in the first place.

Although she spoke and wrote in cosmological terms, Blavatsky herself was little animated by astrology. Inevitably, however, the TS became a magnet for star-gazers, for what was astrology if not part of 'the ancient wisdom'? The popular English astrologer Walter Old, better known under his angelic alias of Sepharial, met Blavatsky in 1888 and fell under her spell, becoming one of her keenest lieutenants. Old was inducted into the élite 'esoteric section' of the society – in effect, Blavatsky's chosen twelve disciples – and was holding the grande dame's hand when she died in London in 1891. Old quit the society a few years later, disgusted by the power struggle that followed Blavatsky's passing – he was to end his life a pentecostal Christian – but he remained one of the period's most widely read astrologers.

It was Sepharial who introduced Alan Leo to theosophy. Leo was instantly smitten. He joined the TS in 1889 and remained a faithful follower until his death. Teetotal and vegetarian, Leo was soon married to an equally ardent theosophist, Bessie Phillips. The marriage was, at her insistence, strictly platonic, so that the energy of their libidos might be focused on higher ends. Bessie soon became an enthusiastic, though leaden, astrological writer herself. Leo realised early in his astrological career – and not for some years could he afford to quit his job – that the age-old traditions had to be tailored to the newly enfranchised masses, that respectable, self-improving suburban class of which he was a representative member. He set about it with evangelical fervour, writing a series of manuals under the title 'Astrology for All' and publishing a series of simple pocket guides to astrology at budget prices.

Leo also made the Sun sign into the astrological catch-all it is today. For him, the Sun was 'the universal principle', the 'primal fount of existence', and one to which all other planetary principles were subsidiary. This cut contrary to much previous astrological thinking, in which the Sun was one planetary energy among seven, and not necessarily beneficial, since it scorched adjacent planets, which were then 'combust' (the principle is still applied in horary astrology). Prior to Leo, the Ascendant and the Moon were more important as indicators of individual character. Leo, thinking along hermetic lines of 'the Sun at the centre' (a doctrine which, as a Sun-ruled Leo, he doubtless embraced with ease), made the Sun the dominant force and can thus be credited, or blamed, for the tabloid astrology that followed him.

Just as presciently, Leo offered a mail-order horoscope service, in which he drew up and delineated a personal birth chart. He had offered this service free to subscribers to *The Astrologer's Magazine*, but the sheer volume of the work involved had overwhelmed him. Following the launch of *Modern Astrology* he devised his 'Shilling Horoscopes', which proved so popular he could once more scarcely keep pace with the demand. So gruelling was their calculation that he eventually took on several staff to maintain supply.

At first his employees did the mathematical spade-work to plot the charts, and took down Leo's dictated deliberations on them. Then one of his clerks had the bright idea of assembling standardised read-outs for particular planetary placings: one sheet for Mars in Cancer, another for Mercury in Leo, and so on. Essentially, Leo was running the equivalent of today's computerised astrological services, but without a computer. Small wonder that his overworked staff became disgruntled enough to stage a walk-out in 1903, an event that Leo ascribed to difficult planetary transits in his own chart. Part of his staff's dissatisfaction seems to have been watching the boss grow steadily rich; aside from his other modernisms, Leo was probably also the first twentieth-century astrologer to become wealthy from his enterprises.

Nor did his innovations end there. Leo also refined and simplified astrological techniques.[1] Most controversially and influentially of all, he introduced theosophical teachings into astrology. These downgraded prediction and instead emphasised the craft's 'spiritual dimension'. Leo talked of the planets as 'star angels' and insisted that 'an astrologer must become an occultist before he can become in any sense of the word an astrologer'. Theosophy's teachings on reincarnation, karma and the evolution of the soul over many lifetimes – ideas that Blavatsky had taken from Hinduism and Buddhism – now became part of modern astrology's domain, and, as in Vedic astrology, discernible from the birth chart.

These were concepts that had never previously figured in the Western astrological tradition, and did not go down well with everyone in the astrological world. Sepharial took mighty exception to astrology being turned into an esoteric pseudo-science and urged it to 'come down from the clouds', as well he might given that he himself was trying to make money by selling an astrological system on horse racing. Even more hostile were such contemporaries as C.T. Pearce, editor of *Zadkiel's Almanac,* who declared theosophical astrology 'nauseating', and Richard Garnett, superintendent of the British Library reading room, who cleaved stoutly to astrology of 'strictly empirical character' and loathed Leo's association of it with occultism.

For his part, Leo was wary of astrology's traditional role as a predictive art. Despite his belief in karma, he disliked the fatalism of traditional astrology, declaring that 'Character, and character alone, determines destiny.' It was ironic, then, that, of all astrologers, Leo was prosecuted by the police in 1914 on the charge of 'fortune-telling' via a postal horoscope. Acquitted on a technicality, he was less lucky when charged again in 1917, and was fined £5 with £25 costs. Leo's defence was that he was concerned only with delineating character from a horoscope; and talked only of the future in terms of 'tendencies'. The case caused deep distress to Leo, who considered himself the acme of respectability, and may well have induced the stroke that killed him a few months afterwards.

There is no doubt that the police action against Leo, the leading astrologer of his day, was calculated to shock other star-gazers into line. Leo's mail-order horoscopes had proved so successful that rival postal charts were on offer from less scrupulous souls.

The influence of Leo on twentieth-century astrology is difficult to overestimate, not least because his books were much translated and widely available – the reach of the Theosophical Society ensured that. The Astrological Lodge that Leo established in London in 1914 (he had already started several other societies) also became the mothership of British astrology, spawning, among other bodies, the Astrological

Association in 1958, which was set up partly to escape the stranglehold of theosophy and establish a broad church for the star-struck.

Leo's influence lingers on. His emphasis on personality rather than prediction, his ideas about karma and reincarnation, his insistence on astrology as a spiritual practice, his occultist language – all continue to ripple through astrology in the twenty-first century.

Leo's ideas have been diffused, consciously or not, by several generations of astrologers. This is particularly true in America, which is now the powerhouse of Western astrology, as in so much else. Most leading American astrologers of the last century were either theosophists or had a pronounced esoteric outlook, among them such popularisers as C.C. Zain and Marc Edmund Jones, both of whose manuals were widely read. The most influential was Dane Rudhyar, the pseudonym of naturalised Frenchman Daniel Chennevière, who in the 1930s started to blend his theosophical outlook with ideas borrowed from Jung to create what he called 'humanistic' (meaning psychological) astrology.

Rudhyar also followed Leo into the speculative realm of 'esoteric astrology'. Leo had written an indigestible tract of the same name which turned on its head the astrological lore he normally followed, redistributing the zodiac's 'ruling' planets in apparently random fashion and applying astrology to such nebulous concepts as 'etheric doubles' and 'the auric egg'. Even more opaque is the esoteric astrology of Alice Bailey, another theosophist, who claimed her books – she wrote a veritable platoon of heavyweight tracts on New Age issues – were psychically channelled from her Tibetan master on the 'inner plane'. More recently has come Alan Oken, another American theosophist, whose *Soul-centered Astrology* follows Bailey in talking about the 'seven cosmic rays' and adding the 'invisible' planet Vulcan to the solar system.

Most star-folk blanch at Vulcan, the 'rays' and the idea that 'Venus is the soul-centered ruler of Gemini', but theosophy's assertion that astrology is there to delve into matters of the soul permeates modern astrological thinking, as evidenced by a popular title like Jeffrey Wolf Green's *Pluto, Evolutionary Journey of the Soul*, which uses the distant speck of Pluto as an indicator of past lives and present incarnation.

Inasmuch as a birth chart has always offered a description of individual personality, astrology can claim to have spoken a psychological language – and by far the most sophisticated – long before Freud formulated his map of the mind, and such Freudian concepts as id, ego, neurosis and subconscious began to slither their way from clinical wisdom to street savvy.

As fellow neo-sciences – one fresh on campus, the other still smarting from its ejection – psychology and astrology made natural bedfellows, and in the twentieth century astrology's role as a psychological tool increasingly became its *raison d'être*, with the ancient art transmuted into a form of self-help and couched in the touchy-feely language of pop psychology.

The birth chart has now become 'a map of the psyche' that enables the therapist/astrologer to probe into the murkiest recesses of the self, and to understand psychological crises in terms of planetary transits. No wonder you're feeling haunted by your relationship with your mother, declares the astro-shrink, Pluto is crossing your natal Moon.

Other than the much-loved and much-reviled Sun sign predictions, astrology's psychological face is the one most often shown to the public in magazines and newspapers, whether as 'Find the right partner for you with our zodiac love guide' or 'The real Princess Diana as revealed by her astrologer'.

Psychology and astrology began their courtship in 1920s Germany, where the astrological revival had arrived late but forcefully. As in Britain, America and elsewhere, theosophy was the major source and conduit of Germany's rediscovered interest in the stars, but there was little popularisation of the sort that Alan Leo had so successfully instigated in Edwardian Britain until after the Great War. In the disillusioned, uncertain aftermath of 1918, Germany developed a passion for astrology that resulted in a boom in popular astro-magazines – one of them, as we shall see, was instrumental in linking Hitler to astrology – and in a growing interest in the subject among reputable intellectual and academic circles. Several leading German astrologers were distinguished *Doktoren*, and there was even an astrological society whose membership was restricted to university professors, something unthinkable in Britain.

Germany's new breed of astrologers took to investigating, modernising and systematising their subject with Teutonic vigour. Adopting a fearsomely technical approach was one way of draping scientific respectability on to astrology, which now became 'cosmobiology' or 'typocosmy' to distinguish it from its medieval ancestor. Such was the enthusiasm for complexity that the 'Hamburg School' founded by Alfred Witte added no less than eight 'hypothetical' (i.e. non-existent) planets to astrological tradition, as if horoscopes weren't already complicated enough. Witte had come to believe in the existence of these planets in the trenches of the First World War, when the timing of Russian bombardments didn't accord to his astrological predictions; clearly the influence of the previously unknown planet Cupido was at work. Later Witte found seven more planets beyond Neptune's orbit, none of which, strangely enough, was Pluto.

The emergent science of psychology was a natural ally for German astrology; psychology's power bases in Vienna and Zurich were near by, and the ideas of Sigmund Freud and Carl Jung were very much in the air in the thinking circles of Central Europe, especially following the publication of Jung's *Psychological Types* in 1921. One of Jung's disciples, the playwright and novelist Oskar Schmitz, seems to have been the first to make the link between Jung's ideas and astrology in his book *The Spirit of Astrology*, published in 1921. Schmitz may even have encouraged Jung's astrological interests, which first surfaced in 1911, when he was thirty-six. In a letter to his mentor Freud in June of that year Jung described his evenings as 'taken up largely with astrology. I make horoscopic calculations in order to find a clue to the core of psychological truth.'

Jung remained fascinated by astrology for the rest of his life, returning to it repeatedly for various reasons: to illuminate his idea of the 'collective subconscious'; to delve into the concept of the Age of Aquarius; and for practical help with individual clients. A letter from 1947 explains that 'In cases of difficult psychological diagnosis I usually get a horoscope in order to have a further point of view from an entirely different angle. I must say that I very often found that the astrological data elucidated certain points which I otherwise would have been unable to understand.'

Jung regretted the absence of objective proof for astrology, and in the 1950s undertook a series of experiments of his own to try to establish its statistical validity. He looked at the birth charts of married couples for three traditional signatures of compatibility between them: Sun–Moon, Moon–Ascendant and Moon–Moon. In each case the results were statistically significant, though they contradicted each other. In effect Jung had found exactly what he was looking for on each occasion. This led him to posit what he termed a 'secret mutual connivance' between the astrologer and his subject; in other words, the astrologer's attitude made a difference to what he or she discovered. Much the same thesis has been a battleground in the experiments of quantum physics; Einstein, in particular, was much vexed by the issue.

Jung's interest in astrology has helped bestow a lustre of respectability on the subject, in as much as Jung himself has remained intellectually respectable, which is questionable. For one thing, Jung's reputation, which during his lifetime rivalled Freud's, has never fully recovered from his alleged flirtation with Nazism during the 1930s,[2] while his extensive interests in the history of esoteric and magical ideas put him beyond the pale for more sober psychologists. For them, alchemy, astrology, Gnosticism and Taoism, all of which Jung studied, are manifestations of what Freud termed 'the black mud of occultism'. Jung saw it not as mud but gold. Occultists and mystics of the past had expressed insights into the workings of the human psyche, he felt, but these needed reframing for the scientific age. Jung himself had psychic experiences throughout his life (his mother's side of the family was involved in spiritualism), and his paranormal interests were one major reason behind the bitter break between himself and Freud, along with Jung's refusal to be bound by Freud's paternalist authority.[3]

Jung also thought Freud's insistence that neurotic and psychotic disturbances all derive ultimately from sexual issues was too narrow. Jung conceived of a far wider psychological matrix. Among his major conceptions was the 'collective unconscious' shared by all humanity and structured principally through the 'archetypes', autonomous, multidimensional images that can take on many shapes without losing their deeper, universal meaning. Jung found the archetypes present in myth and in dreams and conceived of them as the 'organising principles' of the psyche. For example, there is the Senex (the old man), the Puer (the eternal youth), the Trickster, the Universal Mother, and so on; figures who moved through all cultures in different guises. Modern astrology soon saw that its age-old planetary principles and

Jung's archetypes were essentially the same thing: Saturn was, among other things, the Senex, Mercury the Trickster, the Moon the Great Mother. Moreover, Jung's insistence that the individual must disentangle himself or herself from the web of the collective unconscious by undertaking a 'soul's journey' of 'individuation' could be linked to the birth chart, which showed the particular challenges faced by the soul and how to overcome them.

Other components of Jung's thinking were similarly applied to astrology: his assertion that archetypes had a 'shadow side' became another way of viewing badly aspected planets, or the less appealing qualities of signs. His division of personality into 'introvert' and 'extrovert' was linked to how many planets were above the horizon at birth (extrovert) and how many below (introvert). Jung's four psychological types, whose primary mode of experience he defined as sensation, thinking, feeling and intuition, were applied, rather unsatisfactorily, to the four classical elements of earth, air, water and fire.

In 1930 Jung formulated the idea of 'synchronicity', a concept that has proved particularly handy for astrology and which has since entered mainstream language, thanks mainly to rock god Sting naming one of his albums after it.[4] Most people experience synchronicity; the same numbers, names or subjects pop up repeatedly in a short time for no apparent reason. Jung defined synchronicity in several ways. It was 'a meaningful coincidence in time', an 'acausal connecting principle', and was based on the rather tautologous notion that 'whatever is born or done in this moment of time has the quality of this moment of time'. This last definition summed up a major astrological assumption admirably, and handily dispensed with any need for planets to cause events through direct physical interference while instead making them signifiers. Jung gave this quote in an address to the orientalist scholar Richard Wilhelm, best known for his championing of the *I Ching*, the Chinese 'Book of Changes', and synchronicity thus became a way to justify both astrology and such divinatory tools as the *I Ching* and Tarot cards.

Jung later cooled on this definition of synchronicity (though it remains much quoted by astrologers), and instead likened synchronous events to archetypal energies forcing their way from the subconscious into the conscious mind. This notion, too, has been taken up by astrologers to explain how planetary transits operate; as a particular planet in the horoscope becomes accentuated, the archetypal qualities it represents flood the individual psyche, which finds, indeed calls forth, appropriate correspondences in the outer world. The external cause-and-effect world of medieval astrology has thus been replaced by the internal processes of the mind. Sceptical scientism has countered the idea of synchronicity with its own 'probability theory', which uses mathematics to prove that those who find meaning in coincidences are deluded fools; see, for example, John Allen Paulos's *Innumeracy*, which affirms that for 'real science' (theirs) meaninglessness rules.

There is scarcely a modern astrologer who has not absorbed the fundamentals of popular psychology into his or her outlook, with the overwhelming influence coming from Jung. Jungian astrologers have substantially shaped all modern astrological lore, in particular the meaning of the three outer planets, which the Jungians cast as representing the collective conscious, with the seven traditional bodies becoming 'personal planets'. The zodiac and planets alike have been stretched on the psychologist's couch, and their symbolism has been unravelled according to the 'mythopoetic' approach developed by such Jungian psychologists as James Hillman. For Hillman, as for his colleague Thomas Moore (both of whom have written best-sellers), psychology must help in 'the rediscovery of the soul', the psyche banished by materialist science. The loss of soul, in Moore's words, 'is the great malady of the twentieth century . . . implicated in all of our troubles and affecting us individually and socially'. Such ideas pervade modern astrology, and it is interesting to note that both Jung's daughter and Hillman's son became astrologers.

The undoubted superstar of Jungian astrology is Liz Greene, an American who was for many years resident in Britain (she now lives in Switzerland), and who followed up her astrological interests by qualifying as a Jungian analyst. Greene's books, most notably *Saturn: A New Look at an Old Devil,* managed to communicate serious-minded astrology to a wider audience who were familiar with zodiacal basics but wanted to go further, particularly into that most interesting of subjects, themselves. Greene's sympathy for the social and psychologi-cal problems faced by both women and men, her grasp of mythological meaning and her persuasive way with a birth chart gave her ready appeal for the 'me generation', which by the 1970s had become astrology's new audience.

The new public for astrology that in the 1970s and 1980s was tapped by the likes of Greene and other astrologers such as the prolific Robert Hand (a less psychologically absorbed and more fulsome writer) had already been softened up by the explosion of interest in the subject that accompanied the youthquake of the 1960s. Much to the startled delight of the older generation of star-gazers, the baby-boomers provided a much-needed influx of energy into an astrological community that in many ways was still turning over ground bequeathed them by Leo and the theosophists. True, the years between had seen much refinement of astrological technique by such men as Charles Carter, who had been Alan Leo's understudy, and his successor John Addey. But such techniques as 'harmonic charts' and planetary 'midpoints' were arcane matters to a public whose only connection to astrology was through newspaper horoscopes.

The boomers brought a new populism to astrology. Though divided by the best part of a century, they and the theosophists had much in common: a fascination with Indian trappings and mysticism, a pick 'n' mix attitude to world religions, and a repugnance of soulless science and materialism (though in both cases this didn't stop many becoming wealthy). It was the era of 'What's your sign?' and of the Age of Aquarius being proclaimed in the pop charts, though astrology's new converts found few texts that matched their racy, impressionist approach to the subject, Linda Goodman's *Sun Signs* being one of the few.

In terms of dedicated astrology the first major effect of the new interest was a sharp rise in the membership of astrological societies. In general, those who signed up back in the late sixties and early seventies are now astrology's leading lights: its presidents, lecturers, scholars and popular columnists. Go back to the minutes of the Astrological Association convention for 1975, for example, and you will find the names of Russell Grant, now the jolly Falstaff of tabloid astrology, and Liz Greene, now arch-astro-psychologist, side by side, the latter responsible for programme artwork, the former in the improbable role of leading the meditation group.

Although the boomers were preoccupied with the inner realms of the psyche, astrology had not entirely abandoned its claims on the outer, physical realm of the cosmos. As we shall see, the advances of twentieth-century physics and statistical analysis have offered several avenues for the craft to launch its counter-attack on scientific orthodoxy.

5

MEASURING THE UNIVERSE

STATISTICAL SCIENCE VERSUS THE QUANTUM COSMOS

*

Modern astrology's dream of reclaiming its lost status has not only been pursued through psychology, which is itself regarded as a pretender to the mantle of science by the praetorian guards of physics and biology. It has done battle on science's own, empirical terms, attempting to 'prove' astrology by objective, statistical methods. At the same time, astrology has contested with astronomy, its old ally turned bitter foe, the underlying structure of the cosmos, hoping that quantum theory might provide a route back from exile.

The statistical approach was pioneered early in the twentieth century by France's Paul Choisnard, and taken up in the 1920s by the Swiss-German astrologer Karl Ernest Krafft, who would later find a degree of infamy when he was mistakenly named as 'Hitler's astrologer'. Krafft followed Choisnard's investigations into 'astral heredity', trying to show that members of the same family tended to share features in their horoscopes (a standing tenet of astrology from classical times), and investigated the birth charts of some 2,800 musicians whose birth data he extracted from the Geneva registry office. Krafft thought his painstaking analysis proved there was validity in astrology, or at least a scientifically recast version of it he described as 'cosmic influences', but he found few takers among either astrologers or scientists.

The most exhaustive and famous statistical analysis of horoscopes was conducted by Michel Gauquelin (1928–91), a French psychologist who became fascinated by astrology when he was a teenager but who grew increasingly sceptical of its claims as he grew older. As a trained statistician, Gauquelin was well qualified for the exhaustive survey of astro-data that he first undertook for his post-graduate doctorate, and which was to consume him for the rest of his life. Like Choisnard and Krafft – both of whose techniques he cast into disrepute – Gauquelin investigated several astrological theses, starting with the notion that Sun signs are drawn to particular professions; that Librans, being ruled by Venus, make beauty consultants, while Aries and Scorpio, as good Martians, make soldiers. Gauquelin's analysis found no evidence to back up this time-honoured tradition.

His investigations, which he began to publish in the mid-1950s, became more interesting when he classified people not by Sun sign but according to which planets were prominent in their horoscopes. He and his wife Françoise looked at the birth charts of 576 eminent French doctors and discovered a disproportionate number had Mars or Saturn at prominent positions in their birth charts; either 'rising' above the eastern horizon or 'culminating' directly overhead in the sky. A lesser, but still statistically significant, tendency put the planets setting on the western horizon or directly 'under' the Earth.

Gauquelin and his wife repeated this process for other professions, discovering the same tendency for each group (between 600 and 900 in size) to have a particular planet dominant in the charts of its members. Saturn was most powerful for scientists and physicians, but weak for actors, writers and artists. Mars was prominent among physicians, sports champions and executives, weak for musicians and writers. Politicians, soldiers and actors tended to have a strongly placed Jupiter. Gauquelin also extended his research into personality types, and into the same question of astro-heredity that Krafft had explored. For the latter he used a sample of some thirty thousand. In each case his results focused on the position of planets in the individual horoscope, a matter determined by the daily rotation of the Earth rather than the planets' circling of the Earth itself, and produced statistically significant results that corresponded to some (but only some) of astrology's tenets. Astrology has always considered a planet rising or culminating – that is, on a chart angle – important, but the positions of Gauquelin's dominant planets were not quite what they should have been according to astrological theory, falling in the 'cadent' third, sixth, ninth and twelfth houses of charts, rather than in the 'cardinal' first, fourth,

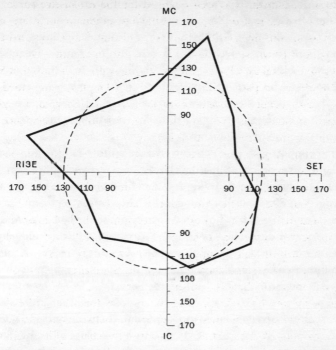

Figure 2: The graph behind some of the most acrimonious disputes between science and astrology. Michel Gauquelin's study of 915 sports champions shows a pronounced tendency for the planet Mars to have just risen over the eastern horizon (the left horizontal axis) or to be just past the midheaven (the upper vertical axis). His findings, known as 'The Mars Effect', remain much contested.

seventh and tenth houses. Gauquelin himself was sharply critical of astro-orthodoxy, although he regularly lectured to astrological conferences, which at least listened to his ideas.

Despite the thoroughness of his research, Gauquelin received little but derision and hostility for his efforts from the scientific world he was most keen to impress. The good burghers of academe found fault with his methodology and called his honesty into question. The Gauquelins' battles with orthodoxy reached a peak in 1976, when they published the full results of their years of research. Almost overnight the Committee for the Scientific Investigation of Claims of the Paranormal (CSICOP) was formed to belittle the Gauquelins' findings. CSICOP's scientists ran a statistical test of their own that was intended to disprove the correlation between sports champions and a prominent natal Mars, but instead found the results backed up the Gauquelins' 'Mars effect', necessitating a frantic fudge of their data to produce a more acceptable – negative – result.

The storm generated by this episode has been rumbling on ever since. One physicist, Dennis Rawlins, denounced CSICOP as 'a bunch of would-be debunkers who bungled their major investigation, falsified the results, covered up their errors, and gave the boot to a colleague [Rawlins himself] who threatened to tell the truth'.[1] A modified rerun of Gauquelin's experiment in a 1997 book, *The Tenacious Mars Effect*, by Suitbert Ertal and Kenneth Irving found in his favour and reignited the controversy in a manner becoming to the red planet's angry character.

Apart from a few psychologists – among them Hans Eysenck, a British professor of psychology who had set out to debunk Gauquelin's findings and instead became persuaded by them – the scientific community remains profoundly antagonistic. The prevailing attitude, as Eysenck put it, is 'Don't confuse me with facts when my mind is made up.'[2]

The reaction of astrologers to Gauquelin was more mixed. Many, including John Addey, the leading British astrologer of his time, welcomed Gauquelin's findings, and thought that inasmuch as they contradicted astrological tradition, the latter should be modified. Others were lukewarm or plain hostile, sensing a threat to astrological order in Gauquelin's marching columns of statistics and a scientific hit squad lurking in the Trojan horse of his planetary graphs.

Gauquelin's studies established a pattern for most subsequent experiments in astro-statistics. If these fail to prove astrological tradition, the sceptics duly crow, 'I told you so.' If they suggest anything different, the sceptics ignore them or cast aspersions on their methodology. Meanwhile, an élite of astrological thinkers debates the significance of the results, while most astrologers simply carry on casting charts and deliberating on them much as ever. For example, in the mid-1970s the New York chapter of the National Council for Geocosmic Research – the grand title conceals an astrological society – conducted an assiduous investigation into suicides in New York City. The birth charts of 2,250 suicides between 1969 and 1973 were analysed, with specific reference to the 311 whose accurate birth times were known, along with charts for the times of their deaths. A randomly selected control group was set in place, and computers programmed to crunch the data in accordance with modern astrological doctrine. The result was that no significant repeating factors were found among the thousands investigated, and the NCGR limped away to the jeers of the sceptics.

Not all astrological experiments have ended so dismally. In 1959 the American psychologist Vernon Clark carried out tests requiring an assortment of fifty astrologers to match horoscopes to biographies, to discriminate between real and randomly generated birth charts, and to distinguish between the charts of people with high IQs and others with cerebral palsy. The astrologers were extraordinarily successful, though the results of this experiment remained predictably unheeded by astrology's opponents, not least because scientific magazines would not publish them.[3]

Statistics are now part of the running war between scientism and astrology, and are one resource which star-folk are increasingly fond of citing. *Astrology Really Works!* yells the title of the 1995 book by the Magi Society, a collective of American astrologers, and, to prove it, they pull out assorted planetary signifiers from the birth charts of the rich and famous and defy astrology's opponents to match them for statistical probability. For instance, the Society cites an improbable number of highly successful sports champions with strong Sun–Neptune aspects in their birth charts, and an equally impressive proportion of captains of industry with powerful Sun–Pluto contacts. Since these Sun–Neptune contacts occur every ten days or so, the Magis demand that the sceptics produce ten times the number of sports champions they have found. Probability, it seems, is a game that both sides can play.

The German business tyro Gunther Sachs is another unlikely recruit to astro-statistics. In his book *The Astrology File* he described how thousands of birth dates were fed into computers to discover which Sun signs married which, which were most likely to be divorced, which diseases each sign dies of, which signs were best represented in professional German football, and so on. Although Sachs's book claims to offer 'scientific proof of the link between star signs and human behaviour', his statistics produce little beyond such factoids as 'Taureans have the most car accidents' and 'Leos are often entrepreneurs', about which it's hard to draw many conclusions and whose relation to astrological convention is not pursued.

What Sachs's book chiefly proves is that statistically significant statistics aren't always significant. Unless, that is, you need to know that Taureans do, in fact, have the most car crashes. This was exactly the conclusion reached when, as a spot of light relief in a 1997 quarterly report, a UK car insurance company, Velo Fleet, ran 25,000 car accident claims through its computers on the basis of star sign rather than age, gender or postcode. The results showed clearly that Taureans were more likely to have a road accident than Scorpios, the signs respectively clocking in at 9.8 per cent and 7.1 per cent of total claims. Virgos, the second most likely to lodge a claim (9 per cent) had the most expensive crashes. In the astrological future, perhaps, insurance premiums will be levied by star sign.

Another report from a non-partial enquirer was that of *Hospital Doctor* magazine, which in 1998 surveyed 1,456 of its number by Sun sign. The magazine found, among other things, that Libra was the most common sign among gynaecologists, neurologists and obstetricians, while anaesthetists were likely to be Gemini. These were findings in complete contradiction to prevailing notions about Sun signs and profession – Geminis are meant to make journalists, not anaesthetists – though they do not take into account the planetary signatures that astrologers look at in birth charts, and which the Gauquelins sought.

Some astrologers are already planning a further step in statistical research intended to subject some of the most cherished and detailed astrological techniques to stringent examination by a computer programmed to become 'an astrology testing machine'. The idea belongs to US astrologers Lois Rodden and Marc McDonough, the latter a cybernaut skilled in statistics, the former the owner of the most comprehensive and accurate set of celebrity birth data in the astrological world. Rodden, who has been collecting rigorously researched birth dates and times for many years, is well known for her books of celebrity charts, which include stars of film, music, TV and media, as well as politicians and murderers. This mass of information has now become an 'astro data bank' that McDonough intends to use for research, looking into the correlations of precise planetary aspects with known behaviour and character. For example, the traditional association of alcoholism with the sign Pisces and the planet Neptune will be examined in the charts of known alcoholics. By allotting a points system to planet and sign – one point for a Pisces Sun, two for a Pisces Moon, two for a 'hard' aspect between Neptune and another planet – McDonough hopes to build up a catalogue of proved astrological signatures and techniques, which he promises will mean 'a lot of pet theories will have to be abandoned'.[4]

No amount of statistically significant correlations, however, explain how astrology might actually work. There remains no known physical mechanism by which Saturn, a giant ball of light gases a few million miles away, might impart a scientific cast of mind to a new-born infant, even if the planet is rising or culminating as Gauquelin's study suggests it should be.

Even in the ancient world, though, planets did not have to be causes of anything; they could be simply 'signs'. This is the basis of both astrology as divination and of Jung's 'synchronicity', though the psychologist was wont to duck and dive around his troublesome theory (sometimes it seems he wished he'd never thought of it) and advised that astrological phenomena could be 'taken as possibly causal in origin'.

Which cause remains a puzzle. Gravity is no real contender, for while the Sun and Moon exert considerable gravitational pulls on planet Earth,[5] the other planets do not, and, as the sceptical astronomer Carl Sagan pointed out, the obstetrician delivering a child exerts more gravitational force on a newly born infant than does, say, the planet Mars. (Sagan's midwife is overshadowed by the gravitational force of Sun and Moon, however, which clock in at respectively 100 and 10,000 times her pull.)

If the planets cannot be called on to exert a physical, causal effect, what chance has the zodiac, whose stars are unimaginably distant, not only from Earth but from each other? Calling a group of stars a constellation implies kinship, but, as Richard Dawkins fondly points out, a constellation's stars are all at different distances from us and unconnected with each other; their pattern 'means no more than a patch of damp on the bathroom ceiling', he chides. Planets are only 'in' constellations inasmuch as they pass before these patterns. Even then, the differences between Sidereal and Tropical zodiacs mean the planets aren't even where Western astrologers put them.

Modern cosmology contradicts astrology at every turn. The advent of space exploration – of men on the Moon, the first view of Planet Earth in its azure luminosity, Mars probes and Voyagers, the clamour of space static and the astonishing shots of deep space provided by the Hubble telescope – has been a black hole for Aristotelian cause-and-effect physics. Little wonder that astrology's principal reaction over the last century has been to shrink from actual star-gazing into spiritual speculation, mythology and the inner cosmos revealed by psychology.

Yet astro-physics has been unable to co-opt the universe completely for rationalism. One reason is that before the good ship Modern Cosmology blasted off, science's excitable and occasionally delinquent cousin, science fiction, had stowed away onboard, and since the late nineteenth century has been beaming its animated reports back to Earth. These have often proved more interesting to the world's populace than official accounts of what's out there, and have filled heads with irrational ideas about UFOs and alien life-forms, many of which bear a marked resemblance to old tales of celestial wonders and the scary land of faerie. Even science's own pilots have been known to return from space speaking animatedly about God and the universe, to the embarrassment of the button-down minds back at Mission Control.

Official accounts of life in the post-Copernican cosmos have made for chilly reading. The stars that inspired myth-makers and shone down on lovers turn out to be vast balls of nuclear fission. As American astronomer Richard Grossinger put it, 'The beauty of space is overshadowed by the sense that it is nothing but a noisy brute. It explodes galaxies and worlds in the way that we build and put out campfires. The planets in our vicinity are not neighbours, they are fires, storms of poisonous gases, and dry meteor-pummelled stone.'

Moreover, the orderly universe that Newton and Laplace thought they were revealing – whether presided over by God or not – has proved an illusion. The greater the success in shooting rockets, probes and people into the deep blue beyond, the stranger have been the dispatches from the front lines of cosmology and its partner, theoretical, subatomic physics.

Two clashing views of the universe emerge from today's astrophysics. The first is that science very nearly understands everything there is to know. Scientists have become 'masters of the universe', knowing how and when the universe started – with a 'big bang' between 8 and 16 billion years ago, depending on which boffin you believe – and the elusive 'Grand Unified Theory of Everything', as it's known in trade circles, is about to get nailed down.

The other view is that the universe is a contradictory place that defies our best efforts to understand it. Out in space, the existence of dark (or 'missing') matter is inferred but cannot be observed. At subatomic level photons and other elementary particles defy mechanistic prediction and can be described only in terms of probability, or as 'a wave function' – the 'principle of uncertainty' established by Werner Heisenberg in the 1920s. As the philosopher Karl Popper put it, 'Through modern physics materialism has transcended itself.'

Quantum theory has offered astrology and other esoteric arts a slender rope at which to grab for scientific validation. Various attempts have been made to paint quantum mechanics itself as a 'spiritual science'. Fritjof Capra, whose The Tao of Physics (1975) drew parallels between Eastern mysticism and modern physics, has been followed by others such as Danah Zohar and Roger Penrose, who have made links between quantum theory and mystic consciousness. Yet the notion, popular among New Age followers, that science is collapsing into post-quantum spiritual enlightenment is erroneous. Far stronger is the tendency to graft quantum mechanics on to a Newtonian outlook which, let's not forget, continues to yield powerful technological results. (Needless to say, Richard Dawkins reserves particular scorn for quantum uncertainty's 'deplorable effects upon popular culture'.)

Many modern astrologers are keen on quantum theory. Dennis Elwell, in The Cosmic Loom: The New Science of Astrology, insists that 'modern physicists ... are describing a universe into which astrology fits quite happily', and in support of this view quotes Bell's Theorem (named after John Bell in 1964), which posits a universe in which everything, from subatomic particles upwards, is connected to everything else, and that interaction between parts is not lessened by distance. The astronomer Percy Seymour pours cold water over Elwell's claims, however, pointing out that if the universe is as unified as Bell's

Theorem proposes, then 'all the hundred thousand million stars which form the Milky Way play just as an important part as the planets and stars which we do see'.

Seymour is a South African-born astronomer who is sympathetic to Gauquelin's claims of planetary signatures and who has posited a theory that can explain them, while remaining unconvinced by astrology in general. In *Astrology: The Evidence of Science* Seymour argues that the planets influence solar activity, creating sunspots, flares and particle emissions. Solar activity travels across space and permeates life on Earth through the planet's magnetosphere, making the planetary imprint on human life not a symbolic but a physical reality. Seymour's theory is essentially an elaboration on the materialist cosmos, offering the planets limited influence, rather than a model of the universe that could explain why Saturn's movement across the top of your birth chart might signify trouble with the boss.

The search for an astrologically friendly macrocosm has increasingly alighted on the 'holographic' universe posited by twentieth-century physicist David Bohm. Bohm was a colleague of Einstein, who was forced to leave America after he had refused to testify against his fellow scientist Robert Oppenheimer during one of Joseph McCarthy's anti-Communist witch hunts. He spent most of his subsequent career in London.

Bohm conceived of the universe as a 'holomovement', a single unbroken matrix of matter and space. Space itself is not an empty vacuum but as real and active as the matter that it contains; the two are indivisibly connected in a way 'which denies the classical analysibility of the world into separately and independently existing parts', said Bohm.

Bohm proposed that there was an 'explicate' and 'implicate' order in the universe. The two are folded together, with the explicate order of Newtonian physics, in which things appear separate, unfolding from an implicate order in which they are deeply interconnected. Essentially this was a manifest order and an unmanifest one, a version of the traditional mystical conception that sees spirit (implicate) as the primary force in the universe and matter (explicate) as its manifestation. It is probably significant that Bohm had a twenty-year dialogue with the Indian sage Krishnamurthi.

Bohm went further and posited that the universe was made up not only of matter and energy but of meaning: 'Meaning is an inherent and essential part of our overall reality and it is not merely a purely abstract ethereal quality having its existence only in the mind, or to put it differently, in human life. Quite generally, meaning is being.' Against conventional quantum theory, Bohm insisted that subatomic particles like the electron have access to information about the rest of the universe. His analogy was of a 747 jet receiving radio signals; the signals don't cause the plane to change course directly but they supply the relevant information that suggests it do so.

Bohm's ideas have been championed by several astrological thinkers, among them Will Keepin, an American astronomer turned astrological convert. Keepin likens Bohm's implicate order to the mass of television airwaves that are broadcast around us, with the explicate order being what's actually showing on the TV screen. Keepin considers that esoteric arts offer a model of the implicate order, though astrology alone is linked to the physically observable universe, and through its readings of the configuration of planets at any time suggests what pictures are likely to flicker up on the screen, what events will manifest themselves.

Others are thinking on much the same lines. The Kentucky astrologer David Thurman proposes that planetary movements can be seen as equivalent to the 'proxy waves' conceived by Heisenberg. These 'are something standing in the middle between the idea of an event and the actual event, between possibility and reality'.[6] Such ideas sing to astrologers because they explain why sometimes astrology works and sometimes it doesn't; why, as star-folk are wont to put it, some planetary transits 'manifest' and some don't.

Such ideas make astrology not the irrationalist, escapist reaction to scientific materialism that its critics claim but part of the shift to a post-Newtonian view of the universe, one with more affinities to Newton's beloved alchemy than to the *Principia* for which he is celebrated. As the modern French alchemist François Trojani puts it, 'for all its great usefulness, science is a very limited, very fragmented, and not very profound way of trying to investigate the mysteries of the universe'. Newton would, it seems, have sympathised.

6

HEADLINES AND HOROSCOPES

NEWSPAPER ASTROLOGY AND OTHER
TWENTIETH-CENTURY TALES

✱

When asked when astrology's golden age was, Carl Jung responded, 'Now!' He was probably right. Astrology at the beginning of the twenty-first century has never been more popular. It may have lost the respectability it carried back in the days when it was taught in the Florentine Academy, but it is once more an indispensable part of daily life for the millions who consult their horoscopes in newspapers and magazines. Surveys enquiring into 'belief' (always a troublesome word) in astrology regularly turn up astonishingly high figures; a recent British survey of 1,000 young people for the *Guardian* newspaper found more credence in astrology (45 per cent) than in atheism (39 per cent), Christianity (23 per cent) or Marxism (15 per cent).

Not all of this interest tallies with what serious astrologers regard as their craft. Many are appalled by such New Age eccentricities as 'Celtic lunar horoscopes', evidence for which is nowhere to be found in astrology's rich tradition, and which has been cooked up from a stew of pagan concepts gathered principally from Robert Graves's *The White Goddess*. The mercurial, capricious spirit of astrology remains out of the control even of its devotees.

While the number of practising astrologers seems to have reached a plateau, to judge by the number of recruits inducted by the major astrological bodies, the burgeoning number of astrological books and magazines testifies to a subject in rude good health.

Of the various illusions surrounding modern astrologers, probably the two greatest are that they spend their time predicting the future and that they make an enormous amount of money from doing so. The opposite is generally true. Astrologers are preoccupied not with the future but with the past, on which they rely to discern the meanings of conjunctions and eclipses. At times it seems that astrology is principally a rear-view mirror rather than a gaze into the future.

Astrology's career structure, if it can be said to have one, is unique. Its most public face is the handful of newspaper astrologers who write Sun sign horoscopes for the tabloid press and are handsomely rewarded for doing so. Well below them in earning power, though higher in kudos, comes an élite of astrological scholars who make a respectable living from a mixture of authorship, lecturing, personal consultations and *ad hoc* work. And a long way below them are the great majority of astrologers who either bump along on fees from personal consultations, blend day jobs with their astrological work or pursue astrology as a passion for which they pay, rather than are paid.

For the fortunate few, the rewards from Sun sign horoscopes can be extraordinary. Newspapers and astrology have been in permanent conjunction since 1930, when the *Sunday Express* celebrated the birth of Princess Margaret on 21 August with a specially commissioned horoscope from the professional astrologer R.H. Naylor (1889–1952). The resultant profile, published three days later, included some general prognostications for non-royals with birthdays in the week ahead. Healthy sales and reader response persuaded the paper to run another column the following week ('Were you born in September?') and a regular column by Naylor from Sunday 5 October.

In this column Naylor warned that British aircraft were in danger, a prediction that was dramatically fulfilled that very day when the R-101 airship crashed in northern France on its maiden flight, killing all on board.[1] Next Sunday, the *Express* replayed its astrologer's prediction in loud headlines, and henceforth handed Naylor a full page for his ruminations. The *People* followed its rival's lead soon after with an astrology column by Edward Lyndoe, whose byline puffed him as 'the most consulted astrologian of all time'.

That title probably already belonged to the popular US astrologer Evangeline Adams, who had launched the first astrology radio show in April 1930, broadcasting three times a week. Like Britain's tabloid press, American radio quickly discovered astrology's appeal: listeners besieged

Adams with requests for horoscopes; she received 150,000 in the first three months, a figure that climbed to over 100,000 per month the following year.

Adams had herself become famous as the result of correctly predicting a tragedy. She had moved from Boston into a New York hotel, the Windsor, on 16 March 1899, to set up her astrology practice, and had obliged the proprietor, Warren Leland, with a reading. Looking at his horoscope, Adams didn't like what she found, and warned him of possible danger the very next day, noting that there had been two comparable periods of danger in the recent past. Leland recalled there had been two small fires in the hotel around those times, but brushed aside her concerns for the next day, which was, after all, a public holiday, St Patrick's Day.

Adams's concerns were horrifically borne out when the Windsor Hotel burned down the next morning, with major loss of life, including several members of Leland's family. The hotelier told reporters that the fire had been correctly predicted by Adams, making the astrologer a celebrity. Leland himself died from shock three weeks later.

Adams's reputation was cemented when in 1914 she successfully defended a public prosecution against her on grounds of 'fortune-telling' – comparable to the case brought against Alan Leo around the same time – during which she demonstrated her prowess to the court by interpreting the horoscope of an unknown 'Mr X'. This was, in fact, the son of the judge, who, upon hearing Adams's delineations, found in her favour, declaring that 'the defendant raises astrology to the dignity of an exact science'.

The scale of astrology's popularity as the ancient art encountered modern media has proved a mixed blessing. Demand for individual horoscopes on such a colossal scale was impossible for Evangeline Adams or any other astrologer to meet; drawing up, let alone interpreting, charts was no small matter in the pre-computer era.[2]

The newspaper Sun sign column proved to be astrology's most potent force in the people's century, providing the newly enfranchised masses of modern society with an entertainment as catchy, democratic and disposable as a pop song, yet, like the best pop, potentially rich in allusive meaning and inspiring fierce loyalties. For most people, the daily, weekly or monthly horoscope *is* astrology, and they feel no need to pursue their stellar destiny further than the hopeful generalisations of their favourite media soothsayer.

For many dedicated astrologers, the pervasiveness of Sun sign columns is maddening, an offensive sell-out of their art in the interests of crass commerce that makes it impossible for 'real' astrology to be accepted. How can we hope to be taken seriously, runs the lament, when we are represented by media showmen whose banal forecasts bear scant relation to the practice of psychological or predictive astrology, and whose methods are suspect?

It's often claimed that newspaper columns are fabrications with no real astrology behind them. A common tale has it that the office junior is asked to dream them up; super-sceptic James Randi claims to have done the job himself while working on a Montreal newspaper, merely reshuffling old columns for credulous readers. Maybe. Yet most national newspapers and magazines take the authorship of their horoscope columns very seriously, even if the usual response of their editors to the contents is a none-too-private snicker (one tabloid editor famously dumped his astrologer with a letter that began, 'As you will have doubtless foreseen, I am sacking you'). Astrology sells papers, and the right astrologer can give a publication a commercial cutting edge.

The career of Patric Walker illustrates the devotion inspired by media star-gazers and the potential financial rewards. With forecasts couched in intimate, purringly elegant prose, Walker became the doyen of Sun sign astrologians, syndicating his column around the world from his home on the Greek island of Lindos, and becoming enormously wealthy – at his death in 1995, his annual earnings were estimated at £500,000. His value to his employers was commensurate; the *Mail on Sunday* would add 250,000 copies to its 2 million circulation when it published Walker's biannual supplements. Small wonder that on Walker's unexpected death there was a none-too-discreet scrabble for his mantle, a contest made sharper by Walker's diverse promises as to who was his chosen heir. 'Patric thought a sorcerer ought to have an apprentice, but he kept on changing his mind about who it should be,' remarked the journalist Miles Chapman, one of Walker's several adopted scions.

Just how high the stakes have become in newspaper astrology was made even clearer on the eve of the millennium, when Jonathan Cainer, the *Daily Mail*'s astrologer of several years' standing, announced he was quitting to join the paper's arch-rival, the *Express*. The *Mail* promptly offered Cainer £1 million to stay, then threatened him with a £2 million lawsuit when he refused. Cainer left, citing personal reasons for his departure, and claiming to have been 'the only voice of tolerance in a newspaper dedicated to the subtle propagation of bigotry'.

One of the sticking points between Cainer and the *Mail* was the split of the enormous profits from the premium-rate phone lines that offer star-struck readers more detailed advice than can be squeezed into a seventy-word soundbite. These, together with media appearances and a web site valued in tens of millions of pounds, had given Cainer an income he put at a million pounds a year, of which around £80,000 was the basic fee for his column. The deal he struck with the *Express* was apparently for no fee for his column, but all the takings from his phone line.

The advent of the astro-phone line has made the celebrity newspaper soothsayer more indispensable than ever, though there's little in the 'star lines' for the public, apart from an inflated phone bill. Some astrologers merely repeat the generalities of their daily forecast word for word; others go into detail about the aspects ahead. Those dissatisfied with what they hear can simply keep punching in the numbers for Tarot lines, runestone readings and clairvoyant consultations until they get the answers they want.

It remains debatable how much any astrologer can tell his or her followers from the techniques used for Sun sign forecasts. Even the emphasis on the Sun above other planets is, as we have seen, a comparatively recent approach championed by Alan Leo.

The most commonly used methodology in Sun sign astrology is the 'solar chart', a specially developed ruse from modern astrology's bag of tricks. The solar chart makes the Sun sign for which the forecast is being written the Ascendant of a chart, and then reads off the planets' positions accordingly. If Aries is the sign under consideration, then Aries becomes the Ascendant. If Jupiter is in Taurus, the planet would therefore fall in the second house of the chart, concerned with money and belongings, and Ariens would be told they are currently beneficiaries of Jupiter's financial largesse.

Yet a Sun sign Aries born at, say, 4 p.m. would in reality have a Virgo

Ascendant, meaning that in their horoscope Jupiter is in the ninth house of travel and religion, an altogether different proposition. For this reason, those who know their birth charts are arguably better served by reading the forecasts for their Ascendant.

Moreover, the number of planetary omens available to the Sun sign astrologer is small. The larger planets, signifiers of major life changes, are so slow-moving that their position changes little from week to week, let alone day to day. This makes Sun sign forecasts heavily dependent on the faster-moving 'personal planets' of Mercury, Venus, Mars and, especially, the Moon, which changes signs every two and a half days. New and full Moons are particular boons to the Sun sign astrologer, since they are sure to make strong aspects to most of the other Sun signs. Hence, a new Moon in Libra means Ariens are cautioned to make a new start with partners (seventh house), while Cancerians are advised to look to domestic affairs (fourth house).

Many Sun sign astrologers enjoy their job, not least because it allows them to pursue full-blooded astrology elsewhere, but anyone who has tried to produce a dozen readings from what is essentially the same chart knows that Sun sign astrology is fundamentally a matter of writing riddles that require the collusion of the reader to become meaningful.

Sun sign practitioners can justly claim that ancient Greek and Vedic astrology use techniques that are similar to those used in the 'solar chart'. Some newspaper astrologers defend their practice as a shopfront for astrology proper, or cast themselves as cosmic song and dance men: 'It's my job to offer a little ray of sunshine to people each day,' summed up Jonathan Cainer, who nevertheless added, 'I sincerely hope to see the end of the twelve-sign formula in my lifetime.'

The fact that most newspaper astrologers use much the same techniques – and there are other, more complex approaches than those outlined above[3] – gives their predictions a surprising consistency. A sample based on a November new Moon, for instance, coupled with a Sun–Mercury conjunction, found six newspaper phone lines telling Sagittarians to shut up and reflect. Reason: the Scorpio Moon fell in Sagittarius's twelfth house, the place of secrecy and hidden enemies. 'There's a lot going on behind the scenes – don't talk too much,' advised the *Express*. 'Bite your tongue,' rapped *The Times*. 'You need to question,' suggested the *Mail*. 'There's a lot going on behind the scenes – collect your thoughts before declaring your intentions,' urged the *Sun*. 'Not a propitious time to push for promotion but one for persistent perseverance,' gushed the *Mirror*.

The audience for newspaper astrology has always been predominantly female, a fact reiterated in all twentieth-century sociological investigations into astrology's popularity. Women's magazines, almost without exception, carry star-sign forecasts, which they supplement with features on love signs, zodiacal diets, planetary beauty tips and so forth. In striking contrast, not a single man's magazine in a burgeoning field of titles has yet felt its readers in need of the unmanly advice of the skies. So far, the egalitarian Aquarian Age is in no need of a blokescope.

Just why are women so much more interested in astrology than men? There are several stock responses: that the feminine psyche is more intuitive and more naturally resonant with the 'queen of sciences';[4] that women are more oriented towards relationships and psychology, and hence more attracted to a subject that deals with both; that in a society in which women are denied real power, astrology offers a way to feel in control of your life.

Whatever answer one chooses, the gender bias within astrological circles remains striking. Historically, it's men who have been astrology's torch bearers; until the late nineteenth century women were as rigorously excluded from esoteric interests as from painting, business and almost every other pursuit (literature was, latterly, very much the exception). Today, most people's image of an astrologer is of a woman rather than a man, be it a hoop-earringed hippie madame, a sober astro-psychologist, or Mystic Meg, the latest in a long line of phoney Romanies. Nor are the public's perceptions wrong – at any astrology gathering, women outnumber men by two to one. (Astronomy, by contrast, is so male dominated that in 1998 the senior astronomer Heather Cooper issued an impassioned plea for more female recruits.)

Astrology's appeal to women is replicated across most areas of the New Age movement, whose rise over the last century has been conspicuously in step with the cause of female emancipation. It is not surprising, then, that the rise of a predominantly secular political feminism since the late 1960s has been reflected in astrology, where women have been responsible for substantial modifications to the astrological canon, writing many of the most popular texts and tweaking astro-tradition. In particular the four largest asteroids – Pallas Athene, Ceres, Juno and Vesta – have been co-opted in the cause of astro-feminism by such writers as Eleanor Bach, Zipporah Dobyns and Demetra George, while Melanie Reinhart has championed the planetoid Chiron as central to 'the feminine journey'.

For many, the rebirth of astrology is part of a far wider shift in consciousness, part of the 're-emergence of the feminine' in a world dominated for millennia by male thinking and behaviour. This view is widespread in the New Age movement, which sees its manifestation in: the ecological movement; the 'Gaia' hypothesis (named after the Greek earth goddess), which considers planet Earth as a single organism; the growing interest in ancient civilisations and indigenous cultures; the growth of alternative healing; the rise of feminism; post-quantum science; and the plethora of new spiritual movements.

The American intellectual Richard Tarnas has described astrology as 'the most feminine science', one that 'reveals a universe that is pervaded by Sophia, by psyche, by soul'. This, he argues, is why male-dominated hard science is so scornful of astrology; it's like 'a military academy citadel trying to keep women cadets from entering'.[5]

While many astrologers are sympathetic to New Age idealism, in Europe, especially, there is a grittier tradition at work that has also made its presence felt over the last couple of decades, principally in the shape of a revival of traditional astrology. It was inevitable that the various attempts to cross-dress the crazy old lady of astrology as a butch twentieth-century science, complete with statistical muscle, or to make her over into a planet-powered psychotherapist, would eventually meet with a reaction. The backlash has come in the form of a 'back-to-basics' campaign that rejects Blavatsky's New Age for the Classical Age of Ptolemy and the Golden Age of William Lilly, a duo who have now become traditionalism's patron saints.

The divisions in astrological outlook that the traditionalists have opened up are, as in architecture, painting and jazz, deep and sometimes bitter. Alan Leo has once more been cast as 'the betrayer of astrology' and his followers as interlopers whose astrology is suspect. The psychologists 'have pitched their yurts at one end of astrology's kingdom', as John Frawley, a leading traditionalist, waggishly put the view in his magazine, the *Astrologer's Apprentice*.

The traditionalists have many lines of complaint. First, there is the importance granted by moderns to the three outer planets, Uranus, Neptune and Pluto, which, needless to say, do not figure large in Ptolemy's deliberations on the 'essential dignities' of the heavenly bodies. Even more irksome is the eager embrace of asteroids and other cosmic jetsam by the moderns' Californian chapter, who are, from the traditionalist view, simply making up astrological meanings for them as they go along. Modern techniques have been the source of some particularly bloody disputes, not least because the traditionalists' rule book is both strict and of arcane complexity.

For traditionalists, birth chart astrology itself has become over-stressed at the expense of the divinatory approach of horary astrology, which offers practical answers to specific problems using time-honoured methods. As it uses a chart cast for the time of a question, and not a person, high-flown deliberations on spirituality fall away into irrelevance. Horary has a chequered history in astrology, being associated with fortune-telling even in the ancient world – both Ptolemy and Al Biruni considered horary practices made astrologers into sorcerers, while scientific types such as Richard Garnett thought it made astrologers easy targets for sceptics.

Traditionalists show little interest in trying to appease science or justify astrology by statistical methods, which, they argue, are mistaken strategies. Instead, astrology should wear its practice, and its history, with pride. British astrologer Geoffrey Cornelius, a champion of astrology as divination, speaks for many when he says that 'Astrology is better left inexplicable if in explaining we lose it.'

The traditionalist approach can be deeply fogeyish. Pluto, after all, is here to stay, and for obscurity there is little to choose between Californian psycho-babble about Juno's aspects and archaic talk of planets being 'under the sunbeams'. Still, for anyone who has waded through endless pages on 'healing relationships on the inner plane', a few paragraphs on a chart demanding 'Will my wife divorce me?' are distinctly refreshing. Traditional methods have also been shown to work on thoroughly modern matters. Australian Bernadette Brady had a very popular spell on television by successfully predicting the outcome of Australian Rules Football matches using the techniques employed by the thirteenth-century Italian astrologer Guido Bonatti to determine the outcome of sieges and battles.

The revisitation of astrology's past has taken another, more scholarly form as the re-examination of astrology's history, which in Britain has come from writers like Patrick Curry, Nick Campion and Nick Kollerstrom. In the early 1990s the American astrologers Robert Schmidt, Robert Hand and Robert Zoller embarked on 'Project Hindsight', an ambitious scheme to translate Greek and Roman texts that had either been ignored or had come down to us as translations of translations, often from the classical world to Arabic to medieval Latin. Apart from their sheer curiosity, these writers shared the suspicion that modern astrology had to some extent lost its way; in the words of Robert Hand that 'astrological terminology had become so vague as to be meaningless'. Perhaps a return to astrological sources could provide a steely corrective to the anodyne musings of the New Age. It was not lost on these three writers, or the wider astrological community, that their 'back to the future' movement was taking place while the two planets most often associated with modern astrology, Uranus and Neptune, were passing through Capricorn, sign of tradition and history. The symbolism could not have been more apt.

That, however, did not stop the three august Roberts from falling out. Desite this, all are still engaged in research, and have published books and papers which show that, in Schmidt's words, 'medieval astrologers in some ways garbled the earlier tradition'.[6] It seems improbable that this will significantly change how modern astrologers handle their craft.

There is a wider feeling that astrology's rich past, and its involvement in the history of ideas, which has been so downplayed by academic convention, might provide the fig leaf of respectability necessary to sneak the subject back into universities. After all, the universities of Glasgow and Edinburgh set up a chair of 'parapsychology' with a bequest left by Arthur Koestler,[7] an institution so far preoccupied with spiritualism and ghost stories. Why not a chair of astrology?

Other astrologers feeling constricted by the theosophical/Jungian nexus of stellar-psychology have found alternative ways to express their dissatisfaction than by marching back to the past. Interest in the astrology of world events – mundane or political astrology – has grown steadily, as has financial astrology.

Most recently, particularly in America, there has been an upsurge of interest in Vedic astrology, or *jyotish*, with adverts for software to access its technicalities now prominent in Western astro-magazines. The attitude towards astrology in India is entirely different to that in the West. It is an accepted part of life, with its practitioners, *jyotishi*, consulted over marriages, baby-naming, business deals and important trips, and while the West was appalled to learn that Ronald Reagan took astrological advice, Indians take it for granted that their politicians consult star-gazers. Shrines to the nine planets – the seven traditional bodies plus the meddlesome duo of Rahu and Ketu, the lunar nodes – flicker in many Hindu temples, presided over by the elephant-headed Ganesh, patron god of astrology.

There are major differences between Western and Vedic astrology, including different planetary rulers; in the West, for example, Gemini is ruled by slippery Mercury, in the East by sensory Venus. Aside from using the Sidereal zodiac, *jyotishi* also employ substantially different techniques to those in the West, particularly pertaining to predicting phases of human life, the so-called *dasas*. The whole tone of *jyotish* is more fatalistic, its predictions couched in blunter terms, its assumptions more saturated in ideas about past-life karma and future destiny.

The impulse that has driven freewilled Westerners to explore *jyotish* seems much the same as that which has impelled them to explore medieval and ancient techniques: a desire to escape the vagaries of much of modern astrology in favour of decisive judgements. For all the advances of science and insights from humanistic psychology, the hunger to predict, to be forearmed against the future, is, it seems, much the same as when astrology first leaped into the world millennia ago. Also unchanged is the desire to believe that a new and better world is imminent. It may even be called the Age of Aquarius.

7

LOVE SHALL STEER THE STARS

THE LONG DAWNING OF THE AGE OF AQUARIUS

*

*'That very next morning, there was nothing left of the Equinoxes
because the Precession had preceded according to precedent.'*
Rudyard Kipling

Whatever happened to the Age of Aquarius? Given that its dawning was
noisily greeted by the cast of *Hair* from the top of the album charts
back in 1969, and on a hit single by the appropriately named Fifth
Dimension, it should surely have arrived by now, ushering in an era of
peace, love, harmony and universal understanding. Instead, the world
has carried on with its customary mixture of cock-up, compromise and
confusion. Is the Aquarian Age really on its way? Has it already started?
What exactly is it, anyway?

The short answer to the last of those questions is that nobody knows.
No piece of modern astrological lore is more fuzzily defined or more
speculatively dated, with a starting point that slides around between the
Renaissance and the thirty-first century, depending on which astrologer
you consult. Oddly enough, the Age of Aquarius is also modern
astrology's greatest hit, a phrase that trips with equal ease from the
tongues of dewy-eyed believers and the word-processors of sceptics. It
even comes with a singalong chorus.

Like much else in twentieth-century astrology, the trail of the Age of
Aquarius leads back to the potted-palm parlours of Madame Blavatsky
and the Theosophical Society. Blavatsky had coined the phrase 'The
New Age' in her 1888 tome *The Secret Doctrine*, claiming this would

commence in 1897, ushering in an era of higher spiritual consciousness. Although Blavatsky didn't identify her New Age as the Age of Aquarius, such theosophist astrologers as Bessie Leo and Dane Rhudyar later did the job on her behalf, letting loose a notion whose wingbeats still resound loudy in the astrological circles of the twenty-first century.

Blavatsky's assertion that humanity was on the verge of a more spiritually enlightened era was not new. Throughout history there has never been a shortage of prophets and movements proclaiming the imminence of what is variously described as the Second Coming, the New Jerusalem, the Age of Horus, the Third Reich, God's Kingdom on Earth and sundry other variations on a spiritually supercharged utopia, for whose arrival it is sometimes necessary first to experience, or even wreak, apocalyptic destruction. Even without a calendar date as ominous as AD 1000 or 2000, the sudden blaze of a comet or the sweeping darkness of an eclipse to superheat the popular imagination, millennial fever has always been contagious. Naturally enough, folk like to think the times they inhabit are charged with especial significance. Sometimes they are right.

What is different about the Age of Aquarius is its astrological character, and its foundation in the astronomical phenomenon of the precession of the equinoxes. Thanks to a slight wobble in the Earth's axis, the zodiac as viewed from our planet is always slipping very slowly backwards in the sky; the simplest way to visualise the phenomenon is to see the globe as a spinning top, with the North Pole describing a small circle as it wobbles. Our present North Star, Arcturus, was thus not always our North Star.

Precession means that each year, when the Sun arrives at the point of the spring equinox – when the ecliptic and the equator meet – the zodiacal background to the event has shifted fractionally backwards; by a degree every seventy-two years, to be precise. Over the course of 25,868 years the equinoctial point slips right round the zodiac to complete a revolution variously called the 'Great Year', the 'Platonic Year' or the 'Precessional Year'. This Great Year can be divided into twelve Great Months, giving each of the twelve signs its own 'age' of around 2,155 years, through which the world is passing backwards.

Precession is a sophisticated but important astronomical concept, since it alters the stars' position in the sky, and means that the star charts of astronomers are redrawn every fifty years or so. Because it is so slow-moving, precession is also very difficult to observe. Nevertheless, it was discovered early on, at the latest by the Greek astronomer Hipparchus around 130 BC, and even he may just have been restating a fact known further back in antiquity. Assorted scholars have argued as much, among them Giorgio De Santillana and Hertha Von Dechend, whose book *Hamlet's Mill* contends that knowledge of precession is present in the stellar mythologies of many world cultures. More recently Earth mysteries writers have argued that numerous ancient monuments are aligned to specific constellations according to the age through which the world was passing when they were constructed. Graham Hancock, for instance, maintains that the Sphinx, which he contentiously dates to 10,000 BC, gazed out on the constellation of Leo, which was then the rising constellation at the equinox and which explains the Sphinx's leonine form. Likewise, Wiltshire's Uffington Horse, first etched into the chalk 4,000 years ago, was purportedly aligned to Taurus, when the Bull was the rising sign at the equinox; the 'horse' was meant to depict a bull.

If the ancients did have knowledge of the zodiacal ages, the concept seems to have disappeared by the time astrology was formulated, since neither Hipparchus nor his successors mention it. Not until the late nineteenth century did astrologers begin to formulate world history according to zodiacal age. According to this idea, for the last 2,000 years or so we have been passing through the Age of Pisces, an era ushered in by the birth of Jesus Christ, its avatar. Prior to that came the Age of Aries and so on. Currently, since 2,000 years have passed since Christ's birth, the Age of Aquarius is dawning. Just as individuals reflect their Sun sign, so each Age reflects the qualities of its sign.

There is certainly a shoal of Piscean imagery surrounding the establishment of Christianity. In the early Church Christ himself was referred to simply as *Ikthos*, Greek for 'The Fish' and an acronym for 'Jesus Christ the Son of God Our Saviour'. The Christian fish, daubed defiantly on the walls of pagan Rome by converts to the new religion, is still floating around, most commonly on the rear end of cars. John and Peter, Jesus' fishermen disciples, were lured with the promise that He would make them 'fishers of men'. Jesus fed the five thousand with fishes and loaves; respectively reflecting Pisces and Virgo, its opposite sign. Jesus also washed the feet (ruled by Pisces) of his disciples, a ritual re-enacted by the Pope on Maundy Thursday. Since Christ's coming marked the end of the Age of Aries, it was symbolically fitting that he was sacrificed as a lamb – 'the last lamb of the Aries era', according to Jung.

To add a further soupçon to this symbolic mélange, Jesus is widely reckoned by astrologers to have been born, if not a Pisces, then under the conjunction of Jupiter–Saturn in Pisces in 7 BC, a year first suggested by Johannes Kepler back in 1603. The conjunction of the two planets fused into one exceptionally bright 'star' which was the 'Star of Bethlehem', an omen whose significance would have been clear to the Wise Men of the East, who were patently astrologers from Chaldea.

There are numerous birth charts on offer for the birth of Christ. Medieval astrologers, when they dared to speculate publicly upon a potentially heretical issue, usually took 25 December 1 BC as Christ's birthdate, making Him a Capricorn. Christmas Day, however, was co-opted by the Church from pagan celebrations at the midwinter solstice of 21 December, which was also the festival of the Roman solar deity Mithras – the rebirth of the Sun god was thus neatly replaced by the birth of God the Son. The date preferred for the nativity by the twentieth-century English astrologer John Addey was 22 August 7 BC, a date arrived at following Kepler's lead and refined by biblical detective work. This makes Jesus a kingly Leo. More recently Adrian Gilbert, in his book *Magi*, offers 29 July 7 BC (Leo again), while Percy Seymour, in *The Birth of Christ*, opts for 15 September of that year, making Jesus a Virgo – a son of the Virgin. The Reverend Pamela Crane, in her book *The Draconic Chart*, settles on 7 May 5 BC at 6.50 p.m. (Taurus), citing numerous portents from Draconian astrology in support of 'the chart of a highly spiritual individual'.

'Gentle Jesus meek and mild' fits in well enough with watery Pisces and its links to mysticism and sacrifice, but the real-life Age of Pisces refuses to conform easily to the symbolism. The history of the last 2,000 years is steeped in war, misery, torture and repression, ending with the prospect of global annihilation by nuclear weapons, chemical warfare and ecological cataclysm. What went wrong? There are several explanations swimming about. One says that since there are two Piscean fish, swimming in opposite directions, the Piscean Age has always been schizoid; for every cheek-turning Christian martyr, selfless saint and kindly Samaritan act there has been a witch burned at the stake for heresy, a victim of the Spanish Inquisition and a corrupt pontiff. Another line similarly argues that the Piscean Age brought with it 'the terrible Shadow of Virgonian dispute', as Alice Howell has it: idolatry of dogma, the accusatory finger, and harsh judgements on sin rather than true Piscean compassion.

Once rolling, the symbolism for the ages has a momentum of its own. Thus the Age of Aries, extending from 2000 BC to AD 1, is seen as dominated by the warrior ethic in the civilisations of Rome, Greece and the Celtic lands, while in Egypt the cult of Amun-Ra, the ram god, held sway. The Age of Taurus (4000–2000 BC) had the bull cults of Egypt and Minoa, and witnessed the advent of agriculture (earthy Taurus being the sign of fertility) and the establishment of cities and towns (Taurus embodying stability). The Age of Gemini (6000–4000 BC), under Mercury's jurisdiction, saw the invention of alphabets and writing. The Age of Cancer (8000–6000 BC) was a matriarchal era, as reflected in the pregnant figurines of the era, while the Age of Leo (10,000–8000 BC) showed its flamboyant character in cave paintings.

There are several problems with all of this, not least the imprecision of the dates defining when one age shifts into another; the Great Year, after all, does not divide neatly into 2,000-year packages. The symbolic associations of the various ages also refuse to tally as happily as the theory suggests. The bull cult of Minoa, at around 1500 BC, falls not in the Age of Taurus the Bull but in the Age of Aries the Ram. The cave paintings said to belong to the Age of Leo come from around 25,000 BC – the previous Age of Aquarius (or Pisces). The 'fecund female figures' of the Age of Cancer were just as common in the Age of Gemini. Moreover, the civilisations featured in the usual depictions of the ages are invariably European, whereas the various ages should surely express themselves on a global scale.

None of these arguments is lost on those astrologers who find the Age of Aquarius and its precedents a pain in the equinox. Nicholas Campion, astrology's most accomplished historian, considers that 'the historical ages bear only the flimsiest relationship to what we know of the history of the relevant period.' Others are even more forthright: 'A shabby pseudo-philosophy of human history, for which there is no evidence other than fancy,' snorts the late astrologer and literary critic Martin Seymour-Smith, who was evidently not a *Hair* fan.

Yet the precessional ages have some heavy guns firing for them. The weightiest is Carl Jung, whose book *Aion* (1951) not only examines the symbolism of the Piscean Age but links specific historical events to the movement of the spring equinox point through the constellation of Pisces. Jung saw the two fishes of Pisces as representing the duality of spirit and matter, and takes the arrival of the equinox point at the first star of Pisces, Al Rischa, in 111 BC as the start of the Piscean Age. As the point moved along the first Piscean fish, 'the fish of spirit', Christianity flourished. Then, as the vernal point arrived at the midpoint between the two fishes in 1427 the religious convulsions instigated by Copernicus (1473) and Luther (1483) began. Since then, the equinox point has been travelling along 'the fish of matter', hitting the first star in its tail, Omega Piscium, in 1817. This, says Jung, coincides with the advent of the Age of Reason at the close of the eighteenth century, and the arrival of the materialist, anti-Christian doctrines of Darwin (born 1809) and Marx (born 1818).

The astronomical basis of Jung's ideas contradicts the conception of the Great Ages adopted by many astrologers. The zodiac is not naturally parcelled into a dozen equal segments. That Pisces is a sprawling constellation means the equinoctial point will not pass through it completely until around AD 2800, taking far longer than the 2,150 years allotted by the symbolic division of the Great Year into twelve equal chunks. This is one reason why estimates of the onset of the Aquarian Age vary so greatly, since allotting the Age of Pisces its strict ration of years from Christ's birth would set the starting point of the Age of Aquarius at around AD 2150. Allowing for a cross-over, cuspal zone where one age blurs into the next – an approach that goes against customary astrological practice when applied to the twelve birth signs – it is therefore possible to argue that the Age of Aquarius is, if not quite here yet, already exerting its character over the present era.

Jung could be as woolly about the Aquarian Age's onset as any star-struck astrologer or wishful theosophist. In *Aion* the grand old man of psychoanalysis suggested 1997 and 2143 as two possible starting dates, though he also speculated that the great UFO flaps of the 1950s indicated a shift in the collective unconscious, and elsewhere spoke out

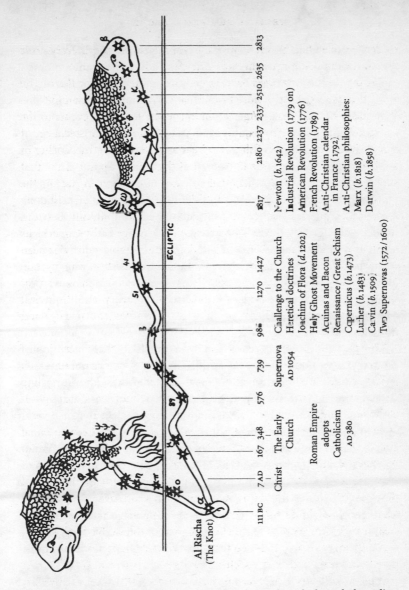

The precession of the spring equinox point as it moves backwards through the zodiac lies behind the idea of the Age of Aquarius. Carl Jung correlated the point's movement through the constellation of Pisces with specific historical events, as shown above. (Illustration by Roland Carter reproduced from *Jung and Astrology* by Maggie Hyde, used with permission.)

in favour of the early 1960s for the beginning of the Age of Aquarius. Perhaps Jung's well-attested sixth sense was quivering at the imminent upheavals of the sixties, or perhaps he was vain enough to associate the end of one age and the start of another with his own passing, which came in 1961, the year before another favoured start-up date for the elusive Aquarian Age. Jung's daughter, the astrologer Gret Baumann-Jung, has expressed the view that her father was 'one of the people sent to prepare us for the Age of Aquarius'.[1]

The year 1962 certainly has plenty of Aquarian symbolism going for it. Most strikingly, there is the grand conjunction of all seven traditional planets in Aquarius in February of that year, a conjunction accompanied by a solar eclipse on 5 February, and a combination portentous enough to have sent several religious sects scurrying up the nearest mountain for refuge from the imminent apocalypse (which, more predictably, failed to arrive). The psychic tremors of the conjunction/eclipse were, however, evidently discernible to the famed American clairvoyant and astrologer Jeanne Dixon, who would later advise Ronald and Nancy Reagan. Dixon declared she had experienced a vision on the day of the conjunction in which she saw a baby born somewhere in the Middle East. This male infant, she declared, would grow to become a world teacher, though one who would lead humanity away from the path of Christ; he was, in fact, the Anti-Christ.

More mundanely, 1962 marked the onset of the 1960s as an age of dissent and cultural and generational upheaval. The year saw the Cuban Missile Crisis, the escalation of the Vietnam War and the intensification of civil rights struggles in the United States; not forgetting the release of the first record by the Beatles, a group who would later become the principal heralds of the Age of Aquarius for the millions of hippies who were by then proclaiming its arrival. Sexual intercourse, as the poet Philip Larkin mused in 'Annus Mirabilis', began the following year: 'in nineteen sixty-three . . . Between the end of the Chatterley ban/And the Beatles' first LP'.

The supposed character of the Age of Aquarius is deeply, indeed hopelessly, entangled with the character and events of the sixties, and raises the question of exactly what is being heralded. Aquarius is, after all, by tradition a rational, philosophical air sign ruled by sombre Saturn, more concerned with science than with sex, drugs and rock and roll. The hippie ethos of the sixties, with its mixture of hedonism, spirituality, pop and ecotopian longing, accords far better with the fluid largesse of Pisces than with sober Aquarius.

Only by admitting the disruptive, electrical energy of Uranus into the equation as the Water Carrier's latter-day ruler can much astrological sense be made of the association between the sixties and the Age of Aquarius. As the planet of revolution, Uranus can be argued to have presided over both the cultural and political upheavals of the time, while the Water Carrier's democratic impulse – the water of life being poured for the benefit of all, regardless of sex, creed or colour – can also be summoned in support of the era of civil rights, Third World independence movements and sexual egalitarianism. This is the view, for example, of Richard Tarnas, who points to the 1966 conjunction of Uranus and Pluto (in Virgo) as the astrological signifier for the upheavals of the sixties.[2]

At the time, however, the dawning of the Age of Aquarius was identified by its propagandists as more or less synonymous with the flowering of hippie utopianism; with what the *Hair* anthem framed as 'harmony and understanding' and 'mystic crystal revelations'. Certainly by 1966 the hippie presses were ablaze with the glories of the imminent, even current, Aquarian Age.

An influential herald of the Aquarian dawn was the Californian astrologer Gavin Arthur, 'the seer of San Francisco'. Born at the turn of the century and the great-grandson of the twenty-first president of the USA, Chester A. Arthur, Gavin Arthur was a quixotic character who had mined for gold in Alaska and knocked around bohemian circles in 1920s Paris, before winding up in 1950s California, where he befriended such beatnik luminaries as Neal Cassady, the star of Kerouac's *On the Road*. Arthur worked as a psychiatric counsellor at San Quentin Prison, where, as an amateur astrologer, he had started using astrology in his work at the jail at the urging of a fellow Jungian therapist. Despite his age – he was in his sixties at the time of California's hippie upsurge – Arthur contributed astrological columns to the underground newspaper the *San Francisco Oracle*, whose eighth issue was devoted to the Aquarian Age, complete with a Technicolor, Tolkienesque Water Bearer on its cover. Among others contributing to the issue was the astrologer Rosalind Sharpe Wall, who later produced the Aquarian Tarot deck.

Although Arthur calculated the Aquarian Age would not arrive until 2260, his propagandising seems to have provided a major impetus for the spread of Aquarius fever through the conduit of Haight-Ashbury and out into the United States and the world beyond.

The underground press elsewhere was likewise spreading the idea of the Age of Aquarius. In Britain's *International Times* John Michell, taking his lead from Jung, presented his dispositions on ufology as part of the shift from the Age of Pisces to Aquarius. The idea even seemed to be hinted at in Stanley Kubrick's *2001: A Space Odyssey* (released in 1969), whose vivid portrayal of a millennial planetary alignment, accompanied by the ominous tones of 'Thus Spake Zarathustra' was one of the film's motifs.

It was natural enough that *Hair*, 'The American Tribal Love-Rock Musical', should include a paean to the new dawn. *Hair* was a collaboration between the Canadian composer Galt McDermot and dramatists Gerome Ragni and James Rado, and was launched off-Broadway on 29 October 1967, becoming an instant success. It was quickly transferred to Broadway proper, and began its 1,750 performances there on 29 April, 1968.[3]

The medley of 'Aquarius/Let the Sun Shine In' became the centrepiece of *Hair*'s disjointed and already clichéd set of cameos from hippie life – draft-card burn-ins, flower-power, be-ins, nudity. Ragni and Rado evidently plucked the astro-jargon for 'Aquarius' from a tabloid horoscope rather than from personal knowledge.

> When the Moon is in the Seventh House
> And Jupiter aligns with Mars
> Then peace shall guide the planets
> And love will steer the stars.
> This is the dawning of the Age of Aquarius.

This is astrological gibberish – Jupiter 'aligns' with Mars several times a year, and the Moon is in the Seventh House for a couple of hours every day (and in an individual's chart for a couple of days each month) – but, hey, the songwriters had their rhyme for 'stars'.

Although *Hair* is usually held up as the acme of hippie cash-ins, it seems to have been conceived in a mood of stoned evangelism by Ragni and Rado. While several years older than most of the cast, the pair donned headband and loincloth to appear in the original off- and on-Broadway productions, and the show's Broadway producer, Michael Butler, self-styled 'Chief of the Tribe', was wont to talk of *Hair* as 'the flowering of a new society'. Astrology was also taken seriously. Butler insisted on gathering the birth data of everyone in the cast, and the original production included a company astrologer (Marie Elise Crummaire) on its cast sheet. The production's errand boy meanwhile doubled as an in-house Tarot reader.

The company astrologer evidently did her job well; *Hair* went on to productions across America and around the world, sold millions of records and was eventually made into a film by Miloš Forman in 1979. Its total receipts were estimated as upwards from $73 million.[4] The evoked spirit of Aquarius didn't last long, however. Within eighteen months Ragni and Rado were in legal battle with Butler, while according to one of the cast's leading lights, Lorrie Davis, cast members were sacked for having the 'wrong' Sun sign. Nevertheless, *Hair* became the vehicle for modern astrology's greatest piece of propaganda, beaming the theosophists' vision of an imminent golden age into the newly founded global village. The Aquarian Age has been gaining ground ever since.

The challenge of finding a birth chart for the age has been one that few astrologers have been able to resist, with many lines of reasoning for the favoured date. For the theosophists, the imminent new age was identified with the coming of the 'World Teacher' whom Blavatsky had predicted, though, according to her, this Messiah-like figure would not arrive until 1975. Blavatsky's successors, however, had other ideas, and in 1909 the World Teacher was identified by one of the society's leading lights, Charles Leadbeater, in the shape of a raggedy Indian boy playing on the beach adjacent to the Theosophical Society's whitewashed headquarters at Adyar, Madras. Groomed for his new role by various upper-class Edwardian theosophists, the boy, Jiddu Krishnamurti, son of an Indian civil servant, grew into a refined young man and a noble thinker, who in 1929 sensibly renounced any claims to the quasi-divine position allotted him by his mentors and declared that 'truth is a pathless land'.

The date chosen for the start of Aquarian Age by American astrologer C.C. Zain was 19 January 1881, on the basis of measurements of the Great Pyramid (in pyramid inches), in which the number 1,881 figured prominently, a date also singled out by Madame Blavatsky as a key turning point in human history, partly on numerological grounds.[5] Alan Leo's wife Bessie, writing after her husband's death, favoured the spring equinox of March 1928 for the advent of both the World Teacher and the Age of Aquarius. Other than 1962, which has already been mentioned, 1996, when Uranus entered Aquarius, and 1997, when there were seven planets in Aquarius, including a Jupiter–Uranus conjunction, are also popular. The year 2000, for obvious reasons, has widespread support, and 2012 is often cited for an apocalyptic shift, a year calculated by New Ager José Aguelles as the end point of the Mayan calendar. The Grand Mutation of Jupiter and Saturn falls in Aquarius for the first time since 1404 in 2020, and this has been proposed as significant by astrologer Adrian Duncan. Finally 2160, using the birth of Christ as a start point and allotting the Age of Pisces its 2,160-year slot of the precessional Great Year, is favoured by Christian astrologer Gordon Strachan.

Whichever date is taken, the intimations of the Aquarian dawn thirty years on from *Hair* are of a decidedly mixed character. Those who wish to dispose of the Age of Pisces can point to the decline of Christianity in the Western world and the ascent of New Ageism as its possible replacement, though sterner minds would argue that the dominance of scientific rationalism over religion fits the Aquarian frame equally well. Aquarian demands for universal human rights as the yardstick for global civilisation – a declaration first heard under newly discovered Uranus back in the 1780s – are enshrined as the abiding ethos of the United Nations, but remain far from fulfilment.

More widespread than Aquarian democracy is the technological innovation ruled over by Aquarius and Uranus, which continues on its giddying exponential curve and now girdles the globe by computer and internet. Other signs of Aquarius' displacement of Pisces include the changing nature of money, allegedly a Piscean invention, which is increasingly being replaced by the techno-finances of credit cards and electronic-finance. Since Aquarius and Uranus have been handed aviation as part of their realms, the growth of flight and space travel are also paraded as manifestations of the Aquarian dawn.[6] One also hears theses such as the argument that the First World War represented the last war of the Piscean Age – mud, rain, mists, gas, mass sacrifice – and that subsequent major conflicts, in which aerial power and technology play much more central roles, have been of primarily Aquarian character.

Modern astrology's preference for describing the current age in Aquarian rather than Piscean imagery is all very well, but does not resolve the issue of whether the new age is an improvement on the old. Modern astrology, after all, holds that all signs are equal but different, all containing their positive and shadow manifestations. Rosy-eyed astrologers of the *Hair* tendency – and there is no shortage – must therefore contend with the unsavoury, shadow side of Aquarius. In place of Aquarian ideals of human collectivism we have dumbed-down satellite television, the global Mc-culture of fast food and consumerism, and the international ambitions of rapacious multinational corporations. Nuclear power, which must also be included as a manifestation of the Aquarian Age, includes the carcinogenic nightmare of radioactive waste (from uranium, mostly), whose decay cycle is a 25,000-year Great Year in itself. What a pity *Hair* didn't warn us.

8

HEAVENS BELOW

GLASTONBURY AND OTHER EARTH ZODIACS

✳

The past is not only another country but a territory whose ownership is relentlessly contested. The extent of astronomical and astrological knowledge in the ancient world has over the last century become a subject of bitter scholarly dispute and fabulous speculation. At essence the dispute is between utopians and social Darwinians, between those who glimpse a now-vanished civilisation in the monuments and beliefs of antiquity, a glimmer of an enchanted golden age, and those who see the world of a few thousand years ago as riddled with ignorance and driven by superstition.

For the utopians, the temples, pyramids, graves and earthworks of Egypt, China, Babylon, Megalithic Europe, India, Meso-America and beyond all show evidence of detailed astronomical knowledge. At one end of the spectrum of prehistoric astronomies are stone circles and passage graves aligned to the solstices of midwinter and midsummer, or to lunar risings and settings. At the other extreme come replications of entire constellations marked out on the Earth's surface on a scale that even now stretches imagination and credulity.

In most academic circles ancient astronomy remains dangerous heresy. Nineteenth-century archaeology's view of the builders of megaliths, for example, was of wode-daubed barbarians whose only apprehension of the heavens was, at best, crude Sun and Moon worship. Sir Norman Lockyer's suggestion at the beginning of the twentieth century that Stonehenge was calibrated to the solstices was greeted with ridicule, despite his position as the grand old man of archaeology. Likewise derided was Lockyer's assertion that the Egyptian temple of Karnak was oriented on the rising of the star Sirius, the representative of the goddess Isis and the most important star in the sky to the Egyptians, not least because its heliacal rising signalled the inundation of the Nile.

Throughout the twentieth century, those who followed Lockyer's drift found themselves similarly rubbished. Among them were Gerald Hawkins, author of *Stonehenge Decoded* (1965), which depicted England's national monument as 'a stone age computer' that could calibrate eclipses, and Alexander Thom, a Scottish professor of engineering whose *Megalithic Sites in Britain* (1967, much expanded 1971) included detailed surveys of hundreds of stone circles and argued their builders were sophisticated astronomers.

The Egyptians' advanced building techniques, hieroglyphic language and profuse art made them undeniably more sophisticated than their European counterparts, but to Egyptologists the subjects of their studies nevertheless remained culturally infantile; superstitious idolaters in thrall to a zoomorphic pantheon. Those arguing otherwise were waved aside as 'pyramidiots', descendants of speculators like Charles Piazzi Smyth, the Victorian Astronomer Royal of Scotland, who believed that the Great Pyramid was both astronomical observatory and contained biblical prophecies.

Over the last quarter of a century, however, the battle for ancient skies has swung steadily towards the heretics. What John Michell dubbed 'astro-archaeology' in 1977 for the theory 'which relates the design and locations of megalithic sites to the observed positions of the heavenly bodies at the time they were constructed' has become impossible to ignore. It's been helped by the arrival of radiocarbon dating – this effectively pushed back the dates of megalithic era monuments by hundreds and in some cases thousands of years, thus scuppering the Victorian theory that culture had been 'dispersed' from the Middle East to the woolly tribes of the West – and by the ease with which the skies of the past can be simulated on computer screens.

Archaeologists have had little choice but to concede ground, and astronomical alignments and large-scale symbolic landscapes have edged towards grudging respectability. Much to the chagrin of academe, the heresies of the utopians have usually bypassed them completely, and been popularised by non-academic tomes. For example, Robert Bauval's and Adrian Gilbert's 1994 best-seller, *The Orion Mystery*, plausibly suggested that the three pyramids of Giza were a terrestrial replica of the three stars of Orion's Belt, and that the Great Pyramids' previously baffling 'ventilation shafts' were alignments to the constellations of Orion and Sirius (Osiris and Isis to the Egyptians). This breakthrough observation, which explained why the three pyramids were almost, but not quite, in line, was dismissed by Egyptologist Robert Chadwick as 'serendipitous' and 'attributed to chance'.

Not all the now lengthy list of best-sellers devoted to unravelling 'ancient mysteries' are as persuasive as Bauval and Gilbert's book. One problem is the tendency of their assorted authors to skate nimbly from Atlantis to the Turin Shroud by way of Jesus' secret birth line and faces on Mars. The most brazen and successful example of sensationalism was Eric Von Daniken's infamous 1969 best-seller, *Chariot of the Gods*, which suggested that humanity had been 'seeded' on Planet Earth by beings from another galaxy. The same notion was served up by science-fiction writer Arthur C. Clarke with Stanley Kubrick in *2001* (later, Clarke was to kibbutz as an earth mysteries expert in a TV series). In tabloid speak it boiled down to the poser: 'Was God an Astronaut?'

The evidence offered by Von Daniken for his arguments was soon dismantled by the experts, but the idea that there was more to the ancient world than a pile of stones erected by savages put down roots. Von Daniken's books have been followed by a succession of best-sellers exploring 'ancient mysteries': Graham Hancock's *Fingerprints of the Gods*, Michael Baigent's *Dead Sea Scrolls Deception*, Adrian Gilbert's *Signs in the Sky* and many more.

If the ancient world was as astronomically sophisticated as its enthusiasts insist, then the origins of the zodiac, and perhaps astrology, may lie several thousand years further back than the Babylonians. Graham Hancock, the most commercially successful of all utopian astro-archaeologists, argues in his book *Heaven's Mirror* that the astronomical alignments of Egypt and later civilisations take account of the phenomenon of 'precession' and the concept of the 'Great Ages'. The concept of the 'Ages' certainly doesn't figure in Babylonian or Greek astrology, but may have existed in the pre-astrological era. For astronomy and archaeology alike, this is a further heresy. Convention has it that it was the Greek astronomer Hipparchus who discovered precession around 130 BC, itself an amazing feat. How could the Stone Age cultures of four to five thousand years ago possibly have known about it? Hancock insists that numerous ancient structures were aligned to constellations according to the 'Age' through which the world was passing: the Uffington Horse to Taurus, the Sphinx to Leo, a cosnstellation also picked out by much later monuments such as the vast temple complex at Ankor Wat in Cambodia. For Hancock, these and other alignments are messages from a vanished civilisation. The message remains unclear, but he discerns within it the cult of an immortality gained from the stars, and the singing out of the spring equinox of 10,500 BC – when the signs of Draco and Orion were respectively at their highest and lowest elevations – as a moment of cosmic significance. Coincidentally, 12,500 years later we have moved almost halfway round the precessional wheel; the same constellations are now at their opposite points in the sky.

Whether antiquity knew about precession or not, its monuments are eloquent testimony to the importance our ancestors attached to stellar-lore. Sometimes the symbolism is obvious. Aligning a chambered tomb like Newgrange so that the rays of the sun at midwinter solstice pierced the darkness brings light into the gloom of the underworld, a seed into the womb of Mother Earth. In other instances, the symbolic intent seems to have been to replicate entire constellations. Several writers have interpreted the gigantic animal drawings on the plains of Nazca in Peru as depictions of constellations, albeit with different figures to those familiar in the West: Orion, for example, becomes a spider.

Nowhere does the lore of 'As Above, So Below' become more literal than with the idea that the land itself assumes the shape of the heavens; that the very rivers, hills and plains of the planet echo the constellations. The Egyptians, for example, saw the River Nile as a terrestial echo of the Milky Way.

Astrologically, the most complete expression of this idea is the Glastonbury Zodiac. Glastonbury is a beguiling nexus of myth. Its ruined abbey stands on what medieval tourist guides called 'the holyest erthe in England', alleged to have been visited by both Jesus (a story echoed in Blake's hymn 'Jerusalem') and his uncle, Joseph of Arimathea, in addition to which there are healing wells, lost grails, ley lines, ancient oaks, Arthurian tales, Bronze Age earthworks and more. The verdant English countryside seems to conspire in the legends: the striking landmark of Glastonbury Tor, an oddly shaped geological anomaly, is visible for miles, its summit crowned by the tower of a St Michael church, whose remainder was destroyed by an earthquake in 1328. Set among the peat marshes of the Somerset levels, the Tor was until the eighteenth century one of several islands protruding above the shifting, flood-prone waters – the 'Isle of Avalon' itself, according to legend and today's tourist brochure.

Glastonbury's importance as a centre of Christian pilgrimage declined after the Reformation, when Richard Whiting, the abbey's last abbot, was dragged to the Tor by Henry's soldiers and hung, drawn and quartered there. In the twentieth century its status as a spiritual epicentre made an astonishing comeback. A succession of mystics, artists, occultists and New Agers have attached themselves to the sleepy little market town and proclaimed its importance. The Christian esotericist Wellesley Tudor-Pole, the novelist John Cowper Powys, the socialist composer Rutland Boughton and the magical adept and writer Dion Fortune were among the 'Avalonians' of the early twentieth century, to be followed in the post-war era by a succession of ley hunters, healers, Arthurians, UFOnauts, druids, hippies and assorted metaphysical hustlers.

It was very much in keeping with the mood of the times, then, when the artist and sculptor Katherine Maltwood 'discovered' the Glastonbury Zodiac in 1925.

Mrs Maltwood's revelation had a suitably Uranian quality. Gazing out over the countryside one day from her summer home in the Polden Hills – the house had a tower where she worked – she was startled to see the shape of a lion clearly delineated by the River Cary and assorted roads and ancient earthworks. Mrs Maltwood soon realised that the lion was not alone, that Avalon's magical vale contained a whole series of figures corresponding to the signs of the zodiac. This was no less than a ten-mile circle of the zodiac's symbols etched into the landscape, with the shapes of Lion, Bull, Fish and the rest outlined by stream, lane and hedgerow. One or two symbols were different – there was a dove rather than Scales for Libra and a ship for Cancer instead of the Crab – but otherwise, asserted Mrs Maltwood, the landscape figures exactly

Madame Blavatsky, founder of the Theosophical Society, sought to 'shape the twentieth century'. Though Blavatsky was not much interested in astrology, her society was highly influential in promoting its cause.

William D Gann
1878-1955

W. D. Gann in the 1930s: astrologer, bible-decoder, and the most successful trader In Wall Street's history, though Gann kept his techniques secret.

Louis de Wohl, astrologer to British Intelligence during World War Two.

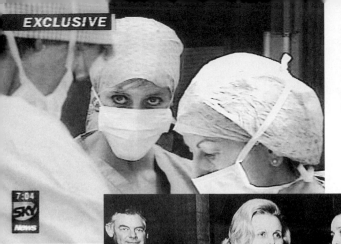

7:04
SKY
News

Neptune in action: Diana's horoscope prominently featured the planet of glamour, martyrdom and anaesthesia.

'What Does Joan Say?' Joan Quigley (left), principal astrologer to Ron and Nancy Reagan during their White House Years, photographed with her sister Ruth in 1975, around the time she was introduced to Nancy by a mutual show-business friend.

Mars on screen: Vivien Leigh as Scarlett O'Hara in the film adaptation of *Gone With the Wind*. Author Margaret Mitchell based her characters on the signs of the zodiac. Aries, ruled by the red planet Mars, inspired Scarlett. Leigh was a Scorpio, also ruled by Mars.

Astrology's greatest hit: The dawning of the Age of Aquarius as proclaimed by the original cast of *Hair* in 1967. The production had its own in-house astrologer and tarot reader.

John Coltrane, jazz giant, in 1966, around the time he turned to astrology for inspiration on titles like 'Leo'.

Carl Gustav Jung. The psychologist, who consulted the birth charts of his patients for insights, believed the UFO flap of the 1950s was one harbinger of the Age of Aquarius.

A pair of magicians and astrologers: William Butler Yeats and Georgie Hyde-Lees, his wife. Yeats married according to a deadline taken by him from his birth chart.

'Married by the solar system': Ted Hughes and Sylvia Plath circa 1959. Hughes' astrological interests weren't to emerge fully until *Birthday Letters* in 1998.

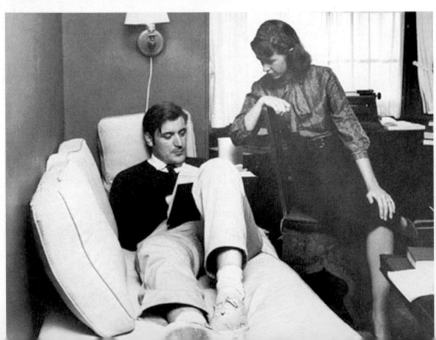

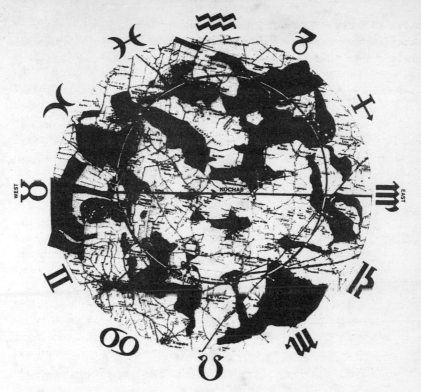

Earthly vision: the Glastonbury Zodiac, as identified by the artist Katherine Maltwood in 1928.

matched their stellar models; a wondrous example of 'As Above, So Below'.

At the time of her discovery Mrs Maltwood was illustrating a new translation of the *High History of the Holy Grail*, a twelfth-century Arthurian romance. Her next imaginative leap followed naturally enough: she had discovered the original Round Table! Moreover, its zodiacal figures corresponded to the characters of the Arthurian saga: King Arthur himself was a horse-riding Sagittarius; Guinevere was the Virgo maiden; Sir Lancelot represented Leo, and so forth. The grail sought by the knights was the zodiac itself.

But how did it get there? Mrs Maltwood concluded that the zodiac had been recognised, and in part shaped, by visiting Sumerians 5,000 years before (she gave an equinoctial point corresponding to 2,700 BC). These antique travellers, laden with Egyptian or perhaps even Atlantean astrological knowledge, she thought, had bequeathed their very name to Somerset, the land of Sumer.

Mrs Maltwood found numerous other place-name clues to support her theory and attributed each sign to an Arthurian hero. If the Once and Future King himself was Sagittarius, Merlin was Capricorn, Perceval was Aquarius, and so on. The monks at Glastonbury Abbey had known about the zodiac, declared Mrs Maltwood, which was a secret handed down over the centuries.

Needless to say, sensible folk thought Mrs Maltwood and her zodiac quite potty. She was undeterred. Married to a wealthy businessman (and Freemason), she was not short of the funds required for a series of aerial photographs that 'proved' her theory. She also wrote and self-published two books delineating her arguments. Although these caused a minor ripple in esoteric circles, Mrs Maltwood's zodiac drifted into Avalonian history, especially when the Second World War arrived and she and her husband fled to Canada.

The 1960s revival of interest in all things Avalonian brought her zodiac back into focus. Hippies gazing out from the Tor, many of them under the influence of more than Mrs Maltwood's ideas, quickly saw it glimmering among the fields and lanes below. It was obvious, man!

The zodiac's most prominent new champion was another artist, Mary Caine, who suggested slightly different configurations for the least convincing signs, like Scorpio, hailed it as 'a revelation of the Aquarian Age' and wrote her own book about it. Caine even came up with her own terrestrial zodiac, nestling in suburban Kingston-on-Thames, discovered after a friend remarked on the number of local pub names with zodiacal associations: Ram, Bull, Griffin, Wheatsheaf and so on. Caine explained earth zodiacs as 'essentially natural contours', helped along by humanity 'acting as an unwitting agent of natural laws'. They are 'the thumb print of the Creator' and we would therefore expect to find them 'at nodal points all over the globe'.

Others were more circumspect. John Michell, most eloquent of Glastonbury's modern mythologists, thought Mrs Maltwood's figures were best seen as 'simulacra' – shapes obligingly supplied by nature to fit expectation. Yet Michell (1990) also found the zodiac 'infectious' and 'effective in waking twentieth-century perception of the large-scale, geomantic works of the ancients'. He noted the curious way that the seven isles of Glastonbury – islands no longer since the levels were drained in the eighteenth century – echoed the configuration of Ursa Minor, the Little Bear, symbol of Arthur.

Elsewhere Michell has championed the views of the French scholar, Jean Richer, who suggested that the major temples of ancient Greece, notably that at Delphi, were conceived as the hub of an astrological wheel which extended across the surrounding landscape, with each of the wheel's twelve sectors corresponding to a sign of the zodiac. Richer claimed alignments from Delphi to other temples constituted the axes of the zodiac; that linking Delphi to Athens and Delos, for example, was the Virgo–Pisces axis.

For a time in the seventies, earth zodiacs were all the rage. Earth mysteries writers Nigel Pennick and Robert Lord added the Nuthampstead Zodiac in Hertfordshire and the Pendle Zodiac, which sprawls thirty miles across the Pennines, and there were others posited at Pumpsaint in Wales, Holderness in Yorkshire, Glasgow, Banbury and Durham. All seem to have since drifted back into the nether realms.

The Glastonbury Zodiac, at least, has antiquity on its side. Unbeknown to Mrs Maltwood, it had already been described three and a half centuries before, by the Elizabethan mage Dr John Dee, court astrologer to Elizabeth I. After visiting Somerset in 1586, Dee noted in his diaries that 'the starres which agree with their reproductions on the ground do lye on the celestial path of the Sonne, moon and planets . . . thus is astrologie and astronomie carefullie and exactley married and measured in a scientific reconstruction of the heavens which shews that the ancients understode all which today the lerned know to be factes.'

Ancient factes or perennial fiction? These days you can buy a map of the zodiac in Glastonbury High Street, or climb the Tor and judge for yourself. 'Too big to be seen, too good to be true!' exclaims Mary Caine. In other words, now you see it, now you don't.

9

RHYTHMS OF HISTORY

THE USA'S BIRTH SIGN AND OTHER TALES
FROM MUNDANE ASTROLOGY

*

Predictions that prove embarrassingly wrong are an occupational hazard in astrology, but few forecasts have been more excruciatingly inaccurate than the reassurances of 1930s astrologers that there was no war imminent. The consensus was extraordinarily widespread. At 1939's Astrological Society conference, held at Harrogate, one eminent name after another declared there would be no war, provoking the Astronomer Royal, Sir Hugh Spencer Jones, to observe that if *he* were an astrologer he would predict war, since the imminent conjunction of Jupiter and Saturn (in 1940) traditionally presaged upheavals, while the two planets joining with insurrectionary Uranus in 1941 must surely spell trouble. It was a shame the king's astronomer did not pursue his stellar insights further, but he at least succeeded in shaming his fellow planet-watchers. Even after hostilities had begun, British star-gazers were consistently caught flat-footed. On the same day that Germany invaded Russia R.H. Naylor was defiantly predicting in the *Sunday Express* that the two countries wouldn't quarrel.

Astrologers were not, of course, the only ones to call the situation wrongly. Even the British Prime Minister, Neville Chamberlain, famously proclaimed 'peace in our time' as Hitler's war machine revved up for its onslaught. Yet the almost universal failure of astrologers to see what was coming was chastening. What planetary signals had they missed or misinterpreted? The more theoretically inclined had several years of grim conflict during which to mull over their failure and reconsider their techniques.

As a result of its failure in the late 1930s, so-called 'mundane' astrology (the study of earthly events) was recast, and over the last twenty years has grown vigorously, being championed by several leading astrological lights. America's Noel Tyl, for example, sees commentary on world events as a way of making astrology respectable, prefacing his 1996 book, *Predictions for a New Millennium*, with the thought that 'Talking about nations and history allows astrology to step forward with its insights into the public arena much more easily than talking about individual personality development.'

Until the aftermath of the Second World War, mundane astrology had languished in the margins of twentieth-century star-lore, despite the central role it had played from Babylon onwards, when predicting affairs of state was astrology's primary function. For modern astrology's creators, the likes of Alan Leo and Dane Rhudyar, personal psychology and astrology's spiritual trappings held infinitely more fascination than foretelling political events or economic upheavals. Even so, the carnage of the First World War had provoked a number of predictions from the eminent names of the time. In 1915 Alan Leo patriotically predicted British victory on the basis of Mars's presence in Leo, where the red planet had also been during the Crimean and Boer wars, both of which had ended in victories for the 'British Lion' (pyrrhic victories, as Leo might have reflected). Meanwhile, Sepharial issued a pamphlet predicting a German surrender in 1917, an event which was to be followed by the dawning of the Age of Aquarius and a new era for humanity. Of the latter in particular there was little sign.

The techniques used for such predictions were scarcely changed from past centuries. Examining the birth chart of a nation's leader, be it Caesar, Kaiser, King or Prime Minister, was one time-honoured method to determine events for a country, on the Arthurian principle that 'The land and I are one.' Another was to look at the 'ingress' charts for the four cardinal points of the year – the equinoxes and solstices, and in particular the spring equinox which is the zodiac's starting point – and read them as a kind of cosmic weather forecast. This practice is what had misled astrologers into predictions of peace in 1939. Since the ingress chart for the 1939 spring equinox showed Venus, planet of peace, rising over London, clearly there would be peace in the year ahead for Albion. Oops!

There was also a tradition that ascribed signs to particular nations or races – Cancer ruled the Chinese, Aries governed England, Aquarius Russia and so forth. Such assignations often stretched back to the ubiquitous Ptolemy; the great systematiser had carved up the second-century atlas according to the four elements, handing fire to Western Europe, water to Africa, air to Russia and earth to the Gulf. Ptolemy also claimed that India was ruled by Capricorn and Spain by Sagittarius. By the Middle Ages, countries and cultures had become variously assigned to planets and signs; Islam was usually held to be ruled by Venus, with Christianity under Jupiter and the Jews under Saturn.

Such shaggy conventions aside, modern astrology had started to study the foundation dates of countries as clues to their destiny. England, for example, had long been considered in the light of the coronation of William the Conqueror at noon on Christmas Day 1066, the resultant chart giving the nation a flinty Capricorn Sun with warlike Aries in the Ascendant. The foundation of the United States of America, timed by the Declaration of Independence on 4 July 1776, was another date that had passed into astrological tradition, though, as we shall see, one which remains a bitterly contested point of astrological lore. By the early twentieth century, German astrologers were also poring over charts set for the establishment of the German republics of 1871 and 1918.

Mundane astrology – which includes not just politics but economics, weather, shipwrecks and similar calamities – also paid great attention to eclipses, and to the intersections of Jupiter and Saturn, the 'great chronocrators' (time lords) whose 19.85-year cycle, from conjunction to conjunction, has from the dawn of star-gazing been considered, if not the solar system's heartbeat (which for humans must be the annual orbit of Planet Earth around the Sun), then the bass line to the music of spheres. This is the conjunction widely ascribed to being the 'Star of Bethlehem' at the birth of Christ, which has presaged the assassination of American presidents and received the blame for all manner of human misfortune. For example, the 1345 meeting of the two planets, along with Mars, all in the sign of airy Aquarius, was blamed by the Medical Faculty of Paris for an outbreak of plague: 'The conjunction of Saturn and Jupiter notoriously spread disaster, while the conjunction of

Mars spread pestilence in the air,' reported the faculty (Saturn showing death, Mars pestilence, Jupiter their vast scale).

That the Jupiter–Saturn conjunction pulses through one element of the zodiac for around a couple of centuries before moving on to another adds a further intricacy to its beat. For example, in 1842 the two planetary giants conjoined in the earthy sign of Capricorn, and thereafter have met in one of the three earth signs of Taurus, Virgo or Capricorn, and will do until 2020, after which their twenty-year meetings will fall in air signs for two hundred years. The shift from one element to another is magniloquently known as the Grand Mutation and carries even more weight than usual. There is a slight aberration in the cycle, which means that the penultimate conjunction in each series moves forward to the next element – 1980's was in airy Libra, for example, anticipating the mutation of 2020 – but the overall pattern is consistent.

By the mid-twentieth century, the mighty Jupiter–Saturn cycle was not the only slow planetary pulse that could be considered. The discovery of the outer planets, which crawl round the zodiac even more tardily than Saturn, brought a more epic dimension to the astrological overview of human history. The past could now be interpreted, and the future forecast, by a slower set of pulses, derived from the positions of Uranus, Neptune and Pluto in different signs of the zodiac, and by their even slower-moving conjunctions, separations and aspects.

The thirty-six-year cycle of Uranus–Neptune, for example, has been much linked to the fate of Russia, whose 1917 October Revolution took place during the two planets' conjunction in Capricorn. When the two planets met again in 1953, the astrologers were waiting, and were rewarded with the death of Stalin. When Uranus and Neptune next met in 1989, the USSR's Eastern Bloc empire crumbled, an event whose accurate forecast by political astrologers is considered further below.

As will be seen in the next chapter, it was financial astrologers, their minds keened by the cycle theories of economics, who first applied the cycles of the outer planets to mundane matters. It took the catastrophe of the Second World War similarly to concentrate the minds of political astrologers on the outer planets. Charles Carter, the leading British astrologer of the mid-century, was so distraught by astrology's failure to predict war – he had been among the culprits proclaiming peace since the mid-1930s – that he denounced the study of ingress (equinox) charts as worthless, and in his 1951 book *Political Astrology* demanded a more stringent approach, using accurately timed charts for nation states and paying more attention to the outer planets.

France's André Barbault was another astrologer who was appalled that his beloved craft had proved so ineffectual in foretelling the Second World War. A precocious eighteen-year-old at the outbreak of war, Barbault quickly put on record that Germany would invade Western Europe on 12 May 1940 (it did so on 10 May) and that the USSR would enter the war on 16 September 1940 (it did so on the 17th, when it invaded eastern Poland). Although he made these predictions by elementary methods (the Sun conjoined Uranus, which he took as Hitler's signifier, on 12 May, and conjoined Neptune, which he took as the USSR's symbolic planet, on 16 September), Barbault was to spend the rest of his life attempting to unravel the complex web spun by the cycles of the five outer planets, from Jupiter to Pluto, and their relation to history. In doing so he attached specific meanings to each cycle and noted the countries to which they particularly applied. These are considered in detail below.

The meanings of the seven traditional planets for political affairs have a far longer lineage. As in an individual's birth chart, the Sun offers an indication of identity, but also represents a national leader. The Moon, by contrast, represents the people. Mercury stands for communications and literature, Venus for creativity, culture and finance, Mars the military, Jupiter the worlds of religion and teaching, and Saturn the legal structure of the state – law and order. As ever, the symbolism is malleable.

Since the identities of the three outer planets have been derived from the events which accompanied their discovery – as detailed earlier – they come even more laden with collective meaning. The associations of Uranus are complex; its revolutionary spirit can lead to freedom but also to bloodshed and autocracy. Neptune is even more ambiguous, being identified with subversion and terrorism as well as with utopian ideals such as those espoused by nineteenth-century socialism, and to such innocent pleasures as cinema. Pluto, discovered on the eve of the Third Reich, comes linked to totalitarianism, fanaticism and the kind of immolation and reconstruction undergone by Germany in the Second World War.

More recently, even the four apparently innocuous asteroids have been called into political and social play, usually by US astrologers. Pallas Athene has been pressed into service as goddess of computers (which are more normally linked to Uranus), on the basis that the goddess was associated with weaving and handicrafts in ancient Greece. The loom, goes the notion, was the first computer. The presence of Pallas Athene next to the Moon in the US chart, both in the technological sign of Aquarius, is reckoned by some to show the country's pioneering role in computing. The grain goddess Ceres is brandished as a signifier of agriculture and ecology. Given that Ceres was conjunct the Sun in the Soviet Union's chart, reckon US astrologers Ariel Guttman and Kenneth Johnson, it is no surprise to find the country had a sickle on its flag, or that agriculture loomed so large in its economic considerations.

How to arrive at the correct 'birth chart' for a country remains a tricky procedure. The usual method is to take the accession of a monarch or the proclamation of a new republic as the equivalent of a nation's birth time, yet most countries have more than one such moment in contention. When considering Britain, should astrologers be looking at the 1066 chart for England, or one based on the United Kingdom, which came into being on 1 January 1801? This, like the 1066 chart, gives the country a Capricorn Sun, but with contrary Libra as its Ascending sign.

France, to take another example, is on its Fifth Republic (a Libra, born 5 October 1958), whereas the four previous republics came into existence under (in order) Virgo, Pisces, Virgo and Scorpio. What sign this makes France and what it says about the country's character is therefore open to debate.

Such vagaries do not much daunt political astrologers, who maintain that national horoscopes have an uncanny way of mirroring if not the country's innate character, then the nature of its current regime, and what is happening to it. Among the most famous examples is the way that the horoscope of the USSR – based on the Bolsheviks' seizure of power in October 1917 – reflected the events of 1989/90, when the Soviet empire fell apart and communist rule was overthrown.

These events had been accurately predicted several years previously (in 1980, and again in 1983) by English author Michael Baigent, using the movements of Saturn and Pluto across the 1917 horoscope as his principal guides. Baigent predicted a power struggle in 1984 (Mikhail Gorbachev became General Secretary the following spring) and in 1989/90 'a revolution which will restructure the country dramatically . . . it would appear the country's tight command structure will disintegrate back into the autonomous states it once was.' This demonstrated substantially more foresight than the expectations of many conventional political commentators.[1] Liz Greene made much the same prediction in 1980, using the same significators.[2]

The problem now facing political astrologers examining Russia is whether the 1917 chart still has any validity – since this was the point when Russian monarchy ended and a republic emerged – or whether the new flag and a new constitution adopted under Boris Yeltsin in 1991 marked the basis for future predictions. If so, was the 'new' Russia born at the symbolic moment when Yeltsin climbed aboard the tank outside the Russian Parliament to give his rousing oration on 19 August and thus thwart the intended Communist coup (making the regime Leo)? Or when the Russian Congress formally adopted the new constitution on 5 September (making it Virgo)? Or when the Soviet Union was finally, irrevocably dissolved on 25 December (making it Capricorn)?

In practice, political astrologers look at several charts that may be relevant and try to find whichever 'works' for unfolding events. The competing charts are also examined for their similarities, in particular if any sign or degree of a sign recurs.

Political astrologers also look at the birth charts of country's leaders for similarities with national charts. Successive national charts for Germany, for instance, show a repeated emphasis on Capricorn and Aries, the latter also being the Sun sign of such national legends as Bismarck, Kaiser Wilhelm and Helmut Kohl. The country's current Chancellor, Gerhard Schröder, is another Aries. Margaret Thatcher's success as British Prime Minister was widely attributed to what was called 'the stunning synastry' between her birth chart and that of the UK.

No national horoscope is more hotly contested than that of the United States, a dispute that owes much to the vitality of America's astrological community at the beginning of the twenty-first century. The Declaration of Independence on 4 July 1776 (in Philadelphia) is the obvious and favourite starting point for most astrologers, giving the fledgling republic a Cancer Sun and an Aquarian Moon; the former said to represent the America of Mom, apple pie and insular self-interest, the latter its democratic, egalitarian instincts.

Yet confusion over the precise hour that the Declaration was agreed and signed by Congress has ensured that the USA's all-important Ascendant remains up for grabs. Should it be nimble Gemini (derived from a 2.15 a.m. chart), warring Scorpio (2.00 p.m.) or questing Sagittarius (5.00 p.m.)? The search for the 'right' answer has generated a prodigious amount of historical research and acrimony. American astrologers have been fairly yoked to their computers to show that their version of the nation's horoscope is correct, correlating the movements of planets and conjunctions across the angles of their favoured chart with such events as the Civil War and the assassination of President Kennedy (the planets, of course, remain at the same points in the zodiac for all the 4 July charts, but the zodiacal wheel rotates in accordance with the time of day used).

There are symbolic associations for each of these Ascendants. Gemini, the most commonly used, has the least going for it, though its champions point to America's versatility, preoccupation with childhood and small-town make-up. Sagittarius is said to describe the country's 'frontier spirit', love of the outdoors and boundless energy. Scorpio has the powerful sign of the eagle (a Scorpio symbol) as the national emblem, along with the USA's Mars-like fixations on militarism, sex, drugs and gunplay.

The dispute over the USA's national chart has at times taken on an almost surreal quality. Champions of the Scorpio Ascendant have cited the evidence of the $100 bill, which has founding father Benjamin Franklin on one side, and on the flip an engraving of Independence Hall, where the Declaration was signed, with a clock tower showing 2.21 (presumably p.m.). Since the Gemini Ascendant requires that the Declaration was signed at the unlikely hour of 2.17 a.m., its supporters have conjured up a scenario in which the founding fathers burned the oil into the small hours to get through their business, or that they deliberately waited up until the most auspicious astrological hour before inking their signatures. Since Thomas Jefferson and Benjamin Franklin were both Freemasons – and therefore conversant with astrological lore – runs this imaginative script, they would have chosen the time of the country's founding with all due care.

This appealing picture is contradicted by the lack of documentary evidence supporting it, and, as persuasively, by the resultant horoscope, which has its ruling planet, Mercury, in retrograde motion, something that any self-respecting astrologer would avoid.

That does not necessarily mean that allegations of Masonic practice at work at the birth of the USA are pure fancy. The American author David Ovason, in *The Secret Zodiacs of Washington DC*, gives a detailed account of the Masonic currents running through the USA's administration, from its founding to the present day. Ovason examines the Masonic affiliations of presidents and founding fathers, the zodiacal orientations involved in the layout of the nation's capital, the timing of the foundation ceremonies of its major buildings, and the copious astrological imagery adorning Washington's public buildings and monuments, to suggest that Freemasonry's ideas about stellar symbolism have been at work since the eighteenth century.

Ovason also makes note that the first person to sign the Declaration on 4 July 1776 – the President of the Congress, John Hancock – was a Mason, and as such 'aware of 4 July as a cosmic event'. The timing of the Declaration, he suggests, was principally motivated by the desire to put the Sun of the new nation at 12 degrees Cancer, in conjunction with the auspicious star Sirius, then at 11 degrees Cancer.[3]

Like several other commentators, Ovason doubts whether 4 July is the correct date for the USA's foundation, suggesting 2 July, when the thirteen constituent states declared their independence, or 5 September 1774, the date of the Continental Congress, as more viable alternatives. The American astrologer David Solte argues for 15 November 1777, when the first US constitution was adopted, giving a Scorpio sun, Gemini Moon and Aquarius Ascendant, and there is no shortage of other contenders. Little wonder that two astrological researchers titled their investigative article 'The Endless Quest for the United States Chart'.[4]

British astrologer Nicholas Campion, author of the compendious *Book of World Horoscopes*, refers to the issue of the US chart as 'a

Gordian knot crying out for a conceptual sword'. The blade Campion applies is to rubbish the idea that a country's horoscope is analogous to an individual's birth chart. 'In historical research it must be recognised that there are no beginnings, only critical junction points when underlying trends of change manifest in major political moments,' says Campion, arguing that the significance of national horoscopes depends on what questions astrologers are asking. For Campion, the 4 July horoscope has significance because it is 'a map of the way the US and its citizens like to show themselves, their beliefs about their own nature and existence'. In other words, pass the apple pie and don't mention the nuclear arsenal.

The USA's founding Masonic patriarchs may or may not have attempted to yoke their country's destiny to the stars, but if the horoscope for a nation's foundation is so telling, it's natural to wonder whether others have attempted to do just that. Coronations and other events of national import were frequently set by court astrologers, a practice followed by Ronald Reagan during his political career. When declaring its independence from Britain in 1948, the incoming government of Burma insisted that the formal handover take place at precisely 4.20 a.m. on the advice of astrologers, presumably because lucky Jupiter would then be ascending. In *An Introduction to Political Astrology*, Charles Carter considered that the founding chart for the Third Reich had been deliberately 'elected' in this manner, although he was probably writing under the widespread illusion that Adolf Hitler took astrological advice. (On the one known occasion when Hitler did consult the stars, it was using a chart set for the proclamation of the German Republic of 1918.)

There is also a suspicion that the state of Israel came into being at a moment set by astrologers (15 May 1948 at 4 p.m.). What is more certain is that Mossad, the Israeli Secret Service, paid close attention to the country's foundation chart when planning its 1977 raid on Entebbe airport to free Israeli hostages. The intelligence writer Richard Deacon, in his book *The Israeli Secret Service*, claimed that the chart 'had been kept up to date since the creation of the state in 1948. Experience had shown that it was astonishingly accurate in regard to both the Six-Day and Yom Kippur wars, and so its indications as regard the Entebbe raid were carefully examined.' Finding Uranus and Neptune well aspected –

both planets are connected to aviation – the raid was launched and was successfully executed.

Political astrology's success in predicting future events using national charts is chequered – as ever, astrology is only as good as the astrologer staring at the glyphs before him or her – but no one can accuse political astrologers of being vague in their predictions. They are often audaciously exact. The forecasts of Noel Tyl, America's self-styled 'Master of Astrological Prediction', are full of gritty detail about time, place and outcome. Tyl has chalked up several notably accurate predictions: as well as the fall of the Soviet Union, he forecast the Israel –PLO peace treaty, and, most famously, the outbreak of the Gulf War.

In 1996 Tyl published *Predictions for a New Millennium*, a giddy overview of turn-of-the-century geopolitics complete with fifty-eight detailed forecasts about what would happen, where and when. A Harvard graduate with a formidable grasp of world history and economics, Tyl gave his predictions after lengthy expositions on, say, Indonesia's history, or the internal politics of the United Nations. So far his score sheet is not impressive, although he's had a few results: Deng Xiaoping died in early 1997 as he forecast; Israel did elect the Likud Party in autumn 1996; Charles and Diana's divorce in July 1996 also arrived, though two months ahead of Tyl's schedule, while Charles's 'personal tragedy' of spring 1997 arrived a little late, in August.

Against such successes are a string of wrong calls: that there would be major upheaval in Spain between November 1996 and June 1997; that Helmut Kohl would triumph in Germany's 1998 general election; that China would announce it was abandoning communism in 1999; that Saddam Hussein's rule would end in 1996. It remains to be seen whether the Vatican will disintegrate early in the twenty-first century, as Tyl predicted.

Putting aside national horoscopes and the history of individual nations, it's possible to make specific forecasts about political and cultural events through the interplay of the outer planets. Under the influence of Jungian psychology, Uranus, Neptune and Pluto have become the carriers of Jung's collective unconscious and signifiers of the zeitgeist. 'There are great movements of ideas and visions which erupt in society and find their way into the mouths of many people all at once,' declares Liz Greene (1983), before speculating which ideas belong to which planet.

The astrological journals are now full of speculation about what is signified by the movement of an outer planet into a new sign, with comparisons to previous periods of history. If Neptune was in Aquarius in 1834, what can be expected now it's back there again from 1998 to 2011? The richness (or ambiguity) of astrological symbolism makes for endless conjecture; for example, the spectre of AIDS is often linked to the arrival of the dark force of Pluto in sexy Scorpio in 1983. Pluto's shift into religious Sagittarius in 1996 was meant to presage a major increase in religious fundamentalism and a shake-up in the world's religious institutions. Yet a moment's reflection shows that AIDS is even more rapacious at the start of the twenty-first century – although in Africa, where Western astrologers tend not to look – while religious fundamentalism was probably stronger in the 1980s than it has been in the last five years.

Symbolic thinking, in other words, can easily drift into vagueness. This becomes particularly apparent when the outer planets are used as generational markers. For example, the baby-boomers are plausibly described as the Pluto-in-Leo generation, born during Pluto's long residency in the Lion between 1939 and 1956, with egocentric, show-off Leo describing the 'me first' generation. The boomers' predecessors had Pluto in conservative Cancer, sign of home and hearth, from 1914 to 1939; appropriately, this was the generation who fought for their homelands in the Second World War.

The symbolism is less persuasive when considering other generations. Why, for example, should the generation sacrificed on the pyre of nationalism in the First World War have been born with Pluto and Neptune in unmenacing Gemini? (The flighty Twins make a better sign for the Roaring Twenties and the 'lost generation'.) Likewise, it is hard to see why the boomers' successors, born with Pluto in health-conscious, purity-seeking Virgo (1956–71), should have produced punk and grunge as a collective expression.

Here, astrologers are inclined to change horses, cross-referring to the presence of visionary Neptune in dark Scorpio between 1958 and 1969 as an explanation. Writing about 'The Cruelty of Today's Youth' in 1977, *Horoscope* magazine thought the punk generation 'faced a life and death conflict in their collective psyche. Uranus in Leo and Neptune in Scorpio translates to mean self-will versus self-loss – an arrogant desire for freedom coupled with a simultaneous longing for death.'

Astrology, though, is no more guilty of cutting its cloth to fit the facts than conventional social commentators. The talking shops of the social scientists and the watering holes of the media are always awash with buzzwords and trite, generational theories which are quickly washed away. Who now talks of 'the Tarantino Generation' (so 1995!) or remembers the eighties description of baby-boomers as 'squeezed radicals'? Astrology, at least, has the solar system on its side.

Between them, Jupiter, Saturn, Uranus, Neptune and Pluto offer a total of ten different cycles, and constitute a formidable, and often contradictory, lexicon of symbolic meaning for the astro-historian. When two or more cycles coincide events of particular magnitude are reckoned to manifest. While the precise meanings vary according to individual astrologers, there is a widespread consensus of interpretation, much of it based on the detailed analysis of André Barbault.

The lengths and connotations of the cycles of the five slowest planets vary from twelve years for Jupiter–Pluto to 492 years for Neptune –Pluto. Since the latter far-flung duo meet so rarely, their encounters have become a yardstick for paradigm shifts in humanity's outlook. Their last meeting, in ingenious Gemini in 1891, is often taken as the starting point of the modern era.

The meanings of the cycles are derived by combining the symbolism of the two planets. Saturn and Pluto, which meet every thirty-three years, make a combination with a sinister reputation. The two planets met in Cancer in October 1914, four months after the outbreak of the First World War, coinciding with the conjunction of Jupiter and Uranus. Contemporary astrologers were, obviously, unaware of Pluto's existence. Subsequent conjunctions took place in 1947 and 1982. The pair next meet in 2020.

The pairing of utopian Neptune and materialist Saturn – they meet every thirty-six years – fits the duo's association with the rise and fall of communism. André Barbault pointed out that their 1846 conjunction was followed shortly afterwards by Marx's *Communist Manifesto*. That the conjunction of 1917 coincided with the Bolshevik seizure of power in Russia, that in 1953 with the death of Stalin and that in 1989 with the fall of communism is the kind of timing of which political astrologers dream. The next encounter is 2026.

The conjunction of revolutionary Uranus and powerful Pluto, which falls between 110 and 140 years apart, is reckoned to mark periods of turmoil and social upheaval. Since Uranus also governs technological innovation, their last conjunction, in 1965/6, is bracketed to both the computer revolution and the revolutionary fervour of the times, which was also present at the previous conjunction in 1850.

Encounters between unsettling Uranus and religious Neptune – the conjunction falls every 172 years – are linked to major changes in religious faith. The Spanish astrologer Jose de Pablos cites the conjunction in AD 622 as signalling the birth of Islam. The 1993 conjunction was the source of great speculation; that this fell in conservative Capricorn suggested to some a reform of the economic world order, though there are few signs of it yet.

The opportunities for decoding history according to these cycles is considerable, but clearly open to the hindsighted grafting of symbolic fancy on to historical fact. And if one cycle does not quite tally with a historical high point such as the Renaissance, it's usually possible to locate the planetary markers elsewhere. The issues are further complicated when not only the conjunctions of planets are considered, but their intermediate aspects, which are interpreted on a rise-and-fall basis. Shortly before his death, André Barbault described a cycle thus: 'When two planets conjunct a current is born. It takes shape with the sextile aspect (60 degrees), becomes a crisis or an internal conflict with the square (90 degrees), asserts itself and takes wing with the trine (120 degrees), and fights or is fought during the opposition (180 degrees), a final challenge during which it either surpasses itself or regresses. The current then moves to a waning phase.' Fanciful as this might seem, it is not that dissimilar to the cycles perceived by some conventional historians, some of whom have linked human history to sunspot activity.

For mundane astrology, the rare arrival of three outer planets at the same point in the zodiac sounds the chimes of the cosmic clock. At around 579 BC Pluto and Neptune were in conjunction, which was followed three years later by conjunctions of Pluto and Uranus, and Neptune and Uranus. This coincidence of the three 'super-cycles' coincided with an assortment of significant beginnings: the foundation of Buddhism, Confucianism, Pythagorean thought and the rationalist school of Greek philosophy. It was, as Charles Harvey observes in *Mundane Astrology*, 'one of the most fertile and creative periods in human history'.

In the 1960s Barbault realised it was possible to combine all the major planetary cycles into one master cycle, which could be expressed as a graph. This plotted the sum total of degrees separating the five most distant planets, and showed, in effect, the pulse of the outer solar system as viewed from Planet Earth. Barbault called this the 'Cyclical Index', claiming it correlated with political and economic events: when the index rose international tension, wars and economic recession waned; when it plunged they increased. In 1914, for example, the index dropped dramatically, and there was an even more precipitous fall in the late 1930s, bottoming out in 1946. More trouble came with another fall from 1950 to 1958 (the Korean War, the Suez Crisis). So far, so good. Yet the steepest fall of all in Barbault's index, from 1975 to 1984, was not met by another world war. Barbault argued this fall showed the economic slump that began in 1974 with the oil crisis, but this scarcely compares with two world wars. Barbault correctly forecast that the world economy would recover in the mid-nineties (at least in the West), and, speaking in 1997, predicted that 1999 would be 'a great year for Europe' and that the new millennium would find 'humanity launching into a constructive future'. The next peak of the index is in 2005.[5]

With all their national horoscopes, planetary cycles, midpoints and other methodology, have today's mundane astrologers fared any better than their predecessors in the 1930s? Not necessarily. The political forecasts of Barbault in the 1960s were subject to rigorous scrutiny by a fellow astrologer, Jacques Reverchon, who concluded that his predictions were no better than those of non-astrological pundits. Yet equally, astrologers do make accurate predictions of political events and, as Charles Harvey pointed out, they identify events, but interpret the symbolism incorrectly. Harvey uses as an example a 1982 prediction that there would be a major air crash, based on a Uranus aspect. There wasn't, but on the day of the supposed crash a major airline went out of business. In 1993 Harvey himself predicted a spring stock market fall, based on a Saturn–Pluto aspect, which didn't arrive; but the New York

Trade Center and the Bombay Stock Exchange were both bombed. Right symbols, wrong events.

Astrologers regularly make correct predictions, and go to great lengths to register them before the event. Among the most famous examples is Dennis Elwell's 1987 prediction of a major seafaring tragedy involving British shipping, a forecast about which he felt so strongly that he wrote to the Cunard and P&O shipping lines, who responded politely but coolly. A few weeks later the ferry *The Spirit of Free Enterprise* sank in Zeebrugge with major loss of life.[6]

Like anyone else peering at probable futures, astrologers get it both wrong and right, and, like others, the correct forecasts tend to be remembered and the erroneous ones quietly forgotten. The major difference is that political astrologers are seldom paid to make their forecasts or rewarded by results. Except, as the next chapter shows, when it comes to money.

10

PENNIES FROM HEAVEN

THE RISE OF FINANCIAL ASTROLOGY

*

For the world's financial traders, 19 October 1987 remains infamous as 'Black Monday', the day on which the global stock markets went into unexpected freefall, wiping billions from their value, provoking comparisons to the Wall Street Crash of 1929, and signalling the end of the 'Greed is Good' era espoused by Gordon Gekko in Oliver Stone's film *Wall Street*. The markets, and greed, survived to prosper afresh, but not before substantial safeguards had been installed to try to forestall a crash of the same magnitude.

For astrology, 19 October 1987 was anything but black. On the contrary, it sealed the acceptance of financial astrology as a predictive tool by the world's financial institutions. Several leading astrologers had accurately predicted the timing of the collapse, and were on record as having done so, among them Wall Street trader Arch Crawford and the British duo of Charles Harvey and Mike Harding, who had correctly called the crash back in the autumn of 1986. The more open-minded executives of the world's banks and trading houses flexed their red braces ruefully and reflected that if they had been listening to the star-gazers, they could have saved themselves and their clients a lot of grief and, more importantly, a lot of money.

Throughout the 1990s financial astrology became an ever more visible player in stock market economics. It is now an open secret that a small but significant number of the world's major financial institutions have an astrologer or two on their payroll. They don't like to parade this too openly, but in an area where a rumour about a minor adjustment to the US borrowing rate can add or subtract billions from the Dow Jones Index, or the hint of a boardroom squabble can send a company's shares racing up or down, factoring in some discreet astrological advice to fiscal forecasts makes sound business sense, especially when the astrologer's predictions can be measured with the same hard-nosed rigour applied to other aspects of corporate activity.

In other words, financial astrologers are judged ruthlessly by results. For once, the customary accusations that astrological forecasts are too vague to be meaningful cannot apply, and since the influence of financial astrology is spreading, it is apparently working. Articles about it now appear regularly in the business sections of broadsheet newspapers. It seems that if anything can make astrology respectable for the age of materialism, it will be its role in the material realm of economics, a realm less interested in soul growth than equity growth, and blithely unconcerned with the objections of sceptical physicists as long as oil prices march dutifully in time with Neptune's orbit, as astrological theory predicts.

At first glance astrology and economics seem at opposite ends of a spectrum running from fanciful to grimly realistic, but in many respects the two are near twins. Both are self-proclaimed sciences that to outsiders look suspiciously like voodoo. Both are presided over by a priestly caste dealing in esoteric mathematical constructs, hieroglyphic graphs, abstract ideas and dubious predictions. The general populus may thumb through the daily financial pages and horoscopes, but otherwise economics and astrology remain hermetically sealed systems from which the uninitiated can glean little beyond such basic concepts as the qualities of a Sun sign or the rate of inflation. To understand the technicalities of Uranus arriving at the Sun–Mars midpoint, of non-indigenous growth theory or of selling short on futures requires more time and study than most of us care to invest.

Above all, astrology and economics share an obsession with time cycles, with getting the disorderly human world on to the smoothly undulating curves of a predictable graph. Most celebrated of all economic cycles is capitalism's boom-and-bust cycle, running on a fifty-four-year average, which was formulated by the Soviet economist Nikolai Kondratieff back in 1931 (for which anti-Marxist heresy Stalin dispatched him to Siberia to die). There are numerous others; for example, the nine-year business cycle identified by the nineteenth-century French economist Clement Juglar and still in use, or any of the thirty-seven cycles at work in the US economy, according to Thomas Dewey, the American economist who established the Foundation for the Study of Cycles in 1941.

To these the astro-economist can bring the same raft of planetary cycles used by other branches of mundane astrology: the twenty-year conjunctions of Jupiter and Saturn; the forty-five-year meetings of Saturn and Uranus; the approximately annual passage of Venus around the zodiac; the waxing and waning of the Moon. There is no shortage.

Such cycles can be applied in both general and specific terms. For example, since jolly Jupiter represents growth, and stern Saturn restriction, their relationship is taken as a primary indicator of economic activity. As in political astrology, rarer planetary events carry even more weight. The 1993 conjunction of Uranus and Neptune (which falls every 170 years) was widely interpreted as the signal for the return of a 'bull' (rising) market, which duly arrived. At the other extreme of frequency are conjunctions of the Sun and slippery Mercury, which arrive every few months and have been doggedly correlated by American astrologer Jeanne Long with the peaks and troughs of soya-bean prices.

Planetary cycles are but one weapon in the armoury of today's financial astrologers, who can also check the prospects of an individual company from its 'birth chart' – either an 'incorporation chart', when the company is registered or incorporated, or its 'first-trade chart', which is set for the moment it was floated on the stock exchange. The incorporation chart is claimed to show the potential and character of the company and can be analysed in much the same way as an individual's chart. A cosmetics firm with a badly aspected Venus is clearly going to be no beauty, whereas a mining company with a powerful Saturn is destined to dig deep. The first-trade chart is concerned more with the company's stock, its fortunes in the market place.

Tycoons and captains of industry can also be subjected to astro-analysis to ascertain the prospects of their economic empires, meaning that the nativities of Bill Gates and Rupert Murdoch are scrutinised as eagerly as the first-trade charts of Microsoft and News International.

That business and financial magnates use astrology is more speculated upon than known. Even arch-geek Bill Gates fell under suspicion of astro-trading following the launch of Microsoft's Windows 98 software at the propitious hour and date of midnight, 25 June 1998, shortly after a new Moon and the summer solstice, with Jupiter ascending.[1] Indeed, if financial astrology continues to gather force, it will be a brave entrepreneur who refuses to consider its advice, simply because astrologically attuned market players are evaluating his or her moves. A dot.com market flotation with a retrograde Mercury would be unlikely to inspire confidence in an investment fund with an astrologer on board.

In Asia and India it is expected that businesses will consult astrologers before making any major moves. Until recently, similar activity in the boardrooms of the West has been likely to bring a curled lip on trading floors, though a number of tycoons have confessed to the astrological habit. Early in the twentieth century the American magnate J.P. Morgan proclaimed bluntly that 'Millionaires don't use astrology, billionaires do.' Morgan's adviser was Evangeline Adams, the most celebrated American astrologer of her day, who also advised two ex-presidents of the New York Stock Exchange, Seymour Cromwell and Jacob Stout.

Around the time Morgan was making his pile, financial astrology was being covertly trailblazed by W.D. Gann, a Texan warehouse clerk who became the most successful stock market trader of his era, and perhaps of all time, making over $50 million from the markets during his career. Gann was a phenomenon, able to predict the peaks and troughs of the market and of individual stocks and commodities with uncanny accuracy. In 1909 a financial journal, *The Ticker and Investment Digest*, published an interview with Gann, along with a record of his dealing transactions for a single month. *The Ticker*'s gobsmacked reporter observed that 'During 25 market days, Mr Gann made, in the presence of our representative, 286 transactions in various stocks, on both the long and short side of the market. Of these transactions, 264 resulted in profits, 22 in losses. The capital with which he operated has doubled 10 times so that at the end of the month he had 1,000% of his original margin.'

Nor did Gann's accuracy end there. He forecast the outbreak of war in 1914 and its end in 1918. Alone, he correctly called the Wall Street Crash of 1929, predicting in the November 1928 issue of his widely read *Annual Forecast*, that 3 September of the following year would bring a market collapse, as indeed it did. He followed this Delphic coup in June 1930 with a warning of imminent depression that also proved soberingly accurate. Shortly afterwards, Gann retired to Florida, though he continued to teach courses and write about his methods.

Unsurprisingly, given his success, there was no shortage of people wanting to know Gann's secrets, and willing to pay handsomely for them, though he fought shy of revealing too much. That he kept charts for the New York Stock Exchange and the 1842 Grand Mutation of Jupiter and Saturn on his office wall was a pretty clear clue to one of his methods. Stocks, he said, had 'their own centre of gravity'. Gann toted graphs and maths as the reason for his success, but only towards the end of his life did he let slip that he relied on a mixture of astrology, numerology and Pythagorean mathematics. Like Isaac Newton, Gann was also an ardent Bible decoder.

Others were less reticent about coming out of the astrological closet. In the half-century following the 1929 crash a number of researchers published assorted astrological techniques that claimed to correlate the markets and national economies with planetary movements, focusing mostly on the cycles of Jupiter, Saturn and the outer planets, with Pluto an added factor in the equations after its discovery in 1930. The consensus that emerged was that while the cycles of the slow-moving planets showed the long-term rhythms of economic cycles, the swifter inner planets – Sun, Moon, Mercury, Venus and Mars – were the catalysts for short-term surges, falls and market turbulence.

Calculating and compounding these multiple cycles, into which aspects, eclipses and other phenomena must be factored, and then allying the resultant astro-statistics with an insider's knowledge of the markets meant that financial astrology remained the preserve of the very few. That it was championed by a few Wall Street high-flyers like David Williams, who for many years worked as head buyer for Consolidated Edison and later became a millionaire by playing the market, kept the market's more open minds sympathetic to planetary signals. It was a 1963 *Wall Street Times* article about Williams that sparked the interest of Arch Crawford, an analyst for Merrill Lynch who subsequently became the first high-profile financial astrologer and started his newsletter, *Crawford Perspectives*, in the late seventies.

Many of today's leading financial astrologers – for example, the Americans Bill Meridian and Ray Merriman – like Crawford, have a background in the markets and came to astrology when they discovered its efficacy as a predictive tool, leading them to combine the twin voodoo arts later in their career. Some have travelled in the other direction, from mainstream or psychological astrology. America's Henry Weingarten, for example, had founded the New York School of Astrology in 1968, and was inspired to set up his investment service, the Astrologer's Fund, in 1988, after noting the success of financial astrology in predicting Black Monday. Weingarten has since chalked up numerous predictive successes of his own, including the 1990 Japanese market crash, and the 1997 collapse of the Far Eastern markets. Among the leading lights in Britain, Christeen Skinner and Graham Bates both come from backgrounds in mainstream astrology, the former having taught for many years with the Faculty of Astrological Studies, the latter having been chair of the Astrological Association.

The arrival of the personal computer at the beginning of the 1980s transformed the scenario, making light of what were previously laborious calculations. That the computer revolution arrived just as the world's stock markets were being deregulated, and were themselves plunging into the brave new world of cyberspace, helped yoke together the worlds of Urania and Mammon in a new and mutually profitable partnership.

There are now a number of sophisticated software packages on the market, most developed and marketed by leading financial astrologers. For example, Bill Meridian and Alphee Lavoie are co-authors of the astro-software *Financial Trader*, while Jeanne Long, a former futures trader, offers *Galactic Trader* and *Fibonacci Trader*, which Long says are sold to 'very sophisticated groups worldwide – banks and financial institutions'. Such programs offer a history of major cycles, can correlate them against the prices of specified stocks or commodities, and give access to thousands of first-trade charts for major companies. Their sophisticated astro-wizardry includes isolating all those companies with specific zodiacal points in their charts so that these can be considered as a helpful/unhelpful planet approaches.

The signifiers and techniques of financial astrology go from the basic to the fiendishly complex. Traditionally the signs most associated with money matters are the pragmatic and acquisitive earth signs of Taurus and Capricorn. Taurus, ruled by pleasure-loving Venus, is thought partial to material comforts and gracious living. Capricorn, ruled by the skinflint planet Saturn, is by repute coldly acquisitive and driven as much by fear of penury as love of luxury. Either way, both the Bull and the Mountain Goat have the determination and stamina to make their pile. Taurus is uncannily common in the 'birth charts' of financial institutions – the stock exchanges of Wall Street (17 May 1792) and Tokyo (15 May 1878) among them – while financial astrologers also regard the Swiss franc and the Bank of England as Taurean.

Jupiter has always been the planet of good fortune and large fortunes, but money-making powers are also attributed to other planets: Venus is traditionally reckoned fortunate, though American astrologer Lois Rodden, author of *Money: How to Find it with Astrology*, demurs. Rodden cites Mars as prominent in the charts of lottery winners, and, like other moderns, considers far-flung Pluto a potential mark of the mogul. 'Pluto is the planet of power and money is power,' reasons America's Magi Society, whose book *Astrology Really Works!* looked at the Forbes list of the 400 richest Americans, and located the combination of Jupiter and Pluto in the charts of the three richest billionaires (Bill Gates, Warren Buffet and John Kluge).

An individual's or company's financial prospects are also shown in the houses of the birth chart; helpful planets in the second house (ownership and money) and the eighth (inheritance and legacy) suggest money comes easily. A combination of Jupiter in Taurus in the second house – money planet, money sign, money house – hence spells serious riches, though if, for example, escapist Neptune was in poor aspect to this combination, the fortune could well be squandered on drugs, drink or gambling, or end up donated to a religious cult.

As in political astrology, the meanings of the planets are adaptable, though many come with centuries-old associations, and will signify different things according to what's under scrutiny: a company, a stock exchange or a national economy. There are also differences of opinion among astrologers.

The major wealth signifiers are Venus and Jupiter, the latter also indicating growth potential, bonds, financial services and banks, while the Sun is traditionally the symbol of gold (though moderns sometimes hand this to Pluto). In a company's chart the Sun shows its central identity and represents its chief executive, who is likely to find himself replaced when the Sun is eclipsed or malignly aspected. The Moon represents the public – either a company's personnel or the consumers of its products – and is likewise linked to everyday products. Transport, the media and telecommunications obviously belong to the winged messenger Mercury, along with trading, deals and mental muscle; a think tank with a weak Mercury is a dim prospect. Mars, which has always been the planet of iron and steel, is also handed heavy machinery, weaponry and sport, and is the yardstick for a company's go-getting attitude. Saturn shows a company's structure, administration, property resources and agriculture. Of the outer planets, Uranus signifies a company's capacity for innovation, technology, computers and aviation, making it a good omen for an arms dealer. Good aspects to Neptune show a company has 'the vision thing', poor aspects that it's susceptible to fraud. In commodity terms the planet is linked to oil, pharmaceuticals and (again) aviation. The murky force of Pluto is, as always, tied to atomic power, though it is also deemed the power planet for tycoons.

In company charts the Ascendant and Midheaven are also vital; the former represents the company's shareholders, the latter its goals and public standing. Once a company chart is in place, current planetary transits are read in much the usual way. If a first-trade chart has an adverse Saturn aspect approaching, then sell! If Jupiter is crossing a company's Sun, buy! Alternatively, it could simply mean the chairman getting an overblown pay rise. 'Saturn will take the stock down, Uranus will split the stock, Jupiter will take it up, Mars will bring high volume,' is Alphee Lavoie's rule of thumb.

As ever, endless techniques can be applied, not all of them complicated. US astrologer Mary Downing cites the case of a communications company that started business with Sun at 29 degrees Gemini: 'The Sun was getting ready to change signs, to do something completely different. Sure enough, it only lasted a couple of months.'[2]

Most astro-financial advisers caution that even a company with a perfectly poised incorporation chart is not a good investment unless its configurations resonate with an investor's nativity; a strongly Libran punter will find a Cancerian company a troublesome addition to his or her portfolio.

Moreover, even individual companies exist only within the larger cycles of markets and economies. For W.D. Gann, the twenty-year conjunctions of Jupiter and Saturn provided the major clue to the markets' behaviour: a boom tended to follow the meeting of the two planetary giants, with a bust occurring at their opposition. Furthermore, observed God's own trader, a major recession arrived after sixty years, with every third opposition, when Jupiter had completed five orbits of the Sun and Saturn two. Gann dubbed this the 'master time cycle', and it is borne out by recent history with uncanny accuracy; in the US economy, at least, major economic downturns accompanied the opposition of the two planets in 1811, 1871, 1930 and 1990.

The absence of records has not allowed the astro-economists to correlate economic activity and planetary cycles with the same grand sweep as their historian colleagues, but there are plenty of theories about these and shorter cycles. For instance, in the 1930s the American astrologer Louise McWhirter showed that the basic pattern of the US economy followed the 18.6-year backward movement of the lunar nodes (eclipse points) around the zodiac with surprising accuracy, peaking when the North Node was in the sign of Leo, and hitting a low when it reached Aquarius. Though this cycle was modified by other planetary factors, the underlying pattern remained sound, though, confusingly, it didn't seem to work for countries other than the United States.

Astro-economists further maintain that planetary cycles work more strongly for some national economies than others. The fourteen-year Jupiter–Uranus cycle has been dubbed the 'free-trade' cycle and is reckoned more applicable to strongly capitalist economies like that of the United States than to the 'mixed' economies of Europe. For stock market trading, shorter cycles of the inner planets are scrutinised. The annual orbit of the Sun, the twenty-five-month cycle between Sun and Mars and the speedy movements of Mercury are all favourites. Oh, and don't forget to keep a careful eye on the lunation cycle.

Financial astrology's complexity explains why it is a service that is hired rather than practised individually. In theory, anyone equipped with some basic astrological nous and a couple of software packages should be able to become his or her own trader, but in practice, as Alphee Lavoie warns, 'If you deal with the stock market and you deal only with astrology you'll get hurt. You have to know the market.'

Several financial astrologers with non-market backgrounds relate getting their fingers, and bank accounts, seriously burned when starting out. A growing trend in recent years has been for groups of astrologically minded small investors to group together as an investors' club, each putting a donation into a common fund, which is then invested according to the collective astrological wisdom of the group.

What, though, does it take to spot a major market crash like that of 1987? Everyone, it seems, has their own method. In *Money and the Markets*, Graham Bates conducts an astro-inquest on Black Monday, noting that several short-term cycles were in their falling phase. Furthermore, the Sun was opposing Jupiter, Mercury had recently turned retrograde, and there were poor aspects to the charts of the United Kingdom and the London Stock Exchange.

Charles Harvey, whose accurate prediction of the crash appeared in the specialist publication *Chartsearch* in late 1986, arrived at his forecast chiefly through considering the long-term cycles of Saturn–Uranus and Jupiter–Uranus. The financial havoc, confessed Harvey, far exceeded his and his co-author's expectations.

Arch Crawford, who also predicted Black Monday, arrived at his conclusions through different means again. He was already operating in terms of his own 'Cycle Sum' – the financial equivalent of Barbault's Planetary Index – which showed post-spring 1987 would be a poor year for the markets. In defiance, they had risen steadily. Crawford, however, had been alerted to another event by the 'harmonic convergence' declared by New Ager José Arguelles for 17 August, allegedly in accordance with the Mayan calendar. This celebrated a planetary pile-up of Sun, Moon, Mercury, Venus and Mars on 24 August. This conjunction sounded alarm bells for Crawford, who advised his clients to be out of the markets by 24 August in advance of a 'horrendous crash'. In fact, markets peaked on 25 August, and were then turbulent for several weeks, during which time there was a solar and a lunar eclipse (on 23 September and 6 October, respectively).

Crawford then suggested 21 October as a turning point, just two days beyond the crash on the 19th.

The predictions of financial astrologers in recent years make chequered reading. Most have inclined to forecasts of bear (declining) markets, which have been contradicted in the West by rampant bull markets. In 1997 Arch Crawford, for example, predicted that a grossly overvalued market would fall by between 33 per cent to 50 per cent before the end of 1998. Bill Meridian predicted a US economic crisis for December 1998. Graham Bates and Jane Bowles, writing in 1994, singled out the total solar eclipse of 11 August 1999 as the signal for 'a disastrous chain of financial consequences' and were quick to claim the credit when the markets dropped dramatically on the eve of the much-heralded eclipse. Yet the markets immediately soared upwards to new levels.

The year 1999 was troublesome all round for planet-plotting economists, as the clash of Uranus, in Aquarius, and Saturn, in Taurus, failed to materialise as a market crash. Henry Weingarten, who started the year predicting that the Dow Jones Index would fall to 7,000 points by the end of the year, watched as it climbed towards 12,000, hauled upwards by the very stocks – technology (Aquarius) and banks (Taurus) – represented by the major planetary configuration – a case of right symbolism, wrong call. At the time of writing, he was still holding out for a major adjustment by May 2000 as Uranus and Saturn made their third square aspect, and a seven-planet stellium arrived in Taurus.

Others suspected that the presence of Uranus, planet of technology, in its own sign, Aquarius, meant all bets were off, and that the 'new paradigm' talked up by Wall Street bulls was indeed in place, this being confirmed by the Internet revolution and booming technology and 'dot.com' stocks.

Where does the boom in financial astrology leave the 'sacred science' beloved of so many astrologers, along with its alleged spiritual purpose? Considerations about the highly dubious ethics of capitalism are conspicuously absent from the considerations of almost all financial astrologers. Modern astrology seems to be moving into two main camps. On one side is the psychological/New Age mainstream, muttering homilies about the Age of Aquarius and healing our souls (while generally going bust). On the other come the financial astrologers, making money while advising multinational corporations on how to exploit the world more efficiently.

Responding to this criticism, Henry Weingarten – who, unusually, stresses 'socially responsible investment' in the manifesto for his Astrologer's Fund – asserted a belief that 'The study of astrology practically demonstrates a divine order which over time eventually transforms most, if not all, serious practitioners. This is a process, not a black and white issue . . . Personal investments energize companies and therefore one shares in their karma in addition to their profits and losses.'[3]

Weingarten's admirable hope is that astrology can combine the best practices of both the spiritual and material worlds. Yet, as ever, astrology is too unruly ever to be fully reined in. In May 1999 firefighters in Greenwich, Connecticut, were called to a mansion belonging to financier Martin Frankel, where they found a smouldering filing cabinet and burning documents. Frankel, it soon transpired, had been running a massive financial fraud, and had embezzled a sum estimated between $200 million and £900 million from various insurance companies. In addition, $2 billion was missing from a Catholic charity he had set up. Frankel himself had vanished. It became clear that Frankel's methods included astrology; among the documents discovered by FBI agents were details of money laundering and several astrological charts, one a horary asking 'Will I Go to Jail?' When the FBI caught up with Frankel a few months later, his first words were, 'All right, you got me,' so perhaps he knew the answer to his question. It seems the world's greatest fraudsters, as well as its greatest traders, are attuned to the stars.

11

BORN TO BE WITH YOU

ROMANTIC ENCOUNTERS AND MATCHES MADE ABOVE

✶

The arrival of the digital age transformed the practice, if not the theory, of astrology. Computers and astrology may seem the epitome of ancient and modern, but have proved a match made in heaven – after all, both are ascribed to the Promethean force of Uranus. At a keystroke, the computer chip has removed the drudgery and mystique of drawing up charts and the necessity for volumes of planetary timetables; today's astro-software will serve up a chart for AD 2150 as promptly as one for 250 BC, taking due account of the troublesome shifts between Julian and Gregorian calendars and other acts of time-juggling. Planetary conjunctions, retrogrades and aspects; solar and lunar eclipses; the positions of fleeting asteroids and other chart arcana; chart comparisons – there is now software for every task and technique. Interpreting the results still needs a human astrologer, of course, but these too come in-built to software that offers a 'cookbook' readout of a birth chart, its transits, and its relations with other charts.

In fulfilment of Alan Leo's Edwardian dream of 'Astrology for All', computerised horoscopes are now available by mail-order and the Internet, with today's £10 predictive printout the equivalent of Leo's 1912 'Shilling Horoscopes'. That doesn't mean the results are any great improvement on the reports compiled by Leo's overworked planetary civil servants. Where their fountain pens laboriously copied out the meaning of Jupiter in Pisces as 'It disposes somewhat to travelling, especially by water', for the same placement today's software offers such platitudes as, 'The study of photography, filming or the history of art may be very rewarding.' As with all computer programs, what you get out is only as good as what's been put in.

Apart from birth charts and predictions, astro-computing now offers numerous other services. There is an 'astro-fashion consultancy' to analyse your horoscope and tell you which colours and 'looks' are right for you, complete with a section on 'Your Fantasy Image' (are you 'Saucy Military Madam' or 'Warrior Queen'?). There is an astro-employment bureau that will spy out the character of prospective employees for employers and assess their chances of fitting in with the company. There are CD-roms that will analyse your love life and the suitability of your partner.

After birth charts, the most popular astrological computer service is chart comparison, specifically to check on romantic compatibility; a more sophisticated version of the 'love planets' guides that feature in women's magazines. Chart comparison, or 'synastry', as it's known in the trade, has a long history, whether it's the charts of prospective wedding partners that are being scrutinised – in India this remains a prerequisite for many unions – or those of family members, dynasties being long reckoned to share signs, planets and zodiacal degrees.

Romantic compatibility is rated chiefly by comparing the 'personal planets' of two charts: Sun, Moon, Venus and Mars. The masculine planets in a woman's chart (Sun and Mars) and the feminine planets in a man's chart (Moon and Venus) are reckoned to reveal what we seek in our ideal partner. Especially valued is a situation where one partner's Sun and the other's Moon occupy the same position; a so-called 'cosmic marriage'. Any planets falling in the same place, in close aspect or at sensitive points in the chart are significant, however. A man's Mercury in the same place as a woman's Venus might be interpreted, for example, as her admiring his intellect. Her Sun opposite his Jupiter suggests he makes her money. Her Moon at the top of his chart means she puts him in touch with a wider public. His Saturn at the bottom of her chart means he provides a secure home. The possibilities are legion.

The ease with which such comparisons can be made by computer has encouraged astrologers to join the soap-sodden world of modern celebrity. Where once synastry charts would be drawn up only on special commission or for royal marriages, in the every-person world of the Aquarian Age the compatibility of TV actresses, boy-band members, sports stars and politicians has become one of modern astrology's principal sports. Are Charles and Diana, or Bruce Willis and Demi Moore, really heading for the divorce courts? What exactly was the nature of the relationship between President Bill Clinton and Monica Lewinsky? Modern astrology knows! Or at least offers some different clues than those supplied by regular columnists.

Bill Clinton's alleged, denied and finally admitted relationship with Monica Lewinsky was, for the onlooking ranks of American astrologers, an open and shut case from the moment they got hold of the birth data of Monica, compared her horoscope with the President's, and found sticky planetary fingerprints all over the synastry chart. Clinton's birth chart is heavily weighted towards two signs; four planets, including the President's Sun, are in royal, obstinate Leo, while four others are sited in charming, strategic Libra (which is also his Ascendant). Mars and Venus joined together in Libra are a perfect fit for an incurable romantic – or an obsessional womaniser.

Like Clinton, Beverly Hills–born Lewinsky (born 23 July 1973 at 12.21 p.m. PST) is a show-off Sun-in-Leo, with blow-dried mane to match. What's more the pair have the same Moon and rising signs (Taurus and Libra, respectively), the odds against this triple coincidence being 1 in 1,728. The astrological overlaps don't end there. That Bill's Sun fell across Monica's Venus – astrologically speaking – is a traditional sign of astro-amour. Monica's Sun conjunct Bill's Saturn suggests Clinton's role as an older man with authority, while the couple's joint Moon-in-Taurus position paints a picture of sensual gratification.[1]

Understanding relationships astrologically no longer stops at comparing two charts. The right software will fuse a pair of charts in an instant, creating planetary positions for a 'composite chart' that represents the relationship as an entity in its own right, distinct from its two participants. The composite chart is created by finding the midpoint of a couple's planets; the midpoint between his 3 degree Scorpio Sun and her 3 degree Pisces Sun would be a 3 degree composite Capricorn Sun. The resulting chart is read like any other: a harmonious Moon and Venus aspect shows a loving relationship, a difficult Mars–Saturn aspect shows cross-purposes and arguments, and so forth.

No-one is certain who originated the concept of the composite chart. The idea was certainly abroad in Germany in the 1920s but it was not until the 1970s that it became an accepted technique. Much the same principle is behind another development, the 'group chart', which synthesises the birth charts of any number of people to create something that is less a chart than a collective planetary graph. This technique has been pioneered by Australian astrologer Bernadette Brady, who developed specific software for the job (JigSaw) alongside computing whiz Graham Dawson, creator of the popular astro-software Solar Fire.

Brady offers five major classifications for her astrological groups – hunting, gathering, play, family and tribal elders – each of which she claims reflects the dominant planets within the collective. Hunting groups, such as business organisations, have lots of Sun and Mars energy; gathering groups rely on Mercury and Venus; tribal elder groups, such as committees, rely on Saturn and Jupiter, and so on. By analysing groups in this way, Brady claims to identify their underlying nature. For example, she claims the collective astrology of the Kennedy clan shows a supportive family group 'with strong hunting tendencies'. That the Beatles' collective chart showed an emphasis towards Cancer and the fifth house reflected their preference for studio rather than road work. 'A heavy 11th house,' she declares, 'would have had them on the road for a far longer time.'[2]

The same open-ended, computer-fuelled curiosity is behind the increasing use of synastry to enquire into actors and their roles. Is it the quality of acting alone that makes some celluloid incarnations of famous figures so resonant, while others shrivel into caricature? Star-struck astrologers argue that actor and subject mesh convincingly because they share astrological signatures. When Madonna, talking of her lead in the movie *Evita*, declared that 'The role of Evita Peron was my destiny, it was made for me,' American astrologer Lois Rodden was quick to investigate the planetary connections between these two powerful, much-adored women. A comparison of the pushy pair's horoscopes proved obliging enough. Madonna is a show-off Leo Sun, with her Moon and Ascendant in Virgo (hence 'Like a Virgin', presumably). Evita was a Taurus Sun, but her Moon was in Leo, while the two share precise contacts between other planets, notably pugnacious Mars and ambitious Saturn.

A trawl round various celebrated big- and small-screen incarnations turns up a fair portion of similar overlaps. Might John Hurt's inspired role as Quentin Crisp in *The Naked Civil Servant* owe something to their shared Aquarian qualities? Hurt's Aquarius Sun obligingly matches Crisp's Moon. It's harder to be certain of overlaps between David Bowie and Andy Warhol (whom Bowie played in *Basquiat*) since Warhol gave out several different birth dates, but Bowie (a Capricorn) can at least muster a Leo Moon to match Warhol's regal Sun.

Lois Rodden, an avid collector of showbiz data, suggests that the astrological interaction between actor and real-life character can be so strong that they 'continue for some indefinite time to play off each other's charts'. Comparing the connections between Madonna and Evita, and between rock star/actress Courtney Love and Althea Flynt (the wife of porn king Larry Flynt, played by Love in *The People Versus Larry Flynt*), Rodden suggests that the acclaim won by the two actresses occurred at astrologically propitious moments in the charts of Peron and Flynt. In other words, astrology carries on working even after death.[3]

The overlaps between the birth charts of Elizabeth I and the various actresses who have portrayed the English queen suggest that Rodden may be on to something. Elizabeth (born 7 September 1533 at 3 p.m.) was a prim and prickly Virgo by Sun sign, which was spun into the myth of the 'Virgin Queen' by her courtiers. Elizabeth also had the Moon in Taurus and a Capricorn Ascendant, a trilogy of earth signs in keeping with her reputation as a practical, hard-headed administrator. The three actresses who have most famously played Elizabeth prove a serendipitous fit for her horoscope. Glenda Jackson, who portrayed Elizabeth on BBC TV back in 1971, is a Taurus Sun; Judi Dench, who played her in 1998's *Shakespeare in Love*, has a Capricorn Moon on Elizabeth's Ascendant; and Cate Blanchett, who played her in *Elizabeth* in the same year, has either a Capricorn or Taurus Sun, depending on which of two possible birth dates one accepts. There are other overlaps, such as the way Elizabeth's Jupiter, the royal planet, in Sagittarius is matched by Jackson's Moon and Dench's Sun. Astrologers could not help but notice, too, that as the Virgin Queen was being portrayed in two different films, the planet of glamour and film, Neptune, was passing over Elizabeth's natal Pluto. Or that on the night of the 1999 Oscars, when the Virgin Queen was hot property on the shortlists and when Judi Dench won Best Supporting Actress for her role, the Moon was passing over Elizabeth's natal Moon in Taurus.

It's possible, as always, that astrology is simply supplying the expectations that its followers bring. Why, for example, was there no TV adaptation of Elizabeth's reign when the mighty conjunction of Uranus, the television planet, and Pluto, the power planet, occurred at the same position of Elizabeth's Sun in 1966? (Uranus did pass over Elizabeth's Libran Venus in 1971, however, when Glenda Jackson commanded the ratings with her version of the Tudor queen's life.)

In a daring leap into the fictional heavens, astrologers have also started to make connections between actors and the fictional characters they play. Lois Rodden has offered case studies on Johnny Weissmuller, the most famous celluloid Tarzan, and Christopher Reeve, the most famous Superman. In the case of Tarzan, Rodden took the time and date that author Edgar Rice Burroughs started his manuscript, *Tarzan of the Apes* (a time handily noted by Burroughs) as the birth-time of the noble savage. Tarzan turns out to be a principled Sagittarian, although his Mercury (speech) is undermined by Pluto – 'he was taught to speak by apes, after all,' points out Rodden. For Superman, Rodden takes the superhero's first appearance on a radio broadcast as his birthday; this makes the Krypton-born do-gooder an unconventional Aquarius with a powerful Mars influence – hence, the 'Man of Steel'. Almost inevitably, Rodden finds potent synastry between the actors and the fictional roles that made their names.

Celebrity synastry, whether romance or role-playing, requires access to the birth data of the famous; not just birth dates but birth times, without which astrologers are compelled to use a 'dawn chart' (set for the moment the Sun rose) or a 'noon chart', when the Sun was at its zenith. The time of birth is not recorded on most birth certificates – Scotland is a notable exception – and mothers tend to be preoccupied at the moment their children arrive, rather than staring at their watch, so sleuthing is often required, probing into family records and rummaging in archives.

Birth times are particularly problematic when it comes to famous people, who, reasonably enough, may not care to have their character and destiny publicly dissected by planetary paparazzi. Even astrologer Liz Greene, while ever ready to peel open a celebrity chart in lecture and book, remains notoriously secretive about her own. It's little surprise that the acquisition of celebrity birth data has become an astrological cult. The undisputed queen of data is Lois Rodden, who has published several books of birth charts covering performers, politicians, eminent women and criminals. The publication of the first, in 1970, introduced a classification system for birth data, according to its accuracy (from AA for family records to DD for 'dirty data' from suspect sources).

As was the case with Princess Diana, the issue of data can become extremely contentious, while Bill Clinton left astrologers with cosmic egg on their faces. When Clinton became a presidential contender in 1992, American astrologers quickly gave a detailed breakdown of his character and career with Leo as his Ascendant, based on a birth time of 3.44 a.m. Then Clinton's mother informed astrologer Robert Hand it was really 8.51 a.m. Clinton's ascendant abruptly went from Leo to Libra, and the faces of astrologers who had examined his career using the 'wrong' chart to bright red. Then again, as Britain's Nick Campion is fond of pointing out, astrologers frequently get 'correct' results and predictions with the 'wrong' chart – the issue seems as much to do with the astrologer as the data.

The data freak has a long history in astrology. Among the first astrology texts is an exposition by Dorotheus that includes sample horoscopes at the back. In the modern era Alan Leo was once again the trailblazer with his *1001 Notable Nativities*. These days, data too is computerised; Lois Rodden's collection, a lifelong labour, is now available as a program. Britain has found a data champion of its own in Frank C. Clifford, whose first book, *British Entertainers: The Astrological Profiles*, presents the charts of scores of celebrities from film, theatre, comedy, TV and pop, with data on hundreds more. Along with the charts of soap-opera stars, Clifford offers charts for the series themselves, based on their first transmission times. *Coronation Street* (born 9 December 1960) falls under cheerful Sagittarius with homely Cancer ascending. Appropriately for anywhere as fishy and pub-bound as Albert Square, *EastEnders* (born 19 February 1985) has Sun, Moon and Mercury conjunct in Pisces. *Dr Who* was born under the sci-fi sign of Sagittarius and *The Avengers* under gender-equal Aquarius.

Investigating the horoscopes of fictional characters and TV series is now one of the proliferating sub-cults of modern astrology. Science fiction, which shares with astrology a passion for distant constellations, spooky planets and dramatic predictions, is a popular choice, with *Star Trek* a particular target for astro-anoraks. US astrologer James Eubanks has assigned horoscopes to the entire crew of the Starship *Enterprise*: the Saturnine Captain Picard as a responsible Capricorn, Commander Data an android Aquarian rationalist, and so on. Californian writer Bruce Scofield meanwhile links the *Star Trek* universe to Pluto's movements, pointing out that *Star Trek: The Next Generation* and *Star Trek: Deep Space Nine* were both born during Pluto's long passage through Scorpio. Pluto's shift into Sagittarius in 1995 for a thirteen-year stay heralded the launch of *Star Trek: Voyager*.

These are games any competent astrologer can play. In *The Sun Sign Reader*, veteran English astrologer Joan Revill recently offered a gleeful romp through the birthdays of fiction's heroes, with thoughtful stop-offs to ponder the horoscopes of their creators. Sherlock Holmes turns out to be a lonely Capricorn with a powerful Jupiter, while Bridget Jones, born late on 21 March, is forever stuck on the cusp of Pisces and Aries.

At least one set of fictional characters has definite Sun signs, however: those of Margaret Mitchell's *Gone with the Wind*. Mitchell, an astrologer as well as a novelist, based the dramatis personae of her celebrated epic firmly on the zodiac, leaving a blatant trail of clues that were only picked up in 1978 when US astrologer Darrell Martinie ('The Cosmic Muffin') was shown photocopies of notes from Mitchell's library while lecturing at a conference in Atlanta. Mitchell's heroine, Scarlett O'Hara, is a dashing Aries, named after the colour of her ruling planet Mars. Her father is a Taurus who not only owns a farm in earthy Taurean fashion but named it the Tara plantation. On it goes: Scarlett's two twittering aunts, Prissy and Pitty Pat, are evidently a pair of Geminis whose names comply with the sign's love of wordplay. Rhett Butler, the great love of Scarlett's life, is a passionate Leo and a fellow fire sign who in true don't-look-back Leo style delivers the line, 'Frankly, my dear, I don't give a damn.' Their daughter, Bonnie, is the third fire-sign Sagittarius and, being born under the sign of the Centaur, meets her end in a riding accident. Ashley Wilkes, the rival for

Scarlett's love, is a wealthy Capricorn whose plantation, Twelve Oaks, reflects both solidity and, perhaps, the twelve signs of the zodiac.

The latest word in fictional astrology is *The President's Astrologer*, a thriller by American writer Barbara Shafferman, whose heroine is an astrologer working behind the scenes for a future US President, much as Joan Quigley worked for Ronald Reagan. Shafferman thoughtfully includes the charts of her fictional President and Vice-President, which enable her aspect-busting heroine to triumph.

12

PUTTING THE STARS INTO THE STARS AND STRIPES

RONALD REAGAN'S STELLAR PRESIDENCY

✴

When Ronald Reagan's former Chief of Staff, Donald Regan, published his memoirs in May 1988, he bestowed on his ex-boss's presidency one of its historical signatures. Along with Reaganomics, Irangate, the chilly confrontation with the 'Evil Empire' of the USSR and the subsequent thaw in the Cold War, the Reagan era would henceforth be remembered for its obsessive devotion to astrology. Or as TV host Johnny Carson joked, for changing the White House theme tune from 'Hail to the Chief' to 'That Old Black Magic'.

What was shocking about the revelations in Donald Regan's book, *For the Record*, was not that Reagan had consulted an astrologer, but that the entire presidential schedule had been calibrated according to astro-diktat. Other world leaders were known to take the occasional consultation – France's François Mitterrand, for example, called on the services of society astrologer Elizabeth Teissier without raising too many eyebrows – but the degree to which the White House timetable was for seven years set by the stars remains staggering even to astrologers. Reagan, it transpired, had not so much as twiddled his cufflinks at a White House dinner without the planetary omens first being consulted via a secret astrologer employed by his First Lady and protector Nancy, who was the conduit for the resultant cosmic counsel.

'Nancy had complete faith in a woman astrologer in San Francisco,' wrote Regan. 'Mrs Reagan insisted on being consulted on the timing of every Presidential appearance and action so she could consult her friend in San Francisco about the astrological factor.'

The media, already gorging on the scandal of Irangate and the possibility of presidential impeachment, exploded with astonishment at Regan's disclosures. Within hours reporters were on the trail of the mystery star-gazer who had helped plot Reagan's term of office, and quickly found her. On a California-bound jet *Time* magazine grabbed the first interview with the astrologer concerned, Joan Quigley, who confirmed her involvement with the Reagans, and who continued to grant interviews to press and television, despite being urged by Nancy Reagan, in her last communication with her confidante, to 'lie'.

For the media and much of the public, the news that the White House had been in thrall to an unknown star-gazer was final proof that the Reagan presidency had been an elaborate and slightly deranged sham, their president a superstitious halfwit. An aura of unreality had always surrounded Reagan's ascendancy from B-movie actor to leading politician. When he first announced his candidacy for the governorship of California back in the mid-sixties the reaction of his opponents was a mixture of scorn and incredulity. Who would take seriously a man whose most famous role was fronting 'General Electric Theatre' on TV, reciting the company slogan, 'Progress is our most important product'?

Against conventional political wisdom, Reagan prevailed, thanks in no small part to the backing of a cabal of industrialists and power brokers from the upper echelons of American society. His good looks, homespun manner and simplistic right-wing politics struck a chord with the American people, if not with the country's liberal élite, who tended to view Reagan and his formidable wife Nancy as vulgar showbiz *arrivistes*. Once Reagan had acceded to the White House he brought more than a touch of Tinseltown's Neptunian illusion to running the country. The 1984 Olympics in Los Angeles, for example, were orchestrated into a pageant of American triumphalism resembling a Busby Berkeley movie, complete with synchronised swimming as a medal-winning sport. Nothing was quite what it seemed with Reagan. Elected as a champion of budget-balancing economics, he ran up the country's biggest-ever budget deficit. He built 'peace missiles', made 'freedom fighters' of the murderous Nicaraguan Contras and financed them by selling arms to Iran, a country he publicly vilified.

Yet despite the turbulence that often surrounded him, despite his age (at sixty-nine he was the oldest President ever elected), and despite his limited intellectual powers, Reagan sailed through, turning in the bravura performance of an otherwise undistinguished thespian career, winning re-election and smiling on while the careers of his staff went down in flames. This was the 'Teflon presidency'. Nothing stuck to Ronnie.

Joan Quigley was quite clear why. 'Astrology was the teflon in the teflon presidency,' she declared in her 1989 book, *What Does Joan Say?*, its title borrowed from Ronnie's customary enquiry to Nancy when confronted by fresh political developments. Quigley may even have a point. Rather than sneering at the Reagans' reliance on astrology one might consider that Ron and Nancy's astrological exactitude helped them survive where more sophisticated political minds predicted they would founder.

Quigley claims she wrote her book chiefly in response to Nancy's disavowal of her astrologer's role in White House affairs. Nancy had vigorously downplayed the Reagans' astrological interests from the outset of Regan's revelations, and in her rapidly completed 1989 autobiography, *My Turn*, claimed she had only turned to astrology in concern for her husband's safety. 'No one was hurt by it – except maybe me,' she simpered. Nancy also accused Donald Regan – one of many White House aides with whom she had clashed and whose dismissal she had engineered – of 'twisting' the story to 'seek revenge'. Regan responded by repeating his accusations in a review of Nancy's book. 'My description of White House life would have made little sense if I had omitted it [astrology]. All those schedule changes, when laid out in black on white pages, would have looked downright senseless in the absence of an explanation ... It was a daily, sometimes hourly, factor in every decision affecting the President's schedule.'

Joan Quigley's account affirmed and amplified Regan's assertions. For seven years Quigley had toiled over her ephemeris and computer charts to ensure the success of the Reagan regime. Without her approval, the presidential jet never lifted off, nor did the leader of the world's leading superpower attend a summit or engage in political debate without his birth chart's transits and progressions first being monitored by astro-control in California. The operation had been shrouded in Plutonian secrecy, using telephone hot-lines and code-words for Nancy and Joan to stay in communication and an intermediary to pass along the $3,000 monthly payments from the First Lady's personal account to Quigley. Knowledge of the Reagans' astro-adviser was restricted to a handful of trusted White House confidants, the main one being Deputy Chief of Staff Michael Deaver, whose job it was to juggle the demands of state and high office with those of the cosmos.

Deaver had worked for the Reagans for many years, and as Nancy's chief fixer had become used to her astrological preoccupations, which were only known to a couple of other aides. Trouble only arose when Deaver left the administration in 1985 and Donald Regan became Chief of Staff. The less accommodating Regan was appalled when he was let in on the Reagans' little astro-secret, as was presidential aide William Henkel, who took over first-line responsibilities for the President's schedule. Arranging the presidential timetable required marathon planning sessions, with details batted back and forth over the telephone between Nancy, her astrologer and Henkel, who then handed the completed schedule to Regan, the Secret Service and others. The process drove Donald Regan to distraction. He resorted to keeping a colour-coded calendar with green for good days, red for bad days and yellow for 'iffy' days, in line with Joan Quigley's prognostications. The pages of Regan's book fairly steam with indignation at having to rely on an unknown 'seer' (a term to which Quigley objects) to know 'when it was propitious to move the President of the United States from one place to another, or schedule him to speak in public, or commence negotiations with a foreign power'. Small wonder that, after Nancy had levered him unceremoniously from office, Regan would choose to expose her astrological fancies.

Long before Regan's revelations, America's astrologers had guessed what was going on. Calling up on to their computer screens charts for Reagan's initiatives, whether it was a trip to China or the invasion of Grenada, they noted that Ronnie swam uncannily in tandem with the cosmic tides. The timing of his announcement that he would seek re-election for a second term in 1984 clinched the issue; after all, 10.55 on a Sunday night (29 January) was not the customary moment for such a declaration, even if it was handy for the late-night news. The *Bulletin of the American Federation of Astrologers* was in little doubt that the time had been carefully chosen by a skilled practitioner of the celestial art. Who that was remained unknown, however.

In retrospect, the outing of the Reagans' astrological fixations should have come as no great surprise. Ronnie had caught the astro-bug back in his movie days as the 'Errol Flynn of the B-movies', while Nancy had consulted an astrologer with her mother while in her teens and presumably renewed her interest with Ronnie early in their relationship (the pair were married in 1952). Even once his political career took off, Reagan continued to steer by the stars in blatant fashion. After winning the governorship of California in 1966, he opted to hold his swearing-in ceremony in Sacramento at midnight on 2 January 1967 rather than waiting until daylight, as California's previous thirty-two governors had done (because New Year's Day fell on a Sunday, the ceremony was put back to the 2nd). Though the Reagans blustered that the timing of the event was to avoid ruining the New Year celebrations, and to get down to business, the real motive for their bizarre timing was obvious enough, at least to the outgoing Democratic Governor, Edmund Brown: 'My only guess is that it's because he believes in astrology.'

The Sunshine State's growing band of star-gazers looked on the chart for the swearing-in and agreed that the time had been 'elected' by a skilled astrologer. While nothing could be done about the day's sticky aspects (and a Saturn opposition to the trio of Pluto, Uranus and the Moon is about as inauspicious as you could conjure), holding the ceremony at midnight put the kingly and presidential planet Jupiter commandingly high in the sky, in the tenth house of leadership. As Gavin Arthur, San Francisco's own prophet of the Aquarian Age, noted in Kitty Kelley's biography of Nancy Reagan, 'No better time could be picked.'

Faced with such obvious deductions, Reagan's press secretary went into denial. 'He does not believe in astrology,' he lied on his employer's behalf, 'nor do we intend to have star-gazers in the administration.'

One of the star-gazers whom the Reagans apparently consulted for the inauguration would certainly have stood out among the wrinkle-proof suits and button-down minds of California's incoming Republican regime. This was the English 'white witch' Sybil Leek, a flamboyant character who had moved to Southern California in the mid-sixties and who, according to the scabrous (and probably unreliable) biography of Nancy penned by Kitty Kelley, was the one who had advised Reagan on the time and place of his oath. (Kelley claims he was told to face west in a part of the capital not previously used for the ceremony – conditions that were duly met.) Leek, who had started life as an antiques dealer before making her mark as a popular occultist in the early sixties, went on to a successful career in the States, writing a string of astrology books on love, wealth and happiness, one of which included the 'Astrological Guide to the Presidential Candidates'. Leek seems to have based her guide, which was written for the 1972 election partly on personal experience.

Jupiter certainly held sway over the Reagans' gubernatorial career, bringing them wealth, prestige and re-election, and Leek may not have been alone in advising Ron and Nancy how to ensure their governorship set off with the right chart. Back in the early 1950s Ronnie had been one of many thespians who consulted the celebrated Hollywood astrologer Carrol Righter, whose clientele included such glitterati as Cary Grant, Lana Turner and Marlene Dietrich (the last was an astro-obsessive). Righter's monthly 'zodiac parties' ran for twelve years and were features of Tinseltown social life, with each sign celebrated in appropriate fashion. Sets of twins were hired to wander round the Gemini party, a live lion was installed for the Leo bash, while snacks were kept in theme – spicy for Scorpio, fishy for Pisces, and so forth.

Righter, a Philadelphia society lawyer before he turned astrologer, became friends with the Reagans. His evening astrology classes were attended by Nancy (a Cancerian whom he nicknamed Moonchild) and he later taught his craft to Maureen Reagan, Ronnie's daughter by his first marriage to the actress Jane Wyman. Righter's daily astrology column would also come to be endorsed by his friend Governor Reagan – 'Nancy and I are always interested in what it has to say. We get a kick out of reading it every morning,' flannelled Ron, whose pronouncement was framed and hung by Righter, a fellow Aquarian.

That Nancy in later years would spend hours on the phone to Joan Quigley may well have been because she had enough astrological knowledge to argue the subtleties of transits rather than simply accept what she was told. The notoriously manipulative First Lady was certainly as rigorous with her astrologers as she was with her other employees, and seems to have always maintained more than one star-gazer in play. Besides Righter, the Reagans also consulted the celebrated psychic and popular astrologer Jeane Dixon, who had won fame with her 1956 prediction that a Democrat would win the presidency in 1960 but die in office. Less famously, Dixon had predicted that the Democrat in question would not be Jack Kennedy.

Dixon, a political conservative and an ardent Roman Catholic despite her psychic and astrological activities, met with the Reagans both in Washington, DC, where she lived, and in California. Neither Dixon nor Righter, however, felt that Reagan had much chance of realising his ambition to become the Republican presidential candidate in the 1976 election. Undaunted, Nancy sought out the advice of another astrologer, Joan Quigley, to whom she was introduced by TV host Merv Griffin, who had featured Quigley and her predictions on his show. Quigley, who came from a grand Republican family (she had been introduced to astrology by her mother) and whose political allegiances were not in doubt, proffered some advice, even though she 'never for one minute believed Reagan would win'. Ronnie's astrological problem at the time was evidently the oppressive presence of Saturn opposite his Aquarian Sun, though plenty of non-astrologically minded colleagues and commentators thought Reagan's bid for the nomination was a mistake for more prosaic reasons, because he was competing against a sitting President, Gerald Ford. On the other hand, Ford could easily be seen as the Saturnian authority figure oppressing Ronnie's self-expressive Sun.

When, four years later, Reagan became the Republicans' choice to run against Democratic President Jimmy Carter (a nice-guy Libran, and prone to his sign's indecisiveness), Quigley offered Nancy an astrological guide to the months ahead. Nancy accepted, though it was not until Reagan blundered in a policy statement about China (on 19 August 1980) that Quigley's advice became part of his electoral strategy; she had specifically warned against making any foreign policy pronouncements on that very day.

In *What Does Joan Say?* Quigley outlines her part in the ensuing months of the campaign that took Reagan to the White House. In particular she cites her role in the important TV debate between Reagan and Carter on 28 October at 9.30 p.m., a time chosen less for its helpful aspects to Reagan than for the disadvantage at which it supposedly put Carter. 'I was definitely responsible for Carter's losing that crucial contest,' she concludes. Quigley's reasoning, which she admits is unorthodox, was that that day's Moon in Cancer would 'activate the grand trine in Jimmy Carter's birth chart'. Since this configuration (usually thought to be beneficial) also had Mercury, planet of communication, opposite Uranus, Quigley reasoned Carter would surely make a faux pas. According to her, Carter duly fell into her trap, becoming overconfident and careless.

In any case, Quigley would have seen that Carter had major astrological headaches during the campaign. With Saturn moving across his Libran Sun and Pluto across his Libran Ascendant, Carter faced a planetary double whammy. Symbolically speaking, Saturn might be seen as confronting him with his own weakness and indecision, a self-inflicted payback. Pluto could likewise be seen to represent the shady deals being cut by Reagan's aides with the Iranian government, to ensure that the American hostages then held by Iran would not be released before a Reagan victory, with arms sales to Iran to follow in return. The release of hostages duly followed Reagan's landslide win on 4 November 1980.

It was a few months into the presidency before Nancy called on Quigley's services again. The spur was the assassination attempt on Reagan on 30 March 1981 that left the President with a bullet through one lung and dangerously near his heart. Nancy wanted to know if Quigley could have foreseen this near miss. Quigley claimed that if she'd been looking, she would have done so. She was hired.

One folk truth that immediately engaged Quigley was the zero-year curse: the fact that every President who had been elected in a year whose date ended with zero had died in office, either from natural causes (like Harrison and Franklin D. Roosevelt) or assassination (Lincoln and Kennedy). Astrologers knew that this pattern chimed with the Jupiter/Saturn cycle, which saw the two major planets conjunct every 19.85 years, an encounter long associated with change and disruption.

Quigley reasoned that because the 1981 Jupiter/Saturn conjunction fell in the air sign of Libra – since 1842 it had fallen in earth signs – it was 'less fatalistic'. She saw her job as protecting the President as much as 'contributing to ... and occasionally influencing' him. Having survived an assassination attempt, Reagan became the only President to defy the zero-year curse, a feat for which Joan Quigley is happy to take some of the credit.

Quigley's first task, though, was to help the new First lady overcome her 'image problem'. Nancy had appalling press. The ex-actress had become a Marie Antoinette-style First Lady, and was seen as a free-spending social climber more interested in her next shopping expedition and hairdresser's appointment than in the problems facing the mightiest nation on Earth. That her first act on entering the White House had been to order a lavish new set of state china at a cost of $200,000 became a minor national scandal. Unveiling its acquisition on the day that her husband abolished school lunches showed Nancy needed all the help that she could get with her timing.

Quigley's strategy was simple and scarcely needed her astrological guile. Nancy was to focus on her charity work. Appearances on behalf of the Drug Rehabilitation Program and the Foster Grandparent Program were to replace interviews with *Harper's Bazaar* and *Vogue*. Needless to say, all Nancy's showcase events were to take place at astrologically propitious moments.

More pressingly, Quigley set to work on the presidential schedule. Since Ronnie's birth time was unknown, she had first to 'rectify' his birth chart, that is, ascertain his ascending sign and its degree by working backwards from his life events. This gave a Sagittarius Ascendant – spot on for a man whose favourite pastime was horse-riding at his ranch, and who radiated geniality. Quigley gives a glowing account of Reagan's horoscope, linking him to Abraham Lincoln and Franklin D. Roosevelt in a trio of 'outstanding' presidents, and reckoning that their leadership of the nation followed easily from the coincidence of their Aquarius Suns and the Aquarius Moon in the United States' national chart. As an Aquarian, Reagan is first and foremost a humanitarian who believes in democracy, equality and brotherhood (all of which would have come as news to Nicaragua's democratically elected Sandinista government). Furthermore, Jupiter in Scorpio lends Reagan his 'incredible natural vitality', while the alliance of Saturn in Taurus and Mars in Capricorn is 'testimony of great physical force, moral strength ... and tremendous executive ability'.

Reagan emerges from his astrologer's deliberations as a veritable colossus, bestriding the world with vision and compassion.

Besides juggling the President's schedule in line with troublesome or possibly fateful transits, Quigley also cast the horoscopes of Reagan's political adversaries and of other world statesmen. The arrival of Mikhail Gorbachev as General Secretary in the USSR presented her with a particular challenge. Reagan had always been a militant anti-communist, ever since his days as president of the Screen Actors Guild, when he eagerly co-operated with Red-finder Senator Joseph McCarthy and the FBI in hunting down the commie menace lurking within Hollywood's ranks. Thirty years later, as President of the USA, he had identified the USSR as an 'evil empire'. Gorbachev, however, was clearly a very different political animal to his predecessors in the Kremlin, a man from a younger generation and bent on moving his country into a new era through *glasnost* (openness) and *perestroika* (restructuring).

Quigley seems to have realised immediately that Gorbachev represented a fresh development in the USSR's outlook. Contemplating his birth chart (again 'rectified' for a missing birth time), she saw not only an undeniably tough character (Saturn in its own sign of Capricorn), but one who was compassionate (Pisces Sun) and cultured (Mercury in Aquarius). She also sensed that he and Reagan would, against apparent odds, be able to establish a close personal relationship. 'From the moment I compared these two incredible charts, I knew that the chemistry between these two great leaders had breathtaking possibilities,' she trills. Later, Quigley would come to believe that Reagan and Gorbachev were continuing a friendship from a past life.

First, though, Ronnie had to be coaxed away from his 'evil empire' mindset. Joan Quigley seems to have been the principal agent in thawing Reagan's personal political tundra prior to the breakthrough in Cold War relations that ensued at the summits in Geneva, Reykjavik, Washington and Moscow. Before the first Gorbachev–Reagan meeting in Geneva in 1985 Quigley spent three hours on the telephone to Nancy Reagan (it was to be their longest call), pounding her with the view that the two men could together make history, and that Nancy should work on her husband to go to Geneva with mind and heart open. Since Reagan was at the time openly musing about fighting 'a limited nuclear war' in the European arena, Quigley's pleas to give peace a chance deserve a significant footnote in history. Naturally, Quigley also set the time for the lift-off of Airforce One to Geneva – 8.35 a.m., 16 November – thus placing 'the planet that represented Gorbachev [Mercury, evidently] on the Ascendant, so that he would be naturally drawn to Ronnie'.

Not all of Joan Quigley's deliberations on world peace were so fruitful. Although the Reykjavik summit was a great success, the Russian visit to Washington was plagued by the Soviets' sudden changes of schedule (Quigley darkly muses that they might have been eavesdropping on her many conversations with Nancy, and changing their timetable to throw her Ascendants into chaos) and she remains fearful about the last treaty-signing governing arms reduction (1 June 1988), which she feels was unpropitiously timed.

By then the Reagan era was drawing to a close, and had in any case been engulfed by the scandals of Irangate and Astrogate, and Reagan's increasingly evident memory lapses; the latter was eventually revealed to be the onset of Alzheimer's disease.

Quigley claims to have foreseen trouble for Reagan at the start of his second term. Some things, she says, are beyond even the capabilities of skilled astrologers to assuage. The transits of Uranus (the 'throne toppler') in early 1987 indicated events that were 'fated and unavoidable', while Pluto's position opposite Reagan's Taurus Moon and the transit of Saturn over Reagan's Ascendant likewise showed unavoidable restrictions. Under the trying circumstances of early 1987, Quigley advised Reagan to go to ground and say as little as possible, a tactic that infuriated Donald Regan but almost certainly helped avoid impeachment.

Unlike the glamour surrounding Kennedy's 'Camelot' court in the early sixties, the era the Reagans so detested, the gloss of the Reagan age and the 'greed is good' materialist eighties faded rapidly. Astrology, which had played so great a role in the Reagans' lives, was not enhanced by its association with their stay in the White House. On the contrary, it was depicted as a delusion of the desperate and demented. John Sears, campaign manager for the Reagans in their 1975 bid for the Republican nomination, may have been right when he told Kitty Kelley that 'Nancy's total dependence on astrology is part of her insecurity.'

The unlikely success of Ron and Nancy's rise suggests that it may also have been rather more.

THE CURIOUS CASE OF MARGARET THATCHER

It may have been the Reagans who suggested to their close ally and friend Margaret Thatcher that she seek astrological advice, for seek it Mrs T did. Shortly after the IRA's bombing of the Grand Hotel in Brighton in October 1984, from which the Prime Minister narrowly escaped with her life, Thatcher's press secretary Bernard Ingham approached Marjorie Orr, the *Daily Express*'s long-serving astrologer, in the House of Commons dining room, where the astrologer was lunching with an MP friend. Unnerved by the IRA's assassination attempt, Thatcher evidently saw the stars as an extra security measure. 'Bernard Ingham said that if I ever heard anything that indicated danger I was to let him know,' said Ms Orr in 1996, when she revealed Downing Street's astrological interests.[1] Ms Orr duly looked at Mrs T's chart and tape-recorded a reading that was despatched to Downing Street and acknowledged. There was no further communication between Downing Street and Ms Orr, which was perhaps as well since the bulldog-like Ingham later described astrology as 'a load of old rubbish'.

With her chemistry degree and no-nonsense manner, Thatcher makes an unlikely astro-fan, yet late in her term of office she did tell a startled House of Commons that 'I come under Libra, which is a very balanced sign.' The Prime Ministerial tongue was doubtless plunged deep in her cheek, but the remark indicates that her Machiavellian mind had, however briefly, at some point strayed heavenwards.

In fact, Libra is not the key to Thatcher's birth chart (born 9 a.m. GMT, 13 October 1925, Grantham, Lincs), though the Scales' aesthetic predilections might have helped elevate her resplendent coiffure. The dominant features of the Iron Lady's horoscope, however, are its adversarial Scorpio Ascendant and the major roles played by the scary trio of Saturn, Mars and Pluto. It as, as Marjorie Orr says, the chart of someone who is 'amazingly strong, ruthless, a powerhouse of energy'. The Thatcher chart is also held up as a good example of Saturn's event-marking capabilities; the planet climbed to her Midheaven when she became Prime Minister, passed her Sun at the time of the Falklands War and crossed her Ascendant, and natal Saturn, at the time of the IRA bomb. Less serendipitously, Saturn squared her Sun nine months before her fall, when Pluto also crossed her Ascendant.

Thatcher's one-time protégé and successor, John Major, may also have indulged in an astrological fling. The fact that Major's authorised biographer, Nesta Wyn-Ellis, is an astrologer led some to wonder whether Major took a few planetary tips from her. If so, few worked out for him. Curiously, Major's successor as leader of the Tory Party, William Hague, appointed a known astrology fan, one-time *Sunday Express* editor Amanda Platell, as his press secretary. At the time of writing, Hague seems more in need of an astrologer than his opponent, Tony Blair, a Prime Minister who remains singly free of taint from stargazers.

13

STARS AND SWASTIKAS

ASTROLOGY AND THE THIRD REICH

*

The conviction that Adolf Hitler took advice from astrologers, or was even an astrologer himself, is widespread. That the Great Dictator didn't, and wasn't, seems almost beside the point; the picture of the mad genius of the Third Reich poised over a desk strewn with battle plans and star charts is just too seductive to abandon. Something about it resonates.

British intelligence certainly felt so. During the Second World War they were sufficiently persuaded of Hitler's stellar interests to employ an astrologer of their own to keep them informed of the likely advice the Führer was receiving. How much attention they paid to his conclusions is uncertain, but the astrologer concerned, one Louis de Wohl, a German/Hungarian émigré who had settled in London in the 1930s, was able to dine out on his reminiscences for several years after the conflict.

As we shall see, de Wohl himself was a major source for the idea of an astrologically obsessed Hitler, but several members of the Nazi élite, notably Heinrich Himmler and Rudolf Hess, did maintain pet astrologers. Astrological interests, however, were a minor part of the often bizarre esoteric notions that helped shape Nazism and contributed to the apocalyptic character of the Third Reich.

For many years after the Second World War the occult streams running through Nazism were confined to the historical footnotes. Mainstream historians noted the Nazi Party's origins among the secret societies and magical orders that were rife in southern Germany in the early part of the century, yet these were not considered to have held any sway over Nazism's character or its subsequent programme of genocide.

Recognition that esoteric ideas helped mould Hitler and his henchmen first burst into popular consciousness with the publication in 1966 of Louis Pauwels's and Jaques Bergier's sensationalist best-seller *The Dawn of the Magicians*, which juxtaposed a breathless overview of the lost wisdom of the ancients – pyramids, Bible prophecies, Atlantean legends, Mayan temples and more – with speculation about the Nazis' occult links. Several subsequent books have purported to unravel Nazi occultism, the most famous being Trevor Ravenscroft's *The Spear of Destiny*, which alleged that Hitler was a fully initiated black magician, whose initiation rites included the use of peyote, gruesome sexual practices and human sacrifice. At the other end of credulity is Nicholas Goodrick-Clarke's scholarly *The Occult Roots of Nazism*, which traces the influence of esoteric thought on Nazi ideology while rejecting the notion that the Third Reich was the product of demonic influence or satanic pacts. Most mainstream historians simply ignore occultism as a factor in the rise and philosophy of Nazism.

Thanks to Steven Spielberg, every ten-year-old now knows otherwise: that the Nazis' drive for world dominion extended to such deeply mystical quests as the search for the Holy Grail and the Ark of the Covenant (in *Raiders of the Lost Ark* the Nazis have already dug it up). With the aid of either of these talismans, the Thousand-Year Reich would likely have become a reality had it not been for the intervention of action-archaeologist Indiana Jones.

Aspects of Nazi theory and activity were just as fantastical as Spielberg's fictions. There was, for example, a section of the SS, the Ahnenerbe, which engaged in historical research to prove that the origins of world culture lay with the Aryan race, a task that included building bogus megalithic circles and mounting searches for the lost continent of Thule (the Northern Atlantis) and Shambala, the lost paradise of the Himalayas. Also on their agenda was the collection of skulls, many from murdered Jews, to establish the 'pure' Aryan physiognomy. Then there was the Pendulum Institute, a collection of seers and psychics whose tasks included dowsing (pendulum swinging) over maps of the Atlantic Ocean in search of British shipping convoys.

The Third Reich's fascist pomp – flags, banners, firelight parades, folk festivals, athletic displays – rippled with magical regalia, from the swastika, an ancient Sun cross hijacked from the Hindus, to the doubled Sig rune, representing power, which adorned the 'Black Order' of the SS. Himmler, a lapsed Roman Catholic turned dedicated occultist, constructed the SS along the lines of a religious order – the Jesuits were his template – with rituals and grades along Freemasonic lines, and castles furnished on geomantic principles. Investigating such obsessions, the English writer Jonathan Meades accused the Nazis of being 'hippies in uniform', a snappy phrase but one that belies the murderous intent that lay behind the Ahnenerbe, whose chief, Wolfram Sievers, was hanged at Nuremberg.

For the Nazi programme of genocide was also informed by esoteric doctrines formulated by clandestine magical societies like the Order of the New Templars (founded 1907), the Germanen Order (founded 1912) and the Thule Society (founded 1918), all of which preached variants of 'Ariosophy' and pan-Germanic supremacy over inferior races, most especially the Jews. In the shadowy realm of this magical underground, the traditions of Rosicrucianism, Teutonic chivalry and anti-Semitism became conflated with the pantheistic spirit of German romanticism, Wagnerian grandeur and the evolutionary theories of Charles Darwin and Madame Blavatsky. Darwin's maxim of 'survival of the fittest' folded easily into Aryan supremacism, while Blavatsky's elaborate scheme of 'root races' and 'sub-races' stretching back to Atlantis was quickly bent into anti-Semitic shape by proto-Nazi occultists like Guido Von List, Jörg Lanz Von Liebenfels and Rudolf Freiherr Von Sebottendorff. The Third Reich's subsequent policy of enslaving and eradicating 'sub-human' races was justified in coldly scientific terms as helping along Darwinian 'natural selection' (in this Nazism shared many ideas with the eugenics movement supported by many respectable European intellectuals), but was also seen, at least by an occultist core, as a prerequisite to the emergence of the Aryan *Ubermensch*, or 'superman'.[1]

Several of the leading members of the Nazi Party had a background in the occult societies, among them Hess, Himmler, Alfred Rosenberg, Dietrich Eckart and Gottfried Feder. Hitler's involvement in them is hazier, but in his penniless days in Vienna and Munich he undoubtedly encountered the *volkisch* (the term has no English parallel but refers to fantastical folklore) ideas that were helping to shape German nationalism, and there is evidence to suggest he was a student of Liebenfels' virulently anti-Semitic magazine, *Ostara*, which later published a 'Kabbalistic horoscope' of Hitler.

Astrology was an inevitable part of the overheated stew of occult thought that gripped Germany in the early twentieth century. As in other countries, astrological activity in Germany was centred on the Theosophical Society, which opened its German branch in 1884, and most astrology books originated with the theosophical press run by one Hugo Vollrath, an unsavoury opportunist who would later join the Nazi Party. Vollrath published several astrology books by Rudolf Sebottendorff, the founder of the Thule Society, and employed him to edit his astro-magazine, *Astrologische Rundschau*. It was also Sebottendorff who acquired a little-known Munich newspaper, *Volkischer Beobachter*, with money supplied by right-wing Russian exiles, on behalf of the Nazis, for whom it remained an official mouthpiece until 1945.

Such was the overlap between Bavaria's occult circles and the brutal street politics and rival militias that flourished in the political turmoil following the First World War. It was natural enough that when Adolf Hitler began to make his mark in the early 1920s, astrology was on hand to chart his ascent. By then Germany was in the early stages of an astrological fever which was to grow steadily until the Nazi seizure of power in 1933 put a swift end to it. At first, though, Hitler and astrology went together. One of those whose head was turned by the charismatic ex-corporal was Frau Elbeth Ebertin, who since 1917 had published a lively and popular astrology yearbook, *Ein Blick in die Zukunft* (*A Glimpse into the Future*). In autumn 1923 Frau Ebertin included an astro-profile of Hitler in her yearbook; he wasn't named, but there was no doubt about the identity of the Aries 'man of action' who was 'destined to play a Führer role' and 'to sacrifice himself for the German nation'. But Ebertin also warned of imminent 'personal danger' from 'incautious action' that could 'likely trigger off an uncontrollable crisis'.

It was a vaguely worded piece of astro-counselling, based on Saturn, then in the late degrees of Libra, moving opposite what Ebertin supposed was Hitler's Aries Sun (in fact, Hitler was born with his Sun just in Taurus, but Ebertin didn't have his correct birth time). Various Hitler acolytes showed Frau Ebertin's prophecy to Hitler, but the future Führer was unimpressed. 'What have women and the stars to do with me?' he scoffed, a remark that almost certainly summed up his contempt for both the opposite sex and for astrology. After all, one of Hitler's guiding principles was that outstanding individuals could forge their destiny by a Nietzschean mastery of the will – the man of destiny was scarcely to be denied by his horoscope. Even if, as writers like Ravenscroft have speculated, Hitler was an adept of the blackest magical arts, he would doubtless consider he was operating in a realm where astrological considerations didn't impinge. For such a man, astrology would seem like a polite parlour game.

However, Frau Ebertin's prophecy was dramatically fulfilled when Hitler led the famous attempted Beer Hall Putsch in Munich on 8 November 1923, a date that subsequently acceded to sanctity in the Nazi calendar. As the National Socialists marched into Munich's Marienplatz Square, the police opened fire, killing sixteen Nazis and dispersing the rest, including the future Führer. For his part in the failed uprising, Hitler was jailed in Landsberg Fortress, where he wrote his personal credo, *Mein Kampf*, with help from Rudolf Hess. Disdainful though Hitler was about Ebertin's warning, any astrologer could have told him that the aspects on 8 November were poor for him.[2]

Frau Ebertin's astrological study of Hitler was the first in a line that continues to this day. There are several versions of Hitler's horoscope proffered, based on different birth times, and with different Ascendants.[3] There is no shortage of portents in his chart for his subsequent tyranny – the overbearing Saturn at its Midheaven, square to Mars, is a favourite signifier – but, equally, not everyone with similar configurations in their horoscope becomes a monster. Frau Ebertin's designation of Hitler as a 'man of action', thanks to what she supposed was his Aries Sun, has had to give way to Hitler the Taurean: the monolithic builder, would-be artist and inspired orator (Taurus ruling the throat).

Not all the leading Nazis were as dismissive of astrology as Hitler. Himmler and Hess, as will be seen, were besotted with star-lore. Others maintained a lively interest. Hitler's comrade in arms, Ernst Röhm, who led the murderous rabble of the SA (Stormtroopers), had his horoscope prepared by his friend Karl Gunter Heimshoth in 1929.

Heimshoth's predictive powers evidently weren't up to much; five years later both men were liquidated by the SS in the infamous 'Night of the Long Knives' as the newly elected Nazi government disposed of internal rivals.

In power the Nazis proved as intolerant of religious groups and esoteric ideas as they were of rival political doctrines and parties – even those apparently in sympathy with them. Assorted religious sects like the Jehovah's Witnesses, the Adventists and the Theosophical Society were banned. Astrology also found itself on the blacklist, evidently too errant a force to be left completely alone; the only description of the world, and certainly of its future, was to be the official Nazi line. It was a similar persecution to that pressed in the past by the Roman Emperors and the Church. Astrological magazines were closed, speculation on Hitler's horoscope made taboo, astro-conferences squeezed shut. Frau Ebertin's yearbook took its last glimpse into the beyond in 1938.[4] Later, Himmler would explain to a captive star-gazer that astrology had been outlawed because, among other reasons, it was a 'universalist' doctrine that claimed to apply to all humanity. Since astrology took no account of the 'specific racial soul' of different peoples, it must be in error.

Old mentors of Nazism fared no better than its opponents. Sebottendorff, who had gone to live in Turkey, was promptly expelled when he visited the Reich in 1934.[5] In 1937, Liebenfels was banned from publication, and his influence disowned. The only occultist ideas that were acceptable to the Reich were those of its warrior élite, Himmler's SS, and even their wilder notions were widely scoffed at behind closed doors by other leading Nazis.

In Britain, where astrologers remained at liberty to say what they wanted, they embarrassingly failed to predict the imminent onslaught. Nevertheless, the dark, uncertain times of the Second World War provoked an upsurge of interest in astrology among the British population, particularly among women, according to reports from so-called Mass Observation, a sociological survey of the time. Concerned questions were even asked in the Commons about whether astrologers were lowering morale with their speculations about the possibilities of German invasion.

A year into the war British intelligence became persuaded that they needed to have the astrological angles of the conflict covered, and hired their own pet star-gazer. The Romanian ambassador to London, one Virgil Tilea, was the unlikely catalyst for this peculiar corner of the Allied war effort. Tilea had asked a Swiss/German astrologer of his acquaintance, Karl Ernst Krafft, for some predictions on the conflict. Krafft's reply, sent from Berlin and clearly slanted to enhance German victory prospects, convinced Tilea that Krafft was in the employ of the Nazis, and was probably advising Hitler himself. On his return to London he suggested to various high-ranking British contacts that they needed a foil for Krafft, a shadow star-gazer who could anticipate the astro-counselling being fed to Hitler. Louis de Wohl, declared Tilea, was their man.

De Wohl was, by all accounts, a likeable character with a rococo sense of style redolent of Sidney Greenstreet in *The Maltese Falcon*. A novelist and screenwriter, probably with Jewish blood in his veins, de Wohl sensed that his prospects under the Nazis were bleak and bailed out of Berlin in 1935, finding a living in Britain as an astrologer, with a clientele that included the upper echelons of society.

In his post-war autobiography de Wohl's account of his recruitment and subsequent role was suitably grand. He claimed that in 1940 he lunched with the Foreign Secretary, Lord Halifax, who over port and cigars quizzed him about Hitler's horoscope. Shortly afterwards de Wohl was installed in an office on Park Lane and made an honorary captain in the British army, a role he took to with panache, strolling through the West End in a tailor-made officer's uniform and swaggerstick, much to the annoyance of his superiors, for whom this be-pipped star-gazer was an embarrassment.

De Wohl's job was not to proffer astrological advice *per se* but to second guess Hitler's supposed astrologers. By then the idea that the Führer was in step with the cosmos had crossed the channel from Germany – where many thought he owed his precipitous rise to astute planetary counselling – and taken root in Britain and America, at least among the popular press. In a 1940 profile of Hitler, for example, *Look* magazine described him as never far from his astrologer. That Hitler made many of his moves in the spring, near to his birthday, was reckoned part of the evidence for his reliance on astrology.

Karl Ernst Krafft would have liked nothing better than to be Hitler's astrologer. An intense, aloof man who prided himself on the scientific basis of his astrology, Krafft was a great admirer of the Third Reich and had a contact in Himmler's intelligence services. Krafft's troubles started when he correctly predicted that Hitler's life was in danger in early November 1939 (possibly because the lunar nodes were passing over Hitler's Sun). When the Führer narrowly avoided assassination by a bomb blast in a Munich beer cellar on 7 November – the sixteenth anniversary of the Beer Hall Putsch – the Gestapo were quick to investigate Krafft. He was cleared, but he was now on the books of Nazi intelligence.

In 1940 Krafft started work for Goebbels's propaganda ministry, as an interpreter of Nostradamus's cryptic prophecies, another of Krafft's passions and one easily bent to propagandist ends to show that Nostradamus had predicted Germany would win the war. Then came Tilea's request for astrological predictions. In replying, Krafft was obliged to compromise his astrological principles for propaganda purposes and he fell out with his employers, who had no time for ethical niceties.

Though de Wohl churned out reports for British intelligence on what Krafft was supposedly telling Hitler, there is no evidence that anyone in High Command took his prognostications seriously. MI6, however, were convinced that there was an occultist angle to Nazism. Even before the war, in 1938, MI6 had approached a West Country white witch, Cecil Williamson, and asked him to supply them with a list of Nazis interested in occultism. Williamson obliged. Travelling under the name of the 'Witchcraft Research Centre', he visited Germany and gave his recruiting officer, one Colonel Maltby, hundreds of names interested in what Maltby called 'this nonsense'. When war broke out, Williamson was given a job by Maltby at Intelligence HQ at Bletchley, broadcasting radio propaganda to U-boat crews: a mixture of jazz and disinformation in which Benny Goodman records were interspersed with commentary on Nostradamus's predictions.[6]

Louis de Wohl's talents were similarly employed in the arts of black propaganda, helping write bogus German astrology magazines that were then smuggled into Germany, and whose gloomy but accurate predictions (they were written after German naval and military reversals) were meant to deepen German despondency. One of de

Wohl's collaborators on this enterprise was Ellic Howe, a Freemason who twenty years later wrote an exhaustive account of the Reich's astrological interests, *Urania's Children*. De Wohl was also put to work on Nostradamus, this time to show that the seer's arcane quatrains predicted Germany would lose. In 1941 he was dispatched to the United States to argue the astrological case for America joining the war, perhaps because US astrologers had concluded that a German victory was likely.

In 1941 came an astonishing event that must have strengthened the idea among the Allies that the Nazi leaders were steeped in astrology. This was Rudolf Hess's ill-starred 'peace mission', his secret solo flight from Munich to Scotland on 10 May 1941. Along with Himmler, Hess was the most metaphysically minded of the Nazi hierarchy, and was interested in homoeopathy and natural diets as well as astrology. Hess's personal staff in Munich included an amateur astrologer, Ernst Schulte-Strathaus, and the Nazi number two would also discuss astrology with Albrecht Haushofer, the son of Hess's old boss and friend Karl Haushofer, a professor at the Geopolitical Institute in Munich. Karl Haushofer, for whom Hess had worked after the First World War, had regularly visited Hess and Hitler while the two were in the Landsberg Fortress following the 1923 putsch, and the professor's contention that Germany's destiny lay to the east, with its *Lebensraum* (living space), was subsequently expressed in *Mein Kampf*. In early 1941 Hitler was poised to fulfil this idea by invading Russia.

Haushofer, however, had become disillusioned with Hitler, and he and his son had been in secret contact with a 'British peace group', said to include Sir Samuel Hoare, R.A. Butler, Lord Halifax (the Foreign Secretary and recruiter of Louis de Wohl had put out peace feelers in 1940, behind Churchill's back) and the Duke of Hamilton, a personal friend of Albrecht Haushofer. The younger Haushofer, who was a professor of political geography in Berlin, was a keen astrologer and student of Nostradamus, and kept a close watch on the horoscope of Hitler. In 1941 he was already active in the underground opposition to Hitler, an involvement that would lead to his murder by the SS in 1945.[7]

The Haushofers were the primer for Rudolf Hess's abortive 'peace mission' in May 1941, for which astrology almost certainly provided the schedule. Early in 1941, Schulte-Strathaus had told Hess, somewhat jokingly, that the world would be rendered lopsided by the upcoming conjunction of six planets in Taurus in May, a configuration that Hess had himself concluded was potentially disastrous for Hitler. There is also a suggestion that Karl Haushofer had told his former student of a prophetic 'big dream' he had had, in which he saw Hess striding through baronial halls in Scotland. Whatever the motives churning through Hess's mind, he requisitioned a Messerschmitt fighter and took off from Bavaria for Scotland, evidently aiming to land at the Duke of Hamilton's residence and expecting to be privy to peace negotiations with the British government. Instead, he was captured and held by the security services until his trial at Nuremberg and lifelong incarceration at Spandau.

The Nazis were bewildered and angered by Hess's flight. Hitler flew into a rage. Clearly the Reichsminister had gone mad, his insanity probably fuelled by some fool astrologer or other. Why an astrologer would advise Hess to choose the full Moon of 10 May for an important mission is a puzzle, since the planetary omens are plainly not good.[8] The obvious conclusion is that Hess was, indeed, advised by an astrologer to take his flight on this powerfully configurated occasion, but that the star-gazer concerned was working against him. Albrecht Haushofer, perhaps with the connivance of his father, whose 'big dream' had influenced Hess, fits neatly into this conspiratorial frame.

In a piece of cosmic serendipity, when British intelligence got their hands on Hess, a noted British astrologer, Brigadier Roy Firebrace, was among his interrogators. Firebrace, who later became the first president of the British Astrological Association but who argued the case for the Sidereal zodiac rather than the Tropical zodiac (he was a Leo by both systems), was the senior military intelligence officer in Glasgow, the nearest base to where Hess was picked up, and after the war claimed he was the first to question Hess. We do not know whether these two astrological minds discussed the ramifications of the day's transits. In any case, Hess remained interested enough in astrology to write to his wife from prison a year after his capture, asking her to send him a copy of the horoscope cast for him by Schulte-Strathaus.

The Nazi hierarchy's conviction that astrological advice was behind Hess's flight led swiftly to 'Aktion Hess', in which the Gestapo arrested and questioned hundreds of astrologers and confiscated their books and papers. The operation was eagerly directed by SS deputy leader Reinhard Heydrich, who, unlike his boss, had no time for esoteric ideas or astrology, and who once compared a prominent general to Himmler with the remark 'One cares about the stars on his epaulette, the other about the stars in his horoscope.'

The arrested astrologers were interrogated about their possible associations with Hess and Krafft, and about their opinions on the Führer's horoscope. Most, including Schulte-Strathaus, were released after a spell in jail and a promise not to practise their art again. Not Krafft, himself, however. After a year in prison he was briefly put to work in Berlin's propaganda ministry in 1942 but, after he once more became uncooperative, he was moved to Oranienburg concentration camp, where he became ill. Krafft was on his way to the infamous death camp at Buchenwald when he died, in January 1945.

So ended 'Hitler's astrologer' that never was. Other star-folk were luckier. One was Wilhelm Wulff, a Hamburg astrologer whose prosperous practice had been destroyed by the Nazi restrictions on astrologers. After spending four months in prison in 1941, Wulff was pressed into service at the Naval Research Institute in Berlin where pendulum dowsing and other neo-magical practices were being investigated. Later, Wulff found himself passed like an astrological totem from one member of the Nazi hierarchy to another, among them Arthur Nebe, head of the SS Kriminalpolizei. Nebe asked Wulff and a selection of dowsers and clairvoyants from the Naval Research Institute to use their powers of deduction to locate Mussolini after the Italian dictator had been abducted by the Badoglio government in July 1943. Wulff claims to have correctly identified the place where Il Duce was being held, which was the isle of Ponza, seventy-five miles south-east of Rome, though Mussolini was soon moved. Eventually he was found and freed by the German forces.

Felix Kersten, Himmler's personal masseur, was Wulff's principal conduit to the SS leadership, and for much of the time after his release from prison Wulff lived on the estate belonging to Kersten, whose influence and contacts went further than his role as Himmler's personal physician suggests.[9] Among those for whom Wulff worked was Walter Schellenberg, head of counter-espionage, who loaded him with astrological assignments. Eventually, Wulff was pressed into the service of Heinrich Himmler himself. In his autobiography, *Zodiac and Swastika*, Wulff describes being summoned to lunch with Himmler, in May 1944, at the Reichsführer's castle retreat in the Alpine foothills. There Himmler engaged him in educated discussion about astrology, ancient Germanic prophecies, Indian philosophy (Wulff was a Sanskrit scholar and knew Vedic as well as Western astrology) and the prospects for Germany in the forthcoming months. He also delivered the Nazi critique of astrology as a 'universalist' doctrine. That, however, did not stop Himmler going into informed conversation about his own birth chart, as well as that of the Führer.

Wulff continued to work for the SS High Command until the last phase of the war. The worse the situation became, the greater was the demand for his services from Schellenberg and Himmler. Wulff met the pair for the final time in April 1945, by which time Himmler was a ghostly, broken man, chewing alternately on his nails and a cigar as he demanded hysterically of his astrologer, 'What's going to happen? What's going to happen?' Wulff advised him to flee the country, and returned to Hamburg to await the arrival of the Allied armies.

Wulff's account of his activities sidesteps the issue of his own political proclivities, and presents him as a reluctant pawn in the power plays of the SS. In fact, Wulff had a background in Ariosophy and in the 1920s was part of the so-called 'swastika circle' assembled by the publisher Herbert Reichstein to preach occult sciences from an Aryan supremacist perspective. Moreover, Wulff says he repeatedly urged Himmler to overthrow Hitler and save Germany from imminent disaster, but that the Reichsführer was wretchedly indecisive (a much-vaunted trait of Himmler's Libra Sun). Perhaps. Yet, if his astrological powers were as accurate as he frequently claimed in his book, one wonders why Wulff had not fled the Reich long before the onset of war. After all, Wulff had cast Hitler's horoscope way back in 1923, when he numbered among his clients Herbert Volck, an early convert to National Socialism who had served alongside him in the First World War. Wulff's interpretation of Hitler's horoscope for Volck was far from flattering. He pointed to Hitler's badly aspected Saturn in the tenth house (a planetary signature shared by Napoleon) and concluded that such a man would 'issue senseless and cruel orders and be feared'. In 1941, when Wulff was arrested under Aktion Hess, this interpretation fell into the hands of the Gestapo, who, needless to say, were not enamoured of it; though, when Wulff was asked by Reinhard Heydrich to elaborate on his interpretation, Himmler, who was also present, 'gave a broad grin'.

In writing his autobiography, Wulff was also responding to the account of his activities outlined by the British historian Hugh Trevor-Roper in his best-selling *The Last Days of Hitler*, where the astrologer is painted as a sound Nazi. Though this ignores the fact that Wulff was a virtual prisoner, keen to stay out of a concentration camp, Trevor-Roper is probably correct. Others also thought that Wulff's sympathies were unambiguous; Henry Miller, an ardent anti-fascist as well as a student of astrology, flatly refused to supply a foreword for his book.

Hugh Trevor-Roper has probably been as responsible as anyone for the continuing fable of Hitler's astrological interests, which are mentioned several times in *The Last Days of Hitler*. Most notably, using an account taken from the unpublished diary of Hitler's minister of finance, Count Schwerin von Krosigk, Trevor-Roper tells the story of how, as the Allied armies encircled Germany in the dying weeks of the war, Goebbels sent for the charts of Hitler and the German Republic, which had been prepared by one of Himmler's departments in 1933. Sunk in the gloom of the Chancery bunker, the two Nazi leaders had been recalling the plight of Frederick the Great, who was unexpectedly saved from defeat at the hands of the Russians by the death of the tsarina. The horoscopes of the Führer and the German Republic were found to indicate a similar imminent reversal of fortune (who was doing the astrological deciphering isn't clear), a prophecy apparently fulfilled soon after by the unexpected death of President Roosevelt on Friday, 13 April. 'It is written in the stars that the second half of April will be the turning point for us. This is the turning point!' the Reich's spin doctor told Hitler. Two weeks later both men were dead.

The end of the Second World War did not lay to rest the story of Hitler's astrological interests. On the contrary, Trevor-Roper's account of the Führer's twilight, the residual associations of Hitler's rise with astrology and fictitious articles in the German tabloid press all helped secure the legend of Adolf the astrologer. So did de Wohl's carefully nurtured reputation as the man who had out-starred Hitler's astrologer – 'the gallant captain with a bandolier full of horoscopes', as Louis

MacNeice mockingly summarised him – which became enshrined in magazine articles and in his 1952 autobiography, *The Stars of War and Peace*. By then de Wohl must have known that Krafft's role in the Nazi era had been insignificant (Krafft's widow wrote repeatedly to him to stress as much), but de Wohl persisted with his self-aggrandisement, even after his conversion to Roman Catholicism (he spent the last part of his life writing religious tracts).

By contrast, the extent of the Nazi hierarchy's involvement with stranger and more sinister fringe beliefs went largely unreported. According to Airey Neave, a British prosecutor at the Nuremberg trials (and later a Tory MP and personal friend of Margaret Thatcher before his murder by the IRA in 1979), the sheer oddity of some of the evidence against the Nazis made it unusable in court as it would have allowed Nazi war criminals to plead insanity and diminished responsibility. The Nazis were portrayed as opportunist gangsters and deranged scientists rather than as calculating practitioners of the dark arts. In reality, they were all three.

When the occult background of Nazism and the Reich was finally dragged into the open, it was in sensationalist and fanciful form. *The Dawn of Magic*, Louis Pauwels's and Jacques Bergier's 1963 best-seller, set the tone for much of what has followed; their allegation that Hitler and his cronies were in reality Satanists or magical adepts has become commonplace, not least among impressionable rock bands and filmmakers looking for a plot. Was Hitler an astrologer? Not according to the planetary set-up of 1 September 1939, whose three retrograde planets and void-of-course Moon would, as author Michael Baigent has argued, have been avoided by an astrologer at all costs.[10] Rather than persist with the fiction that Adolf Hitler used astrology, historians should perhaps give thanks that he did not.

14

MOON QUEEN

THE ASTROLOGICAL REIGN OF DIANA SPENCER

*

With the possible exception of Adolf Hitler, the most studied of all twentieth-century birth charts must be that of Diana, Princess of Wales. During her life Diana's horoscope was subject to endless in-depth analysis, its transits dissected, its progressions pronounced upon. Her birth time, artfully disguised by Diana herself, became the subject of widespread speculation and rumour in the astrological community. Was she really Sagittarius rising? Or was her given birth time disinformation, and her true Ascendant Libra? What would happen when Uranus moved opposite Diana's Sun? Or Pluto over her Ascendant? The obsession was as strong in the USA as in Britain.

Astrologers were struck by Diana for the same reasons as everyone else. She offered a unique alchemy of royal tradition, designer glamour and high drama. As a wife struggling to find an identity independent from her husband's, and a mother of two pitted against the patriarchy, she was a feminist exemplar. She was variously victim, heroine, neurotic, pin-up, martyr, media manipulator and romantic. On top of all this, she was a devout follower of astrology, at one time employing the services of three different astrologers to help her run her affairs.

Principally, though, she was the queen-to-be, and astrology's ancestral love affair with royalty showed few signs of waning in the twentieth century. The relationship has become a tad lopsided over the last few hundred years – the last British monarchs to take astrological advice seem to have been Charles II and James II back in the seventeenth century, though Edward VII briefly rekindled the romance when he had the time of his 1902 coronation set by the famous palmist and fortune-teller Cheiro, confidant to the ruling classes of Europe and America. Cheiro chose 9 August for Edward's crowning on the basis that – blow the transits! – August was the seat of regal Leo and Edward's lucky number was nine. Otherwise, post-Newton royalty seems to have blanked the royal art. There have been rumours of assorted Windsors having their horoscopes cast by celebrity star-gazers like Russell Grant, but these encounters, if they happened, seem to be end-of-the-pier flings rather than serious consultations.

In any case, Elizabeth II, unlike her sixteenth-century namesake, who put the master astrologer and mage John Dee to good use choosing her coronation date, reputedly frowns on astrology. As head of the Church of England, she is rumoured to have been warned off star-lore by the former Archbishop of Canterbury Michael Ramsey. Even so, astrologers couldn't help but wonder whether Elizabeth's auspiciously starred coronation in 1953 was entirely down to chance (that Sun–Jupiter conjunction!).

Despite the one-way nature of the love affair between monarchy and astrology, the royal art has kept the torch blazing for the old romance. Each successive royal birth has found a poised pen and open ephemeris ready to cast the chart of the latest blue blood issuing from the House of Saxe-Coburg-Gotha, or Windsor, as the family restyled itself in 1917, when dissociation from its German roots became a painful necessity. Each coronation and royal marriage has likewise been scrutinised for omens, and for correlations with the zodiacal patterns of the royal line. Rarely, if ever, has any dynasty been the subject of such exhaustive astro-analysis.

If nothing else, royal horoscopes have kept astrology before the public. Twentieth-century astrology's invasion of the popular press was, let's not forget, launched by R.H. Naylor's ruminations on the birth chart of the newly born Princess Margaret in the *Sunday Express* in 1930, establishing an equation that tabloids and women's magazines subsequently took to their hearts: royalty + astrology = sales.

The engagement of Prince Charles and his blushing teenage fiancée duly rang in a series of gushing astrological profiles of the royal pair. Charles's birth chart was well known (and reckoned less than satisfactory), but the advent of his future queen opened up new vistas of speculation. From the outset, though, Diana posed a major, and still unresolved, problem: her birth time. Upon announcement of her engagement to Charles, Buckingham Palace gave her data as 2 p.m. (on 1 July 1961, on the royal estate of Sandringham). This gave her a Libra Ascendant – perfect for pretty 'Shy Di'. Alas, a week later came a corrected birth time of 7.45 p.m., yielding an Ascendant in sporty, adventurous Sagittarius; harder to equate with the retiring Diana of the time, who, unusually for a member of the British upper classes and annoyingly for the Centaur symbolism, didn't even like horses (she'd been thrown in childhood and had broken her arm). Under this new time, Libra became Diana's Midheaven.

Whatever her Ascendant, Diana's chart told a complicated story. Her Cancer Sun was emotional, nurturing and traditionalist, her Aquarius Moon independent and unpredictable. The hazy glamour of Neptune was also prominently placed at the top of her chart. For most astrologers, though, the most powerful signature in Diana's chart was the triangular configuration of Moon–Venus–Uranus, with its points in the fixed signs of Aquarius, Taurus and Leo, respectively. With the two emotional planets of Venus and Moon in conflict with incendiary Uranus, this was at best an intense, excitable combination, at worst a stormy Bermuda Triangle of passions. Since the Moon represents the mother, it also chimed with Diana's broken home.

Synastry of Diana's and Charles's charts still suggested a union made in heaven to most astro-commentators. Both had Suns in water signs: Charles's in intense Scorpio, Diana's in emotional Cancer. Both had fire-sign Ascendants: his in royal Leo, hers in questing Sagittarius. Her Aquarian Moon fell in his seventh house of relationships. That Charles's Scorpio Sun made a rectangle of Diana's triangular Moon--Venus–Uranus triangle suggested she found completion in him, and there were several other encouraging overlaps.

The chart for 'the wedding of the century' confirmed the idea of a union blessed by the cosmos. This is not surprising, since the timing of the wedding (29 July 1981 at 11 a.m.) was almost certainly astrologically chosen to do just that. It's a remarkable chart. Most striking is the once-in-twenty years conjunction of Jupiter and Saturn sitting exactly astride the chart's Libra Ascendant. In the sky above, the Moon (the bride) is in its own sign of Cancer while the Sun (the groom) is in its own sign of regal Leo. What's more, the Sun, at 5 degrees Leo, falls exactly on Prince Charles's Ascendant, re-enforcing his blaze of royal show. Surely all this couldn't be coincidence?

Yet would any astrologer worth their bag of sovereigns feel happy about putting gloomy Saturn on an Ascendant square to angry Mars at the pinnacle of the chart? (Misery and arguments!) Worse, two days after the wedding the Sun was eclipsed by the Moon, an obvious omen to avoid (the monarch loses his light!). John Dee would not have been impressed.

One explanation for the contradictions of the chart is that this time was, indeed, astrologically chosen, but by an amateur. High on the list of suspects must come Laurens Van der Post, mystic, author, friend and biographer of Carl Jung, and spiritual mentor to Prince Charles ever since the murder of Earl Mountbatten by the IRA in 1979. As an avid student of Jung, Van der Post would have known plenty about astrology, and about the 'Sacred Wedding' of Sun and Moon, of male and female principles, the *Mysterium Coniunctionis* described by Jung. Sun in Leo–Moon in Cancer, and the Jupiter and Saturn conjunction fit in beguilingly with this concept. To re-enforce the symbolism, as Charles and Diana paced down the aisle of St Paul's Cathedral, Holst's 'Jupiter' blasted forth to the world, pulsing its regal refrain down the geomantic alignments radiating from Wren's masterpiece on Lud Hill, out to the last shores of Albion and beyond. Clearly this was designed to be not just a wedding but a cosmic coupling. Sadly, it didn't work.

But then the *coniunctionis* presumably requires that male and female share a mutual attraction, and Charles, as we learned later, had explicitly told Diana he didn't love her just the night before the wedding, prior to disappearing into the night, allegedly to his once and future mistress, Camilla Shand, alias Mrs Parker-Bowles. Such a scenario could arguably be glimpsed in the wedding-day chart, where Venus was locked forlornly away in the twelfth house of confinement.

At the time, most astrologers were swept along by the tide of royalist sentiment that accompanied the wedding, a tide still swollen from the red, white and blue razzmatazz of 1977's Silver Jubilee. For example, Martin Freeman, a distinguished ex-president of the Faculty of Astrological Studies, devoted a thirty-page chapter of his 1982 book *Forecasting by Astrology* to scrutinising the charts of Charles and Diana without a murmur of alarm about their compatibility. To Freeman's credit, he does single out the years 1991–2 as extremely difficult, yet cannot bring himself to draw the obvious conclusions. In the charts of mere mortals, he suggests, the passage of gloomy Pluto at this time would indicate 'turbulence in the marriage aggravated by broader life changes'. Yet, because this is royalty, 'a less parochial interpretation must be considered'. His comments offer a measure of how much the status of the House of Windsor has subsequently declined, thanks in part to Diana's insurrectionary influence. Everyone now knows that royal marriages are no less turbulent, and no less likely to end in divorce, than anyone else's.

Not all of the astrological community were as convinced that all would be well. In her 1982 book *Synastry* Penny Thornton compared the birth charts of Charles and Diana and forecast trouble. Although she found many 'karmic' and 'harmonious' links, Thornton also foresaw 'powerful cross-currents' and 'block-busting rows', 'marathon icy silences' and 'sexual problems'. The composite chart for the pair (a blend of both charts into one) was worse. Its sixth house Moon suggested a partnership in which, according to Robert Hand's manual on composite charts, 'One person may feel like a doormat for the other; he or she is likely to get tired of that position and revolt.' *Touché!* Moreover, like Martin Freeman, Thornton saw in the distant future of the early 1990s 'by far the most troublesome time' for the couple.

Thornton did not have to wait that long to have her prognostications affirmed. In March 1986 she picked up the phone to find Diana herself on the line, asking after her services.

The call was not unexpected. Thornton had been primed by Diana's friend and soon-to-be-sister-in-law Sarah Ferguson. 'Fergie' had already consulted Thornton about her imminent marriage to Prince Andrew and knew that Diana 'wanted her chart done'. Thornton, who was a friend of friends of Andrew, was obviously the person to do it, especially after she had given the planetary go-ahead to a Fergie chafing at the bit to marry into the Windsor 'firm'.

The astrologer was uncertain when she could fit Diana into her schedule – she was writing a book – but once the seductive, unhappy tones of Diana herself came down the wire, wondering 'if there was a light at the end of the tunnel', she found the necessary time.

Thornton remained Diana's astrologer until 1992. A former dancer with the Royal Ballet, she had studied with the Faculty of Astrological Studies, gaining their diploma in 1977. Thornton's account of her role, *With Love from Diana* (published in the United States in 1995, it remains unpublished in Britain), contains some stark insights into Diana's despair in the mid-1980s, when the fiction of the 'fairytale marriage' was still being effectively maintained by the Palace. At her first meeting with Diana (4.00 p.m., 6 March 1986), an appalled Thornton learned that in reality this marriage came from the darker realms of faerie. The Princess was distraught, and ready to leave a husband whom she felt had betrayed and belittled her. She was bulimic, and had made a pass or two at suicide. Meanwhile, she felt a wicked Queen on a cold throne showed indifference to her plight.

The astrologer assured Diana that her position was not hopeless, that one day she would be 'allowed out', and that there was much she could do for herself, rather than remaining a passive victim of circumstance. For the next year Thornton was in close and constant touch with the Princess, principally by phone, sometimes driving to Kensington Palace in her battered Volkswagen.

That Diana was seeing an astrologer remained a well-guarded secret, one which did not emerge until 1992, when two biographies of her let it spill. The first was *Diana in Private* by upper-crust hostess Lady Colin Campbell, whose detailed account of the relationship between Princess and astrologer was presumably leaked to her by Diana herself, just as it was Diana who had supplied most of the material for Andrew Morton's throne-shaking *Diana: Her True Story*, which appeared a few months later. Both books dealt favourably with Diana's use of astrology. The 'friend' quoted by Lady Colin Campbell says that 'She [Thornton] helped Princess Diana get in touch with the spiritual part of her personality. She helped her see that her role as Princess of Wales was important.' From the Princess's encounter with her astro-counsellor, continues Campbell, 'Diana the Good was born.'

Diana: Her True Story and its post-divorce sequel, *Diana: Her New Life*, made the same point: 'The application of astrology to her personal life is a weapon in her armoury as she attempts to take control of her life,' asserted Morton.

All of Diana's astrologers seem to have acted as much as psychological counsellors as soothsayers. Thornton in particular seems to have advised her that there were roles she could play other than dutiful wife. Many of the abiding images of Diana – champion of the disadvantaged; the royal who threw tabloid homophobia in its face by cuddling AIDS patients; caring, sharing Di who kissed her kids in public; Diana the dancer, twirling her gown imperiously on stage with Wayne Sleep in defiance of Hanover's iron protocol – are self-expressive acts that followed her encounter with astrology. This, with its language of archetypes, undoubtedly helped the sequestered Shire Sloane to engage with the grand role she had imagined for herself from an early age. Perhaps it should have done more.

What sort of astrological advice did the Princess receive? In *Her True Story*, Andrew Morton quotes Diana saying of her last astrologer, Debbie Frank: 'She doesn't advise, she just tells me her angle with astrology. I listen to it but I don't believe it totally. It's a direction and a suggestion rather than it's definitely going to happen.'

Advice about specific troublesome dates obviously came in handy, however. In 1987, for example, Penny Thornton warned Diana that 'everything you do in the months ahead you will pay for' (Saturn crossing her Ascendant and moving opposite her Sun), a prediction that proved accurate when Diana was berated for such frivolous behaviour as wearing leather trousers to a David Bowie concert and poking a brolly up someone's backside at Ascot. 'I learned a lot,' she said afterwards.

By this time the influence of Diana's old friend and new sister-in-law, Sarah Ferguson, was also at work. The Duchess of York brought succour to the beleaguered Diana in the shape of her jolly hockey humour and a disregard for the stuffy etiquette of the Palace. Yet Fergie's Libra Sun liked to play diplomatic softball with 'the firm', and Penny Thornton paints an unflattering portrait of the Duchess. 'Be careful who you trust' was the nearest the astrologer felt she could say to Diana.

As the Duchess herself became estranged from her husband, who was preoccupied with naval duties, and tired of the dowdy correctness of royal life, she increasingly turned to the New Age market place for comfort. Seances, Tarot cards, astrology, channelling, sitting beneath plastic pyramids with Madame Vasso (who had secretly wired up her pyramid to a tape-recorder): the Duchess approached them all in the same cavalier spirit that had won her membership of the Dangerous Sports Club (badge: a pair of golden crutches). Fergie did, after all, have a sporty, high-powered Mars conjunct her Libran Sun, a show-off Aries Moon opposite it, a reckless Scorpio Ascendant and a volcanic Pluto on her Midheaven. These are not the astrological signifiers of a mystic but of a daredevil and an emotional insatiate. For Fergie, the New Age became a lifestyle prop, whether it was ringing her astrologers every few hours, or dealing herself endless Tarot spreads in her sitting room.

Diana was also drawn into esoteric pursuits. Besides astrology and Fergie's Tarot deck, she tried spiritualism and mediums. She was certain she had contacted the spirit of her grandmother, and her private policeman who had died in a road accident. She took reincarnation seriously, and told Penny Thornton that in a previous life she had been 'a martyr', a role she seemed determined to pursue in this existence.

As rumours about the royal marriage swirled across the tabloids, Diana's and Charles's charts became the subject of increasing scrutiny. A royal astro-ratpack followed their transits, which, like Mrs Thatcher's, kept remarkably accurate pace with their careers, particularly Diana's. As transformational Pluto passed over her Midheaven at the time of her wedding, Diana mutated from private Sloane to public Princess. As Pluto moved on to Diana's Neptune in 1986, she started to transform herself from psychologically battered wife and victim to self-expressive rival to her husband. By 1989, when Saturn, Neptune and Uranus were making their historic conjunction in Capricorn opposite Diana's Sun, it became brutally apparent that the happy marriage was a threadbare myth, at least to those who cared to see. Just as the broadsheets dismissed tabloid reports of the marriage as vulgar sensationalism, so some astrologers looked at the horoscopes of Charles and Diana through Venusian glasses. In 1988 Penny Thornton wrote a piece for the *Daily Mail* questioning whether Charles would ever be king and forecasting a divorce for the Waleses early in the next decade. The Faculty of Astrological Studies promptly accused her of bringing astrology into disrepute, while leading astrologers, Jonathan Cainer prominent among them, lined up to rubbish her predictions and proclaim all was well with the House of Windsor.

Thornton's predictions were quite correct; the bubbling royal cauldron finally boiled over in 1992, a year famously described by the Queen as her 'annus horribilis'. It was the year when two royal marriages foundered as the 'Squidgygate' and 'Camillagate' tapes mysteriously surfaced, and the 'Fergiegate' photographs of the Duchess of York cavorting with her Texan lover splashed down in the tabloids. *Diana: Her True Story* appeared to an aghast reception from the world's media. Finally, a year of royal scandal, when the republican cause prospered, came to a climax as a sizeable chunk of Windsor Castle went up in flames, a piece of symbolism not lost on the royals themselves.

The Queen might have been better prepared if she'd used an astrologer rather than berating her daughters-in-law for doing so. The year 1992 had long been fingered as meltdown for the Windsors. The basis for the prediction was simple enough: Pluto, crawling through the sign of Scorpio since 1983, would then cross Charles's Sun. Shortly afterwards it would reach the Scorpio Midheaven of the Queen's chart, where Saturn had held iron sway over her horoscope since her birth in 1926; a case of irresistible force meeting immovable object.

Shortly after that, the rare conjunction of Neptune and Uranus in Capricorn would fall on the Queen's Ascendant. This same passage of the slow-moving outer planets had already been linked to the collapse of the Berlin Wall, apartheid and the dissolution of the USSR. Now it was the turn of the English monarchy to face the forces of insurrection (Uranus) and dissolution (Neptune) as they acted on tradition and hierarchy (Capricorn). The Queen's annus horribilis duly arrived, though unlike apartheid and the USSR, the English monarchy survived.

Though she fared better than the in-laws, 1992 was not easy for Diana, either. The revelations in Morton's book, although in great part supplied by her, had to be parried with some fancy media footwork. Confirmation that she was using astrology also needed careful fielding. Diana had occasionally dropped the word 'psychic' to her policemen, and watched them 'freak out', and knew that she would be depicted as a crank when her astrological interests were divulged. Diana handled it with a mixture of disavowal and disinformation. By this time, Thornton had become astrologer with *Today*, one of Rupert Murdoch's tabloids, writing regularly about the planetary prospects of the royal family. Astro-portraits of Charles, Andrew and Sarah Ferguson had also featured in her 1990 book *Romancing the Stars*. Once *Today* learned that they had Princess Di's personal astrologer on their payroll, they naturally expected an exclusive payoff (the *Mail* had paid handsomely to carry extracts of Campbell's book) and were furious when Thornton refused to betray her Princess. Still, Thornton's by-line in *Today* henceforth came with the tag of 'Princess Diana's astrologer'.

Except Thornton wasn't any longer. Diana had moved on. Andrew Morton's book quoted another astrologer about Diana rather than Thornton; this was Felix Lyle, who talked of Diana's proneness to melancholy and self-destructiveness. That Lyle was Thornton's ex-lover led some to believe that she had simply 'passed on' Diana to him, though both parties adamantly denied this. In any case, by this time Diana had a third astrologer in play, Debbie Frank, whom she had started to consult in February 1989.

Muddying the zodiacal waters further, Diana once more changed her story about her birth time, pronouncing that 7.45 p.m. was wrong, and the original 2 p.m. correct – something she had told Thornton back in 1988. (Later Felix Lyle would claim a third time of 4.15 p.m. as accurate, this yielding a Scorpio Ascendant on which Neptune beamed forth ominously.) The astrologers were stumped, though the Piscean ingenuity of Nicholas Campion suggested a get-out clause: Libran Di, he posited, was private Diana. When she became Princess, questing Sagittarius became appropriate. Both charts and identities were relevant.

As 1992 drew to a close, it was clear that Charles and Diana could not continue. Penny Thornton had predicted an announcement of separation for 9 December, on the basis of that day's total lunar eclipse (this fell at 18 degrees Gemini and was therefore on the Descendant of Diana's 'wrong' 7.45 p.m. chart!). Again, she was proved correct, when Prime Minister John Major told a hushed House of Commons of the split. It's a curious fact that many of the key events in Diana's life took place around eclipses: her marriage, the birth of William, the announcement of her separation and her death.

Diana had a sting in her tail for Thornton. No doubt incensed by Thornton's bragging by-line, she told *Today*'s royal correspondent that she had only seen Thornton once, back in the mid-eighties, and that 'she has never been my astrologer – perhaps your editor should know that'. Though Thornton was able to demonstrate otherwise from greetings cards, she did not last much longer as *Today*'s astrologer. But then *Today* itself didn't survive for long.

After their separation, Charles and Diana took up media cudgels for a protracted war of image and reputation that was to continue until Diana's death, and beyond. While the Princess's use of astrologers was brandished as evidence of her mental instability by some, the astrological community continued to speculate feverishly on her horoscope and identity. Neptune, with its cocktail of glamour, martyrdom and fantasy, was a popular choice as the defining planet of her horoscope. For others, and not just astrologers, Diana was primarily a creature of the Moon – in 1992 the American intellectual Camille Paglia wrote that she resonated with the archetype of Diana the huntress.

Diana continued to have her horoscope read by Debbie Frank. According to Frank's own accounts, delivered via the *Sun* and elsewhere shortly after Diana's death, the Princess called her frequently, often a couple of times a day. Apart from her own developments, she was keen to know the signs of the figures whom she met: the likes of Nelson Mandela, the Blairs and the Clintons. Once every few months throughout the nineties Frank and Diana would have lunch at Kensington Palace, followed by an in-depth look at Diana's and other charts, for Diana remained obsessed by her husband's affairs, and kept a gimlet eye upon the planetary prospects of her rival, Camilla, a fellow Cancerian. The last meeting between Princess and astrologer took place on 30 July 1997. The upcoming solar eclipse of 1 September was mentioned, and Diana, looking in her diary, noted that she was getting 'her boys back' that day. The car crash that took her life, and that of her lover Dodi and their chauffeur, intervened on 31 August.

The news of Diana's death was as big a shock to astrologers as to the rest of the world, sending them scurrying to their computers to find out what they hadn't foreseen. For despite all the intense scrutiny of Diana's chart, there had been no suggestion that August 1997 was a difficult, let alone dangerous time for her. For example, Shelley Von Strunckel, one of Britain's best-known newspaper star-gazers, foresaw 1997 as a year in which 'Diana remains radiant'. America's Noel Tyl, writing two years previously in his book *Predictions for a New Millennium*, had predicted a royal death for spring 1997, but it's clearly not Diana he had in mind; more likely the enduring Queen Mother (whose Leo Sun faced a major opposition of planets in Aquarius early in the year). True, the forecasts for August 1997 in *Old Moore's Almanack* did include 'Attacks upon the monarchy', but this prediction came true principally because of the Queen's graceless refusal to accord the dead Diana due regal ceremony and pomp until public opinion forced her hand.

In retrospect, of course, astrologers soon detected the ill-omens that accompanied the grisly crash. There was, for example, disruptive Uranus passing over Diana's ruling planet Jupiter, and the Sun and Mercury poised over doomy Pluto the day before a solar eclipse. It was noted that she was born under the sign of the Moon, and died at the dark of the Moon.

Diana's funeral, finally accorded full state pomp after furious disputes between Elizabeth and Charles and the diplomatic intervention of Prime Minister Tony Blair, was rich with symbolism. As at her wedding, Holst's Jupiter rang out: 'we had the Goddess of the Moon in the temple of the Sun having a hymn to Jupiter played for her,' remarked the distinguished American astrologer Robert Hand in a lecture at the Astrology Association Conference held on the afternoon of the funeral. Even so, it was Elton John's 'Candle in the Wind' that captured the public mood, written for one Neptunian, Marilyn Monroe, and recast for another. Diana seemed to be worshipped less as the People's Princess as the People's Goddess, and the Arthurian overtones of Diana's last journey could scarcely be missed.

Diana's funeral took place on the weekend of the annual conference of Britain's Astrological Association. Here the mood was subdued, with the Saturday morning's lectures suspended. At the first session of the afternoon Robert Hand opened his talk on medieval techniques with some observations on the event. No other nation, he opined, could handle a collective ritual of this sort with such aplomb, and while he was not going to engage in the debate about the monarchy, such displays 'would be harder if you didn't have a royal family acting as magical head of state to direct this energy'. At this point a sudden squall of papers blew up at the back of the hall; clearly the ghost of William Lilley had been aroused from his republican grave.

Later Nick Campion, the Association's president, articulated the mood and the realities: 'Astrology is inadequate to the moment. Diana's destiny was written larger than anything in her chart. The idea that astrology can predict an event like that is wrong; it's more a case of peering through a glass darkly – you can only see shadows.'

The idea, widespread at the time, that Diana's passing signalled the demise of the Windsors has yet to be borne out. 'The firm' has simply closed ranks and carried on with familiar Saturnine dreariness. Diana was a devout monarchist, in any case, fully expecting her son to accede to the throne. Like the media, astrology has turned to other royals to fill the void left by Diana, particularly Princes William and Harry. Here, while Buckingham Palace has made a polished job of setting up the teenage princes as heralds of a touchy-feely, people's monarchy, with Dad basking in reflected glory from his buttoned-down neo-DiCaprios, it has yet to convince astrologers all is well with the House of Windsor. On the contrary, long before Diana's passing astro-royal watchers had noted problems of succession facing both Charles and William. In terms of kingship, it seems, Harry is the one to watch.

Even when Prince Charles was born in 1948, the leading British astrologer Charles Carter questioned whether his horoscope was 'of a royal character'. For Carter and others since, Charles's astrological problem is that he lacks a powerfully placed Jupiter. The planetary symbol of 'the divine right of kings', a doctrine to which Charles is known to be attached, languishes miserably in his birth chart.

In 1995, Noel Tyl boldly prophesied that 'Charles will not be King', based on his study of the last ten monarchs, from George II to Elizabeth II. Tyl thinks the succession will pass to William, whose reign 'could well begin precipitously between September 2001 and March 2002'. Even so, he doubts whether King William will last long. 'He will be confused, disappointed and constricted by affairs of the heart,' he asserts, drawing watery parallels between William (Sun and Moon both in Cancer), his father Charles (Scorpio Sun, Taurus Moon) and Edward VIII (Cancer Sun, Pisces Moon), who abdicated the throne after less than a year rather than give up his life with divorcee Wallis Simpson.

The Windsors and their predecessors show several zodiacal patterns in their birth charts (the fixed signs of Taurus, Leo and Aquarius, for example, recur). The so-called 'Curse of the Stuarts' that blighted an earlier branch of the Anglo-Scottish blood line has also been identified with the recurring combination of Mars and Pluto in their horoscopes. Astrologer Paul Wright found this aspect looming large in the charts of nine of the twelve Stuarts, almost all of whom experienced exile or execution (the decapitated Charles I did not have the aspect). The two planets were in conjunction at Diana's birth.

In *Born to Reign*, an astro-historical survey of the royal family down the centuries, Nicholas Campion unravels the patterns of royal stars, and expresses doubts about Charles and William. 'More often than not, the heir to the throne does not succeed,' he argues, pointing out that of the eighteen monarchs who have reigned over the thrones of England and Scotland since 1605, 'only five could have expected at their births to inherit the throne'.

William is blessed with Jupiter appropriately high in the sky, but everything else in his horoscope is stacked against him becoming king. Being born hours after a powerful solar eclipse on midsummer's day doesn't help. Campion also finds few connections between William's birth chart and those of previous monarchs – the unfortunate Edward VIII aside – and suggests that 'his inheritance is that of a Spencer, not a Windsor'. For Campion, 'William's entire horoscope is romantic', suggesting he will, like Edward VIII, be forced to make a choice between private feelings and public duty.

Harry (a practical Virgo with his Moon in Taurus) is astrologically a more convincing candidate for king, with plentiful overlaps between his horoscope, those of the Windsor dynasty and the chart of Great Britain itself, and while Harry has Saturn rather than Jupiter atop his birth chart, this only makes him 'old school effective rather than new school popular', according to Tyl.

Opinions differ whether the United Kingdom will ever be rid of its monarchy. Most royal watchers agree that the period between 2011 and 2017 is critical, thanks to the tension between Uranus, which will be letting rip in headstrong Aries, and Pluto, which will be melting down the authority represented by Capricorn. If this fierce planetary combination does not topple the House of Windsor, it may at least persuade it to turn to astrology.

15

THE MUSIC OF THE SPHERES

HOLST'S *PLANETS* AND OTHER CELESTIAL SUITES

✶

'Space is the place.'
Sun Ra

Among the most resonant ideas bequeathed to the world by Pythagoras of Samos was his conception of the Music of the Spheres, the celestial refrain that the great mathematician imagined was made by the movement of stars and planets as they whirled along their courses. Composers, musicians and listeners have been trying to tune in ever since.

Pythagoras famously came to his theory while listening to the sounds of hammers beating on anvils in a smithy's forge, a moment of discovery celebrated in Handel's 'Harmonious Blacksmith'. The mathematician noticed that a heavy hammer produced a frequency twice as long as one half its weight, an octave lower. It was a short step to see that the musical scale worked in accordance with mathematical principles. Music and the cosmos, reasoned Pythagoras, were organised on the same harmonious, mathematical basis.

The Music of the Spheres became part of the hermetic conception of the world, reiterated by the likes of Plato and Ptolemy, and famously illustrated by the English alchemist Robert Fludd. Then, two thousand years after Pythagoras, Johannes Kepler showed the theory was also a physical reality – that the planets did indeed move according to the same mathematical template that operated in music. Kepler's measurements showed, for example, that the ratio between Jupiter's maximum and Mars's minimum speed corresponds to a minor third; that between Earth and Venus to a minor sixth. In his work *Harmonice Mundi* (1619) Kepler exalted in 'the song which the cosmos sings to its lord and centre, the Solar Logos'. Even modern astronomy accedes that the correspondence between musical ratios and planetary velocities is, in the words of Fred Hoyle, 'frighteningly good'.

The concept of the Music of the Spheres carries an important corollary: that if humanity were to create music in tune with the celestial laws of harmony, the perfection of heaven can be replicated on Earth in the time-honoured principle of 'As Above, So Below'. One can catch a glimpse of the notion in the Christian Church's insistence on appropriate music for different services and the tradition of plainsong. John Michell (1991) has suggested the latter a remnant of the strategically sited 'perpetual choirs' with which Druidic geomancers and, later, the saints of Celtic Christianity attempted to 'enchant the landscape'. The Pythagoreans were similarly interested in the healing and civilising power of music, which, as Shakespeare observed, can 'soothe the savage breast'.

The idea that music can and should represent a higher, universal order has proved no less resonant in the modern era than in previous ages. Twentieth-century music is full of it, from Stockhausen's cosmic epic *Licht* to the spiritual quests of John Coltrane's jazz and the interplanetary rock of Jimi Hendrix. Astrology's role has usually been secondary and suggestive, though it looms large in the post-Coltrane jazz of Pharoah Sanders in pieces like 'Capricorn Ascending'. Most strikingly, astrology became the direct inspiration for Gustav Holst's *The Planets*, which adopted its planetary symbolism intact to become a modernist masterpiece whose roots lie deep in antiquity.

Holst came to astrology via theosophy, through which he also encountered the Hinduism that kindled his other major works, the Indian operas *Sita* (1906) and *Savitri* (1908–9), and the Gnostic Christianity of *The Hymn of Jesus* (1917). In his theosophical leanings the composer was far from alone. Madame Blavatsky's cornucopia of esoteric lore poured into the work of many European musicians and painters intent on fashioning a new art for a new century and, of course, 'a new age'. The Russian émigré Wasily Kandinsky, painter of the first abstract canvas in 1910, was much influenced by esoteric ideas gathered from theosophy and anthroposophy, as was the Dutch abstract painter Piet Mondrian. Both Kandinsky and Mondrian were to make common cause with the Bauhaus school founded by Walter Gropius in 1919, and though the Bauhaus soon shifted into purely functionalist mode, in its early years it, too, was infused with esoteric ideas, many of them stemming from the overseer of the school's foundation course, Johannes Itte.

In music theosophical concepts were also active, notably among composers keen to break from traditional structures, particularly of harmony, and embrace new, modernist forms. The Russian composer Alexander Scriabin, who gave Kandinsky Blavatsky's *Secret Doctrine*, combined an extravagant and sensuous mysticism with musical radicalism. Scriabin dreamed of translating music into colour and his grandiose plans included building a colour organ for his symphony *Prometheus* (first performed in 1911), with the scale matched to shades: C was red, C sharp violet and so forth.[1]

In Vienna Arnold Schoenberg came under the influence of his teacher and friend Oskar Adler, a doctor by profession but also a keen musician, theosophist and astrologer. Schoenberg's radical ideas on atonality and twelve-tone technique ('serialism') were to prove highly influential on twentieth-century composers, beginning with his disciples, Webern and Berg. In Britain theosophy's recruits included the composers John Foulds and Cyril Scott, as well as Holst, the composer who was to translate theosophical astrology into music.[2]

The debt owed to astrology by Holst's masterpiece is acknowledged only vaguely by most musical historians, partly because most are uninterested in astrology but also because Holst himself was circumspect about the source of his inspiration. When *The Planets* received its first public performance in February 1919, and its début proper the following year, Holst referred only to its 'poetical basis' being 'the study of planets', as though he had been peering through an astronomer's telescope for ideas. In reality Holst had undertaken an intensive study of astrology in the years prior to writing *The Planets*, between 1914 and 1916, and the different parts of the suite were written entirely according to the astrological character of the planet in question.

Holst's pains to conceal the identity of his muse are easy to understand. To confess that he had been courting Urania would doubtless have brought a critical belittlement in which the musical qualities of *The Planets* came a poor second to his astrological interests. The successful prosecution of Alan Leo, the very astrologer whose books had provided Holst with his planetary template, lay only two years in the past. Far better to stay in the closet, while leaving the door ajar for those who could recognise the tell-tale message in the titles Holst bestowed on each planetary movement. These went beyond any mythological association; 'Neptune The Mystic', for example, had nothing to do with the jolly Roman sea god, but everything to do with the planet's astrological meaning.

Even after *The Planets* became a *cause célèbre* – it was hailed as a masterpiece from the outset – Holst remained coy about its astrological basis. In 1926, his reputation secure, the composer would say only that *The Planets* was 'a series of mood pictures', though the following year he acknowledged, only slightly less vaguely, that the suite deals with the 'seven influences of destiny and constituents of our spirit'. It was not until 1993 that the extent of Holst's astrological interests and their musical expression were fully unravelled by the classical critic Raymond Head in his perspicacious essay, 'Astrology and Modernism in *The Planets*', published in *Tempo* magazine, a piece to which this author is indebted.

The son of a Swedish émigré family (his stepmother introduced him to theosophy), Holst was virtually alone among eminent British composers in having no private income on which to rely (Elgar was the only other exception) and undertook teaching and orchestral jobs to pay his way – he met his wife while conducting the Hammersmith Socialist Choir.

Holst's output, however, was indifferently received, despite the advocacy of his friend Vaughan Williams, and the composer became increasingly dispirited, his depression not helped by overwork and money worries. Around 1912 Holst turned to astrology for guidance. There was no shortage of stellar advice within his circle; his friend Clifford Bax, another theosophist and brother of the composer Arnold Bax, was an amateur astrologer. Holst's friendship with George R.S. Mead (1863–1933), the Sanskrit scholar and theosophist, was doubtless also influential in turning Holst towards astrology. Mead had been Blavatsky's private secretary and remained a leading light in the Theosophical Society until Annie Besant's accession to its presidency in

1908 drove him out in disgust. Mead then formed his own society, called The Quest, which quickly attracted a following which included Holst, the poet John Masefield and A.E. Waite, whose Tarot deck, drawn by Pamela Colman Smith, remains perennially popular.

Holst had learned Sanskrit in order to pursue his fascination with Indian religion, and he now immersed himself in astrology. The obvious place to start was with Alan Leo, and Holst duly acquired a couple of books from Leo's *Astrology for All* series – *How to Judge a Nativity* and *The Art of Synthesis* – which Raymond Head singles out as the inspiration for *The Planets*. Holst also owned *Raphael's Mundane Astrology*. He was soon contemplating his own birth chart, and, as Raymond Head sums up, 'By meditating on the nature of the planets ("my planets" as he called them, in other words his chart) he began to discover new worlds of sound.'

Leo's *Art of Synthesis* offered chapters on each of the nine astrological planets (Pluto was still in his invisible realm) under such headings as 'Mars the Energiser' and 'Mercury the Thinker', a lead which Holst followed, adopting Leo's description of 'Neptune the Mystic' intact while modifying the titles of the other six planets on which he composed (he left out the Sun and Moon). Mercury became the 'Winged Messenger', Mars 'Bringer of War', Venus 'Bringer of Peace', Jupiter 'Bringer of Jollity', Saturn 'Bringer of Old Age' and Uranus 'The Magician', the last apparently inspired by the Tarot trump of the same name.[3] Holst shaped his music accordingly; the jagged 5/4 rhythm of Mars, the romanticism of Venus, the merry dance and magisterial horns of Jupiter and the serene, wordless choirs of Neptune.

As Holst contemplated his birth chart, what might he have discovered? That, with Sun in Virgo and Moon in Aries, he was, in the unflattering words of Leo's astrological cookbook, 'a little difficult to get on with', with 'too much tendency to live in the head' and inclined to 'sarcastic and bitter speeches'. He would also have observed that in March 1914, just as he started work on *The Planets*, the conjunction of Jupiter and Uranus in the sign of Aquarius took place within a degree of his natal Saturn, a transit linked by astrologer Robert Hand to 'a sudden release of tension'. Furthermore, Holst would have seen that 1914 marked the halfway point of his Uranus cycle (i.e. the planet was opposite his natal Uranus), a time associated with a major shift in goals.

Holst certainly seems to have identified with the Promethean, liberating energy of Uranus, for, as the critic Malcolm MacDonald observed in 1987, the opening brass incantation of 'Uranus the Magician' sounds the musical letters of Holst's name in German (GuStAv H.): G, E flat, A, B.[4]

The Planets did not signal the end of Holst's astrological interests. The composer continued to cast charts for others, which he referred to as 'my pet vice', and remained good friends with the astrologer Vivian E. Robson until the end of his life; Holst's copy of Robson's book, *A Beginner's Guide to Practical Astrology* (1931), is dedicated 'To Gustav Holst, the inspirer of this book, with kindest regards'.

After Holst's *Planets* astrology was not to make any major impact on music for almost half a century, when the Music of the Spheres suddenly started to sound from very different constellations in the cultural firmament. Jazz, classical, rock and pop – as the 1960s unfolded, all began to echo with the sounds of outer and inner space.

In jazz a rare conjunction of ancient Egypt and the space age was manifesting in the music of Sun Ra. The name concealed the identity of a misfit pianist from Birmingham, Alabama, Herman 'Sonny' Blount (born 22 May 1914), who, after moving to Chicago in the 1940s, had reinvented himself as Le Son'y Ra, or Sun Ra, and assembled his big band, the Arkestra.

Although Blount was rooted in jazz tradition, he was a musical radical whose compositions went beyond the modal forms of most post-war jazz, using unusual keys, odd tunings, chants, African drumming and proto-electronics. To most people, the Arkestra's sound was discordant cacophony – it was too way out for the jazz circuit – but Ra and his talented musicians insisted their music was from 'the atonal tomorrow', the space age, and they were in tune with the cosmos.

Onstage the Arkestra dressed in a resplendent mixture of African robes, Tibetan hats and space glitter. Amid the mohair suits of the time they looked as if they had landed from another planet, as indeed Sun Ra claimed he had; he was not from Earth but Saturn, and his mission was to awaken humanity, and in particular the black race.[5]

The mythology in which Sun Ra wrapped himself and his music was a complex synthesis of esoterica, space age and science fiction. Raised as a Baptist, he was steeped in the Bible, but from his teenage years he had read avidly, consuming Blavatsky, Egyptology, Steiner, Ouspensky, Gurdjieff – the whole canon of 'illuminated' thought. In music his tastes included Tchaikovsky and Scriabin, whose 'mystical chord', on which the Russian composer had based his *Prometheus* symphony, was eagerly taken up by Ra and his saxophonist Marshall Allen.

The planets evoked by such Sun Ra titles as 'On Jupiter' and 'Next Stop Mars' were literal rather than astrological, but the sense of a cosmic destiny shared by humanity and the heavens clearly owed much to his astrological studies. In the late 1960s and early 1970s the same mixture of cosmic consciousness, musical innovation and cultural radicalism was gripping other jazz musicians, among them John Coltrane and Pharoah Sanders.

Coltrane, the most gifted of all jazz saxophonists and, alongside Charlie Parker, the most influential, was an artist of deeply religious bent. Shocked by being sacked from Miles Davis's group on account of his heroin habit, he renounced drugs early in 1957 and embarked on a spiritual quest that was to dominate his life until his death in 1967 at the age of forty.[6]

Coltrane's religious search was most eloquently expressed on his 1964 masterpiece *A Love Supreme*, a record whose appeal reached far beyond the confines of jazz *aficionados*. In the last few years of his life his music became increasingly experimental, and it was during this final phase that his interest in the cosmos, and in astrology, came into play. In 1966 Coltrane released *Cosmic Music*, and in the following year *Interstellar Space*, a duet with drummer Rashied Ali, whose tracks included 'Saturn', 'Mars', 'Jupiter', 'Venus' and 'Leo'. On the sleevenotes to the 1968 album *A Monastic Trio*, Coltrane's widow, Alice, described a mandala-like map her husband had created: 'The chart John used was a musical one with twelve tones correlating to the twelve zodiacal signs.'

After Coltrane's death both Alice and his former sideman Pharoah Sanders pursued Coltrane's cosmic and spiritual ideas (Alice Coltrane later converted to Hinduism), with Sanders using astrological themes for 'Capricorn Rising' and 'Sun in Aquarius'. By the early 1970s much jazz was suffused with the cosmic imagery and Afrocentric attitudes pioneered by Sun Ra and Coltrane. Soul band Earth Wind and Fire likewise co-opted his Egyptian imagery, while the sci-fi persona of

George Clinton's Funkadelic, whose space-glam shows featured a flying saucer landing onstage, also owed him a substantial debt.

In the pop world the Age of Aquarius had dawned, shone and passed, lasting substantially less than the two thousand years of astrological theory. *Hair*'s anthem, 'Aquarius/Let the Sun Shine In' had topped charts across the world in 1969, although, given astrology's honoured place in the hippie lexicon, alongside the *I Ching*, Tarot and other chunks of arcane lore, the hippie era produced surprisingly little astro-pop aside from oddities like 1967's *The Zodiac* by Cosmic Sounds, a session group who played torrid West Coast rock while a vocalist intoned Sun sign characteristics along the lines of 'Virgo the Perpetual Perfectionist' and 'Libra the Flower Child'.

Mostly, rock musicians have been more inclined to consult girl-friends and groupies about their horoscopes than to use astrology for inspiration. An exception was Jimi Hendrix, another innovator for whom 'cosmic music' and spiritual vision were entwined, and whose esoteric interests found their way into his creations. 'If 6 Was 9', for example, draws on his fascination for numerology, while in 1967 Hendrix was already expressing a Scriabin-like desire 'to play a note and have it come out as a colour'. A couple of years later Hendrix had, like Sun Ra, decided he was not Earth-born at all, and had come here 'from an asteroid belt off the coast of Mars'.[7]

While Hendrix was interested in astrology – at the Rainbow Bridge concert he played on the Hawaiian island of Maui a few months before his death in 1970, the audience was invited to divide themselves according to star sign – most of his cosmic interests were expressed in imagery picked up from his preferred reading matter, science fiction. His songs were accordingly full of visits from UFOs and interplanetary travel. Like Sun Ra, Coltrane and Stockhausen, Hendrix saw the universe as fundamentally benign; the very axis on which the world turned was 'Bold as Love'. The task facing the musician was to translate the universe into sound, to match microcosm and macrocosm. To match the immensity and awe of the planets in numbers like 'Third Stone from the Sun', Hendrix conjured from his Fender Stratocaster cataclysmic power chords and arcing solos, with gentle melodies and chimes for the lunar powers of 'Moon Turn the Tides ... Gently, Gently Away'.

Similar (and more astrologically based) ideas have propelled the music of Karlheinz Stockhausen, electronic music pioneer, mover and shaker in the classical avant-garde, and another composer in whom esotericism, innovation and cosmic longing converge. After taking up his studies in music in Cologne in the early 1950s, Stockhausen was taken with serialism, in particular the compositions of Webern. He subsequently developed his own musical theories, variously describing his work as electronic music, spatial music, aleatonic music, variable music, scenic music, cosmic music and, more recently, simply as spiritual music. Stockhausen's musical philosophy is often highly reminiscent of Scriabin, Hendrix and Coltrane. He has spoken of the correspondence between music and the chakras, and the consequent need to listen to music that vibrates with our 'higher' centres. His esoteric interests have become more apparent as he has grown older. With 1975's *Tierkreis* (*Zodiac*), he created the first overtly astrological work of modern classicism since Holst's *Planets*, a piece divided into four main sections based on the cardinal points of the year – Aries, Cancer, Libra and Capricorn.

His mammoth space opera *Licht*, on which the composer has been engaged since the mid-seventies and which he expects to complete early this century, is also imbued with astrological symbolism. *Licht* is divided into seven separate works, each corresponding to a day of the week, and relates the struggle between good and evil, light and dark, through the eternal triangle of the archangel Michael, Lucifer and Eve. Much of its inspiration comes directly from *The Urantia Book*, a curious tome of cosmic lore first published in America in 1955, though Stockhausen didn't encounter it until the early 1970s, around the same time that Sun Ra was exploring its five hundred pages (he can be seen reading it in the 1972 film *Space is the Place*).[8]

Each day of *Licht* corresponds to the planetary symbolism and colour of the planet after which it is named. Monday, which features Eve on the beach, is infused with the watery symbolism of the Moon. Tuesday (Mars) takes war as its theme. Wednesday (Mercury) is 'collaboration day'. Thursday (Jupiter) is Michael day and is swathed in purple. Friday (Venus) is Eve's day of temptation by Lucifer. Saturday (Saturn) is Lucifer's day, black and full of death. Sunday (Sun) is the 'mystical union' between Michael and Eve.

Stockhausen's conception for *Licht* is suitably gargantuan, with each of its seven works lasting up to five hours and entailing phenomenal feats of performance and staging. Tuesday, for example, requires the members of a string quartet to be dispatched into the skies in four separate helicopters, where they continue to play in perfect time via a radio link-up while pictures are beamed down to the audience on four TV monitors arranged onstage. The performance of Sunday (which, along with Wednesday, is yet to be unveiled) will require a massive set in which the solar system's planets revolve around a central Sun, while singers, dancers and musicians equipped with radio mikes and speakers flit between them in interplanetary traffic.

While Holst, Coltrane and Stockhausen have found ways to describe astrology through music, astrologers remain divided about how best to describe music. By tradition, music belongs to the creativity of Venus and to the fluid, artistic sign of Pisces (music invariably 'flows'), but the advent of new music, and new planets, has posed problems. To what sign and planet, for example, should jazz be attributed, quicksilver Mercury or the innovative Uranus?

In her mammoth tome on Neptune, Liz Greene argues that its nebulous, impressionist qualities make it the planet *par excellence* of the artist and musician, or at least of the classical composer. Greene finds Neptune prominent in the birth charts of 'most composers who are considered great', and gives a seventy-strong list of names to back up her point. In particular, Greene cites the English Romantic composers as expressing 'Neptunian feelings of mystical yearning, melancholy and boundlessness'. For Greene, Holst (whose birth chart had Neptune–Saturn and Neptune–Moon in square aspect) 'understood the symbolism of the planet not only intellectually but at a profound emotional level'.

Other astrologers are not persuaded that music can yet be handed over to Neptune's mysterious force. Many of the Neptune aspects cited by Greene as active in composers' charts are certainly so common as to be meaningless; because the outer planets move so slowly, an aspect like Neptune–Saturn, for example, will be active for several months at a time. Paul Wright, in *Astrology in Action*, rightly observes that music, far from being formless, relies on the order and shape supplied by rhythm (Mercury) and by melody and harmony (Venus). Moreover, in the birth charts of musicians he finds no great emphasis on Neptune, or indeed on any planet, since 'music is not one but a number of things'.

The advent of a generation of astrologers weaned on popular music has brought much speculation about how astrology's symbolism might apply to modern music. A British 'Rock and Astrology' group briefly flourished in the 1990s, and there have been numerous examinations of the birth charts of pop stars and groups.[9] Increasingly, the conjecture is about which of the outer planetary cycles might correspond to the zeitgeist shifts articulated by pop; indeed, to which planet one might attribute pop itself. Here Uranus has emerged as the prime candidate. The move of the planet of revolution into the exhibitionist, youth-oriented sign of Leo in August 1955 coincides obligingly with the arrival of rock and roll and the phenomenon of the teenager. The numerous candidates for 'the first rock record' date to 1954, but it was Bill Haley's 'Rock Around the Clock' which became the clarion call for 'teen rebellion', arriving in the US charts in July 1955 and sitting atop them for several weeks. A few months later, Elvis Presley recorded the hits that would turn him into the first rock star of the twentieth century. A chart set for the recording of 'Heartbreak Hotel' has become just one of the proposed 'birth times' for rock. On the principle that the electric guitar is the *sine qua non* of rock music, for example, British astrologer John Frawley has proposed the birth of its inventor, Les Paul (9 June 1915), as a significant astrological date, though Frawley finds Mercury (invention), Saturn (weight) and Mars (sexuality) prominent, rather than Uranus.

The incendiary force of Uranus proves obliging in several other speculative dates for pop's evolution. The planet finally left Leo for Virgo in early 1962, for example, just before the Beatles launched the second wave of the 'youth revolution'. Though prim Virgo makes a poor fit for the arrival of the 'beat boom', rocking astrologers can point to the seven-planet pile-up in Aquarius in February 1962 as a harbinger of the revolutionary times to come. A more apt set of symbolism for the upheavals of the 1960s is provided by the conjunction of Uranus and Pluto, which occurred in October 1965 and again in April and June 1966. In his tract on Uranus, *Prometheus the Awakener*, Richard Tarnas describes this conjunction as 'a profound manifestation of the Prometheus archetype being empowered and compelled by Pluto on a massive scale across the world', finding it emblematic of the era's 'pervasive spirit of rebellion' and 'the spectacular musical creativity of the decade'. In terms of rock music, psychedelia, which boomed suddenly in 1966, must belong astrologically to this once-a-century conjunction (Tarnas cites psychedelics as 'an apt example of Prometheus's fire').

It's possible to freewheel through pop history finding similar, though far less striking, planetary correlations. Punk rock's arrival in 1976, for example, might be assigned to Uranus's presence in destructive Scorpio opposite Jupiter. In musical terms, however, the mighty conjunction of Uranus, Neptune and Saturn in the sign of Capricorn – widely held by astrologers to be the harbinger of the collapse of the Eastern Bloc – seems to have heralded only the arrival of acid house. It's similarly difficult to find much musical excitement coincidental to Uranus's conjunction with Jupiter in Aquarius in 1997, unless one counts the short-lived phenomenon of the Spice Girls.

The astrology of pop, however, is still in its infancy, awaiting a computer search through the birth dates of musicians to isolate the planetary aspects that produce great guitarists or flat-voiced lead singers. Several leads already dangle enticingly: the uncanny number of jazz musicians with Libra Suns, for example; witness John Coltrane, Ray Charles, Leon Thomas, Yusef Lateef, Abdulla Ibrahim, Thelonious Monk, Art Blakey, Lester Bowie, Pharoah Sanders, Wynton Marsalis and Dizzy Gillespie, to name but some.

Pop itself continues to conduct its celestial love affairs in promiscuous, non-astrological fashion; swinging among the stars, breakfasting on Pluto, visiting the Dark Side of the Moon, courting Venus in Blue Jeans, rocking out with the Spiders from Mars and perpetually greeting the Sun. Astrological themes still occasionally surface: in Des'Ree's 'What's Your Sign?', in Erykah Badu's Piscean homage 'What a Day', in the ferocious electro-squall of Björk's 'Pluto' and in Goldie's drum'n'bass epic 'Saturnz Return'. So far there is no sign of Bryan Ferry's promised zodiac concept album, which may be as well.

Record companies have also caught on to the idea that astrology can be used to sell their wares. In the late 1990s EMI began packaging classical music in zodiac-shaped bites: a 'Libra' album, for example, featuring such Scales subjects as Shostakovich and Liszt; while MGM promoted their vintage musicals by commissioning *Cosmo* astrologer Maggie Hyde to allocate them by sign, giving us the confrontational *West Side Story* for Aries fans, the navy larks of *Anchors Aweigh* for Cancerians, and so forth. TV campaigns for pop compilations called *Now That's What I Call Taurus* and *The Greatest Leo Album in the World, Ever!* can't be far away.

16

PINNED TO MIDHEAVEN

TED HUGHES, SHAKESPEARE, YEATS
AND OTHER CELESTIAL POETS

✳

On 29 January 1998, the day of the new Moon, the world of English
literature was jolted by a current of Neptunian energy. Its origin was
Ted Hughes's *Birthday Letters*, a volume of poems addressed by the
Poet Laureate to the long-dead Sylvia Plath, his first wife. The book's
publication was utterly unexpected. There had been no fanfare of
publicity, no hint that Hughes had been preparing a collection that he
and his publishers knew was sensational by virtue of its subject matter
alone, irrespective of its literary merits.

The story of Hughes and Plath, two poets entwined in passion,
betrayal and death, had become one of the most chronicled and bitterly
contested sagas of twentieth-century literature. The two lovers had met
at university, and after a marriage of six years and two children,
separated in 1962. Hughes had been unfaithful, and left to live with his
lover, Assia Wevvil. Plath was a long-term depressive, who had
attempted suicide before she met Hughes, and who, within months of
her husband's departure, had gassed herself. Six years later, Wevvil also
killed herself by gassing, along with her two-year-old daughter by
Hughes.

It was a forlorn, tragic tale, in which Hughes was subsequently cast in
the role of villainous male oppressor by the champions of Plath, who
was soon canonised as a feminist saint, with her novel, *The Bell Jar*, and
posthumous poetry collection, *Ariel*, as her sacred texts. That Hughes
had destroyed some of his wife's journals – to spare their children, he
said – compounded his devilry for Plath's worshippers. For the most

part, Hughes refused to engage in the literary wars that raged round his name; Sylvia should be left in peace, he insisted, with her work as her testament. Now, twenty-five years after Plath's death, there were these, some eighty-eight poems, all but a couple addressed to the wraith of his troubled wife.

The reaction to *Birthday Letters* was a mixture of astonishment and admiration. Far from seeking to settle scores with Plath or his critics, Hughes had delivered tender laments for a woman whom he had clearly loved deeply, whom he loved still. The confessional tone and almost conversational style of the poems resembled little in Hughes's lengthy canon, most of which is inspired by the animal kingdom and comes steeped in the feral imagery of tooth and claw, hunter and hunted. *Birthday Letters* became an immediate hit, not only with literati but among a wider public who made it a best-seller; almost unprecedented for a volume of verse. Shortly after the book had started to win a series of prizes, its creator died of cancer. Since Hughes's death the saga of Ted and Sylvia has ascended to another level of literary legend, with a flurry of competing biographies seeking to capitalise on it, a projected biopic and, doubtless, revelations from the poets' friends and lovers.

Among the surprises that sprang from the pages of *Birthday Letters* was the image of the Poet Laureate as an accomplished astrologer. One poem, 'Horoscope', addressed astrology directly, while others made passing reference to it. In '18 Rugby Street' Hughes describes Plath's particular beauty in zodiacal correspondences, finding Scorpio's influence in her retroussé nose ('Scorpio's obverse to the Semitic eagle') and that of her Ascending sign on 'your little chin, your Pisces chin'. In 'Horoscope' he turns to Plath's own astrological interests, and her apprehension of the stars' 'Babylonish power sprach'. Plath, says Hughes, was right to fear that the stars could spell her fate, while she, finding omens of fate so readily around her, had no need of astrology. Best of all there was 'St Botolph's', which as an account of Hughes's and Plath's first meeting was among the most keenly studied poems in the book. The poem is unapologetically stuffed with astro-jargon: 'The conjunction combust my natal Sun/Venus pinned exact on my midheaven.' What were the champions of Eng. Lit. to make of it?

Disappointingly little. Out of embarrassment or indifference, the literary establishment studiously avoided commenting on the astrological references that pepper *Birthday Letters*, not even deigning to point out that the current Laureate shared his interests with the first, John Dryden. There was the odd reference to Hughes's 'dottier beliefs', and the poet's friend Seamus Heaney, in his review of *Birthday Letters*, described Hughes and Plath as 'mythopoetic' writers, borrowing a term from the Jungian psychologist James Hillman. That Hughes had a long-standing interest in Eastern religions, Renaissance magic and mythology was well established, but such interests wear the cloak of reputable scholarship more easily than astrology. 'Mythopoetic' sounds a grand note of respectability; while 'The laureate believes in astrology' does not ('Queen's poet is star crazy,' as a tabloid might put it). Even *Ariel's Gift*, the posthumous, biographical study of *Birthday Letters* by the critic Erica Wagner, manages to avoid using the word astrology anywhere in its two hundred-page consideration of the poems. It was ironic that one of the few literary critics to share Hughes's astrological outlook was Martin Seymour-Smith, author of *The New Astrologer*, who was one of Hughes's fiercest opponents. In his *Guide to Modern World Literature*, he accused Hughes of 'lack of ear' and 'sheer stupidity and unpleasantness', among other things.

The foreword to Hughes's book of stories *Difficulties of a Bridegroom*, acknowledges its foundation in *The Chymical Wedding* of Christian Rosenkreuz, a famous Renaissance text that had supplied the doctrinal basis for assorted Rosicrucian societies down the centuries. Hughes's sprawling critical study *Shakespeare and the Goddess of Complete Being*, likewise shows his obsession with the archetypal realm and the system of correspondences that seek to describe it. Beneath the 'surface glitter of the plot [in Shakespeare]', wrote Hughes, 'all archaic mythological figures and events are available as a thesaurus of glyphs or token symbols'.

Despite such declarations and some references to his astrological interests in Plath's journals, Hughes the planet-plotter was a revelation to most of his readers. It was as if, after years of foraging in the undergrowth of Darwinism, jousting with pike and staring down death's-heads through the eyes of ragged crows, another Ted had finally come into the open, a blast from his twenty-something past: Ted the undergraduate astrologer, 'his pockets stuffed with horoscopes', as Sylvia described him.

When, exactly, Hughes became interested in astrology and from where he learned it remains unknown. His interest in esoterica was long-standing, and must have been fed by the copy of *The White Goddess*, Robert Graves's extravagant survey of Greco-Celtic myth, which he received as a school prize. As a student of archaeology and anthropology at Cambridge, his Greek encounters may have included astrology. Or he may have been taught it by his elder sister, Olwyn, whom he acknowledged as the real expert on the subject. Perhaps it was during the idle hours of his National Service years, stationed high on the empty Yorkshire Moors at the remote RAF station at Fylingdales, when Hughes was reading and rereading Shakespeare, that he taught himself the skills of ephemeris and chart-wheel. Certainly by the time he met Plath in 1956 Hughes was well immersed in astrology, coercing 'oracular assurance in my favour out of every sign', as he writes in *Birthday Letters*.

'St Botolph's' reveals the extent of Hughes's astrological interests at the time of the couple's first volatile encounter at a Cambridge literary party on 25 February 1956, a night which left the hulking young poet bleeding from a love-bite incised on his cheek by Plath. The poem's opening section – incomprehensible without detailed astrological knowledge – outlines the planetary alignments for the night, and how they fell on the birth charts of himself and his future wife.

> Our Chaucer, I think, would have sighed.
> He would have assured us, shaking his sorrowful head,
> That day the solar system married us
> Whether we knew it or not.

The evening's omens, the young Hughes seems to have decided even then, were not good. It was the night of the full Moon, which was conjunct Jupiter, leading Hughes to predict 'disastrous expense' since the money planet was amplified by lunar power. Nevertheless, as 'a wait-and-see astrologer', he braves the 'touch of a bat's wing' about the astro-forecast, and sets off, whereas Chaucer, another eminent poet-cum-astrologer, would have stayed home. After reciting a litany of significant aspects to his and Plath's horoscopes – 'that day's Sun in the Fish/Conjunct your Ascendant exactly/Opposite my Neptune and fixed/ In my tenth house of good and evil fame' – Hughes's conclusion is striking. Despite the bitterness and recriminations that had raged around their relationship, this was a marriage that was made in heaven; he and Plath had been 'married by the solar system'.

The passage contains one or two inaccuracies; the night's Moon/ Jupiter conjunction (in Leo) did not oppose Venus (in Aries) but the Sun. Nor is it possible for Venus (in Aries) to be 'pinned' to Hughes's Midheaven if the Sun (in Pisces) is in his tenth house; if the Sun is in the tenth, then Venus must be in the ninth, or if Venus is at the top of the chart, the Sun must be in the eleventh house.

Whichever way round is correct, it raises the question of Hughes's own horoscope (he was born on 17 August 1930 in the serendipitously named Mytholmroyd in Yorkshire). No birth time is available for him, but 'St Botolph's' suggests Hughes considered himself to have either Leo or Cancer as his Ascendant. Either could arguably fit. The main features of his birth chart are an obdurate combination of Leo Sun and Taurus Moon, along with a Jupiter–Saturn opposition, traditionally a difficult combination, indicating trials of faith, an inflated ego and success through toil.[1]

Though Hughes gives Plath a Pisces Ascendant, most astrologers settle for the last degree of Aquarius for her, yet his delineations of the synastry between their horoscopes are entirely accurate. Was the stormy marriage between the two poets really made in heaven? The ill-matched combination of their Suns in the fixed signs of fiery Leo (Hughes) and watery Scorpio (Plath) would cause most astro-matchmakers to blanch, but elsewhere the overlaps between the charts match their emotionally compulsive relationship. Most glaringly, Plath's Moon (feelings) falls exactly on Hughes's Venus (love) in the romantic sign of Libra, while Hughes's Sun (self) is sited exactly with Plath's Mars (sexual energy).

Plath's own writing, and its obsessions with death and sex, accords all too well with the character of her Scorpio Sun ('Red was your colour,' recalls Hughes in Birthday Letters). In The Literary Zodiac Paul Wright thinks suicide and early death 'fall disproportionately on those strong in this sign', and lists Plath alongside fellow poetic Scorpios Thomas Chatterton, Anne Sexton and John Berryman (all suicides) and

Dylan Thomas, who drank himself to death at the age of thirty-nine. Plath's much-examined horoscope has also been correlated with her fixation on finding a husband (four planets in the seventh house), with her morbidity (Saturn in the twelfth house opposite Pluto and square Sun), and her literary gifts (a much-aspected Mercury in Scorpio).[2]

Outside of *Birthday Letters* astrology scarcely figures in Hughes's poetry, but the titles of two youthful plays, *House of Taurus* (1959) and *House of Aries* (1960), attest to his early interest, and Plath's journals from 1956 and 1957 make several references to the couple's fascination for astrology, Tarot and the Ouija board. Hughes hoped their glass-pushing experiments with the last would win them a pot of money from gambling on the pools, though, as he says in 'Ouija' in *Birthday Letters*, it was 'Always bad news from the Ouija board.' He moved on to sterner stuff: meditation, magical invocation, Rosicrucianism and the *Tibetan Book of the Dead*.

The Hughes scholar Dr Ann Skea, one of the few to deal comfortably with the poet's metaphysical passions, has suggested that Shakespeare and Renaissance poetry provided the spur for Hughes's explorations into astrology, alchemy and magic, and that his animal poems cast him as a shamanic figure, shape-shifting into the creatures of the poems. Skea has also convincingly suggested that *Birthday Letters* is structured on kabbalistic lines, with its eighty-eight poems arranged according to the twenty-two pathways on the kabbala's 'Tree of Life'. There are four poems for each pathway, corresponding to the kabbala's four overlapping worlds of Atziluth, Briah, Yetzirah, and Assiah. Hence poems two and three in *Birthday Letters* – 'Caryatids (1)' and 'Caryatids (2)' – represent the apex of the two outer pillars of the kabbalistic tree (a caryatid is the female statue which supports the portico of a Greek temple).[3]

Plath's musings that she and Hughes might become 'a team better than Mr and Mrs Yeats, he being a competent astrologist, reading horoscopes, and me being a Tarot pack reader' (*Journals*, 23 October 1956) are a reminder that the pair were far from the first writers to take an interest in the esoteric arts. Chaucer, to whom Hughes compared himself, was the first in a long line of poet-astrologers, among them Dryden, Yeats and MacNeice, while Sidney, Spenser, Shakespeare, Blake, Coleridge, Kipling and Masefield certainly knew about astrology and were sympathetic to it. For all these poets, as for Hughes, astrology was but one part of a wider body of hermeticism, neo-Platonism or other aspects of the 'perennial philosophy', yet in making their personal gnosis, and sometimes in creating their art, astrology had an important part to play. Rich in symbolism, offering a language which enabled the ancient gods and goddesses to reappear in contemporary life, and often of practical help, astrology has proved a natural ally to English poetry down the centuries.

That Chaucer's *Canterbury Tales* are threaded through with astrological references is no surprise; the founder of English poetry lived in an age when astrology was securely accommodated in high culture, was indivisible from astronomy and played an important part in medical diagnosis. Chaucer praises his 'Doctor of Physic', for example, precisely because he was 'grounded in astronomye' and 'wel koude he fortunen the ascendant/of his ymages for his pacient'. In other words, the doctor's skill in casting a chart for the illness (a 'decumbiture') helped him cure his patients.

Chaucer's interest in the stars greatly exceeded what might be expected of a man of his class. Among his writings is 'A Treatise on the Astrolabe', which advises how this, the central instrument in early astronomy, could be used to ascertain the zodiacal degree of the Sun and the planets, the houses of the zodiac, and so on. Chaucer modestly describes himself as an 'unlearned compiler of the labors of old astrologiens', but then goes into particular detail on the subject of Ascending signs and their importance to astrologers, although he declares his spirit has 'no faith' in such matters of judicial astrology, he remains on the fence about it.

In general, the custodians of English literature are leary about the extra-curricular interests of their subjects. The Masonic affiliations of Robbie Burns are downplayed, the immersion of W.B. Yeats in magic treated as an embarrassment ('the price we must pay for the poetry', remarked one critic), while the visionary genius of William Blake has only recently emerged from the slur that he was plain mad (how this madman functioned as a busy artisan engraver throughout his life is never explained). Astrology played only a tangential role in the formation of Blake's personal mythos as expressed in his epic prophecies, *The Four Zoas* and *Jerusalem*, but its symbolic framework undoubtedly helped shape the poet's work. Blake drank in copious draughts of esotericism; from Boehme ('the astrologer's philosopher'), Swedenborg and such radical Protestant sects as the splendidly named Muggletonians. Blake also numbered among his best friends the landscape painter and astrologer John Varley (1778–1842), a maverick presence in London society who was encountered by the painters John Constable and Samuel Palmer, among others. In 1819 and 1820 Varley and Blake undertook a project in psychic research at the former's home. While Blake drew the various historical personages that appeared from the spirit world (Richard the Lionheart among them), Varley checked the Ascending sign at the time of their portraiture; he was particularly interested in 'zodiacal physiognomy' and wanted to correlate appearance and Ascendant. Among the results of this odd exercise are Blake's drawings of 'The Man Who Built the Pyramids' and 'The Ghost of a Flea', which was given a Gemini Ascendant and is sometimes held up as an example of the Mercury visage.

The most contested case of a poet's astrological allegiance is that of William Shakespeare, the source of many frequently quoted edicts both for and against astrology. Rare is the astrologian who has not had Julius Caesar's line flung in his or her face: 'The fault, dear Brutus, is not in our stars/But in ourselves, that we are underlings.' Nevertheless, the astrological community has long claimed the Bard as one of their own. According to them, Shakespeare was not only conversant with star-lore, as one would expect of any literate Elizabethan, but an active subscriber to its tenets.

How well based are astrology's claims on the Bard? Shakespeare's writings are notorious for supplying whatever those reading them wish to find, be it proof that he was a Marxist, a Christian, a Rosicrucian, a bisexual (the sonnets' 'Dark Lady' as lad theory), an accomplished sailor, Italian traveller, lawyer or falconer. Or that his plays and poems were in fact penned by Francis Bacon, the Earl of Oxford or another of the candidates eagerly advanced against the plain playwright from Stratford-on-Avon, whose life remains so exasperatingly (and invitingly) out-of-focus.

The plays are undeniably studded with astrological references – over a hundred of them, according to most reckonings – yet because

Shakespeare wrote in character, his attitude to star-gazing is ambiguous. In fact, the plays' most famous astro-allusions are damning putdowns. Expanding on Caesar's celebrated line comes the eloquent denunciation of Edmund in *King Lear*, making the same point – that we are masters of our own destiny: 'This is the excellent foppery of the world, that when we are sick in fortune – often the surfeit of our own behaviour – we make guilty of our disasters the sun, the moon and the stars: as if we were villains by necessity, fools by heavenly compulsion.'

Yet, as astrologers have noted, Shakespeare's dismissals of their craft are invariably delivered by villains, usually in the first act. John Addey (1963) claimed that Shakespeare's astro-references distinguish two sets of characters: 'those who acknowledge in their lives Universal Order and Harmony and the rule of Justice, and those who believe that Man is the sole arbiter of his destiny'. Addey's point is well made. Shakespeare was writing at a cuspal moment in human history, when the Renaissance was overturning the medieval sense of a fixed order in which everyone knew their predestined place. That he put his anti astrology speeches in the mouths of villains is not to deny the point they make – in literature and cinema, everyone knows the bad guys are usually more fascinating than the goodies – but nor is it to endorse it. Just as strong is the sense of a divine order underpinning nature, one on which 'the stars in secret influence comment' (Sonnet XV) and which one defies at peril. As Ulysses puts it in *Troilus and Cressida*, at the end of a long astrological speech: 'Untune that string, and, hark, what discord follows'. In the endlessly contested dialectic between freewill and destiny, England's greatest writer articulated both sides of the argument.

Where Shakespeare learned his astrology, or indeed any of the subjects on which his characters hold forth, remains unknown. The Elizabethan astrologer Simon Foreman is alleged to have shared a mistress with Shakespeare – none other than the Dark Lady herself, according to some. The nearest we get to such a figure in the plays is the magician Prospero in *The Tempest*, whose model is usually assumed to be John Dee. Tales about the age's most celebrated magician were doubtless familiar to Shakespeare, even if he didn't meet the Queen's favoured magus personally.

Astrologers have, needless to add, sought to unravel the mysteries of

Shakespeare's life and plays through his horoscope, undeterred by the fact that the Bard has no clear birthdate; all we know of the Stratford Shakespeare is the date of his christening (26 April 1564), which in his times usually took place within two or three days of a birth. Shakespeare's birthday is usually taken as 23 April, a date that may owe something to its also being St George's Day, making him a Sun Taurus, both artistic and practical. The Irish astrologer Maurice McCann exhaustively explored several options for Shakespeare's birthday, trying to match the events of his life with his horoscope. He settles on 24 April as the Bard's birthday, giving him a Taurus Sun and Ascendant, a Libran Moon and Neptune in the first house signifying 'the unfathomable mystery surrounding Shakespeare – the man, the authorship, the conflicts with tradition'. But while this horoscope 'works' for events in Shakespeare's life, McCann concludes that 'It does not, however, appear to be the horoscope of a genius.' The mystery lingers on.

The association between Shakespeare and astrology received a major boost with the completion of the Globe Theatre in 1996, the recreation of Shakespeare's long-lost headquarters and the inspired brainchild of the American film director Sam Wanamaker. By an act of heavenly grace, the Globe's charge was handed to the gifted actor and director Mark Rylance, who, like Ted Hughes and others, sees the plays as expressions of hermetic philosophy. 'The theatre plays very much with the statement "as above, so below",' remarked Rylance, 'and the many references to the stars in Shakespeare support that.'[5]

Accordingly, the Globe's completion was celebrated on 14 June, Wanamaker's birthday (just under a year before the official opening), with a feast of astrologically inspired theatricality. In 'The Masque of Heaven and Earth' actors incarnated the five planets, from Mercury to Saturn, as modern-day tourists – Mercury, for example, was always on the phone. Groups of banner-carrying schoolchildren represented the signs of the zodiac, moving rapidly for Gemini, martially for Scorpio and so on, under the stage's painted heavens, complete with planets. The following year the Globe's opening, on 12 June, was elected by the astrologer Su Rose.[6]

No one disputes the astrological sympathies of William Butler Yeats, though these are normally overshadowed by his membership of the Hermetic Order of the Golden Dawn, the magical society established in

1887 by a group of English Freemasons. The Golden Dawn occupies a pivotal place in the Victorian occult revival. Stranger, more élitist and infinitely more mysterious than Blavatsky's Theosophical Society, it drew into its ranks a number of eminent figures such as the writers A.E. Waite, Arthur Machen and Yeats (Bram Stoker also flickered around its fringes), the tea heiress Annie Horniman, the actress Florence Farr (mistress of George Bernard Shaw), the painter Moina Bergson (sister of the philosopher Henri and wife of MacGregor Mathers, one of the order's founders), and, not forgetting the Great Beast himself, Aleister Crowley.

Unlike the Theosophical Society, to which Yeats belonged in the 1890s, the Golden Dawn was secret and engaged in applied ritual magic, something expressly forbidden by Blavatsky, probably because she had tried it herself in Cairo and knew of its dangers (both Mathers and Crowley, for example, became troublingly unhinged figures who assumed God-like status for themselves). The order's extreme secrecy, to which members were sworn on pain of being omitten by 'a current of energy' raised by the group, meant that for many years its influence on Yeats's thought and poetry remained speculative. In the second half of the twentieth century, however, details of the order's activities came into the open; those jealously guarded rituals can now be downloaded from the Internet.

Yeats the magus has also come into sharper focus through biographies sympathetic to, or at least intrigued by, the esoteric interests that most Yeats scholarship has preferred to bypass, concentrating instead on his exoteric activities as poet, man of letters, playwright, political activist and Irish statesman.[7] Among those bothered by Yeats's occultism were T.S. Eliot, Stephen Spender and W.H. Auden, who spoke for many when he asked 'How on earth, we wonder, could a man of Yeats' gifts take such nonsense seriously?' Auden's question can be as easily inverted: if a man of Yeats's gifts took such nonsense seriously, maybe it is interesting.

Yeats's esoteric explorations were extensive, entwining Celtic and Greek myth, Indian religion and spiritualism (he often attended seances), in addition to which the Golden Dawn's first-grade teachings included visualisation, contemplation, meditation, Tarot and astrology. (The requirements for first-year students included the ability to raise a horary horoscope and read it. Further astrological training was voluntary. Other requirements included students making and painting their own Tarot deck in accord with GD designs.) All of these provided much-prized sources of imagery and symbolism for his poetry, and a way to articulate the invisible realm that lay beyond surface reality. Blake figured large among Yeats's poetic influences (he edited an edition of Blake in 1896), just as Yeats was to be an inspirational figure for Ted Hughes.

Yeats may have taken up astrology even before he joined the Golden Dawn in 1890, and he remained a lifelong devotee, assiduously following the transits and progressions of his horoscope. Like many astrologers, he found the mechanics of calculation tedious, and sometimes hired professional astrologers to do the spade-work. In 1907, for example, he had his 'Primary Directions' and 'Secondary Progressions' drawn up for the next ten years. As late as 1934, when Yeats was sixty-nine, Virgina Woolf noted in her diary that 'He believes entirely in horoscopes. Will not do business with anyone without having their horoscopes.'

Yeats's astrological interests are there in his poems, but were above all practical and predictive. He wanted to know the most auspicious times for his undertakings. The earliest horoscope we have for him (he was born in Dublin on 13 June 1865, at 10.15 GMT) is from 1893 and was drawn up by his favourite uncle, George Pollexfen, who also joined the Golden Dawn. Yeats himself and, later, his wife Georgie Hyde-Lees both drew up Yeats' chart. With an Aquarius Ascendant and Aquarius Moon to go with his Gemini Sun, the chart has several striking features: a 'Grand Trine' in air signs, a Jupiter–Sun opposition, and a Venus–Mars square.[8]

This last aspect was a source of some vexation to Yeats, the clash of the two personal planets of romance and sex being a poor omen for successful relationships, one that could 'menace the affectional life', as Georgie Hyde-Lees put it later.[9] Yeats, a virgin until he was thirty, was racked by sexual uncertainty and his close relationships with women were intense and difficult. It was this particular aspect in his birth map that helped finally propel Yeats into marriage in autumn 1917. He was, as his biographer Brenda Maddox has noted, meeting 'an astrological deadline', since Yeats had known for many years that his progressed

Sun (self) would reach his natal Mars, in the seventh house of marriage, at this time. He went through the year in a state of emotional turmoil, torn between his unrequited love for Iseult Gonne, the daughter of his greatest love, Maud Gonne, and the willing Georgie Hyde-Lees. The last, like Iseult Gonne a much younger woman, was also a member of the Golden Dawn, and a more skilled astrologer than Yeats. Like Hughes after him, Yeats noted the overlaps between his own birth chart and his wife's, and seems to have chosen an astrologically propitious day on which to get married.[10]

From the outset, the marriage of William and George, as she liked to be called, was based as much on their overlapping esoteric interests as on any mutual physical desire (Iseult still held his heart). Within days of the marriage they had embarked on the experiments in 'automatic writing' that would hold Yeats spellbound for years, and would culminate in *A Vision*, an exposition of Yeats's personal cosmology and philosophy. The book was published in 1926 and again, much revised, in 1937. *A Vision* is a cryptic, complex work, which tries to correlate the mysteries of incarnation according to phases of the Moon. As such it has a clearly astrological perspective, but the twenty-eight 'Mansions of the Moon' which it describes are not given by the Moon's phase at birth, being instead stages in the soul's evolutionary path through incarnation. One's present life might be, say, in phase 23 'the receptive man' or in phase 10, 'the image-breaker'. Yeats and Hyde-Lees often discussed the people they met in this way.

Both the concept of the Mansions of the Moon and the enormous time cycles on which they are founded (the 'gyres') clearly owe much to Indian thought; Vedic astrology has twenty-seven lunar *Nakshatras* which represent the journey of the soul, while the vast *yugas*, or time cycles, had been outlined by Blavatsky. Whether the contents of *A Vision* were, as Yeats and Hyde-Lees maintained, dictated by spirit forces, represented the outpourings of the couple's unconscious, or, as Brenda Maddox suggests in *George's Ghosts*, were written with conscious guile by Hyde-Lees remains a matter of conjecture. As so often with the paranormal, deciding what is 'from outside' and what 'from inside' is not easy or necessarily profitable. Whatever their origin, the messages from beyond furnished Yeats with extensive material for his writing and poetry.

Astrological influences come to the surface in Yeats's work most forcefully in the most famous of all his poems, 'The Second Coming', which was written around 1919, in the midst of Georgie Hyde-Lees's channelled outpourings:

> ... but now I know
> That twenty centuries of stony sleep
> Were vexed to nightmare by a rocking cradle.
> And what rough beast, its hour come round at last,
> Slouches towards Bethlehem to be born.

That so many meanings have been read into the poem is a mark of its greatness. Clearly one of its mainsprings is the concept of the 'Great Year', the complete precession of the equinoxes, of which one month is, for convenience sake, twenty centuries. Like any theosophist astrologer, Yeats knew all about the New Age that was supplanting the Age of Pisces, which had in its turn supplanted the Age of Aries at the birth of Christ; hence the image of the rocking cradle. Brenda Maddox cannily points out that Yeats and his wife were expecting their first child at the time the poem was written, and suggests that the couple considered that their own child might be the Maitreya, World Teacher, the role for which Jiddu Krishnamurthi was being unsuccessfully groomed by the theosophists.

What sort of new age was Yeats describing here? The poem rings with millennial expectation, and the 'rough beast' carries an echo of Revelation's Beast of the Apocalypse. Yeats was living in turbulent times, in the aftermath of the First World War and the Russian Revolution and amid ongoing turmoil in Ireland. Yet he may not have been describing apocalypse and the collapse of civilisation but the birth of the much-expected new age; what theosophical astrologers were beginning to describe as the Age of Aquarius.

Astrological imagery appears elsewhere in Yeats's poetry; his depressed lyric 'Under Saturn' is an example (though when it was written, late in November 1919, Saturn was not especially prominent in Yeats's horoscope). There is also, for example, a couplet such as:

When Jupiter and Saturn meet
Oh what a lot of mummy wheat.

This is playful mythology. 'Mummy wheat' refers to Osiris, the
Egyptian god of the underworld, who is sometimes shown painted
green, with wheat sprouting from his belly (wheat, as in many cultures,
was considered a divine gift in Egypt). The twenty-year conjunctions of
Jupiter and Saturn, suggests Yeats, bring plenty with them. Such was
the manner of Yeats's cross-cultural symbolic thinking and its enriching
effect on English poetry.

It is difficult to discover what particular fascination astrology held for
Louis MacNeice, a fellow Irish poet and astrologer, but one of a
different generation and of very different outlook from Yeats's. The two
poets met on one occasion, when MacNeice was taken to tea with the
elderly Yeats by a mutual acquaintance, but the younger man, hoping
to talk about poetry, was disappointed when his host rambled off into
discussions about phases of the Moon.

Like his contemporaries W.H. Auden and Stephen Spender, with
whom his name is usually linked, MacNeice wrote under the long
shadow cast by Yeats. Their poetry, by comparison, was studiously
modern and engaged in the hurly-burly of industrial life and political
events; the literary establishment of the 1930s soon had them pinned
down as the 'Pylon Poets', a tag MacNeice detested. In surveying the
unfolding political drama of the times, MacNeice proved an independent voice. Like Orwell, he was sympathetic to the left but refused to
follow the communist line taken by many of his contemporaries. The
son of an Anglican Ulster bishop, he was, in the way of many ministers'
sons, not much taken by religion either.

MacNeice was, then, an unexpected convert to astrology, the subject
of his last book, which he had just about completed by the time of his
death in 1963. A thorough introduction, with a substantial historical
background, MacNeice's *Astrology* is still a commendable overview of
the subject, and is written with a fluency rarely encountered in
astrological texts. It is usually explained by commentators as a way for
the then cash-strapped MacNeice to raise some money. Doubtless this
was partly his motivation, but a much-honoured poet and dramatist
might be expected to choose some other commission than one for
which his peers were sure to mock him.

It may have been MacNeice's schoolboy enthusiasm for astronomy which led him to its less respectable sibling; in his autobiography he describes astronomy as combining 'the excitement of collecting with the glamour of the church' and enthuses about 'bagfuls and bucketfuls of stars'. Alternatively, while he was working for the BBC during the Second World War, he may have become intrigued by the phoney astrological war being waged between London and Berlin; the curious case of Louis de Wohl and Karl Ernst Krafft is given lengthy coverage in *Astrology*. In any case, by 1947 MacNeice was already disowning 'realism' in favour of myth and parable: 'Man does, after all, live by symbols,' he wrote in the introduction to his radio play *The Dark Tower*.

MacNeice only occasionally used astrology in his poetry; the title of *Solstices*, MacNeice's 1961 collection, gives a clue to his orientation. When astrological references pop up, they usually prove to be unhappy conceits; railing against the blight of modern urban planning, he writes:

> Bulldoze all memories and sanctuaries: our birthright
> Means a new city, vertical, impersonal,
> Whose horoscope claimed a straight resurrection
> Should Stimulant stand in conjunction with Sleeping Pill

With the passing of Yeats, MacNeice and Hughes, English poetry seems no longer enchanted by the muse of Urania. It has, in short, never been so shorn of myth, magic and metaphysics. Hughes's interests seem unlikely to be pursued by his successor as Laureate, Andrew Motion. The main mythological poet at work is Tony Harrison, who is also president of the UK's Classics Society. A poet who has often addressed gritty social issues, Harrison can, as his 1999 film and poem *Prometheus* showed, illustrate the present through classical myth.

CONCLUSION

*

From time to time astrology turns its predictive powers inwards and attempts to forecast its own future. What is invariably foreseen is a new era in which its maligned art takes its rightful place in the cultural firmament, and its practitioners are afforded respect rather than derision.

Back in 1971, for example, John Addey, president of Britain's Astrological Association, delivered a keynote lecture to the association's annual conference which opened with the confident declaration that 'From being an outcast from the fraternity of sciences, it [astrology] seems destined to assume an almost central role in scientific thought.' Writing in 1987, the late Charles Harvey, Addey's successor as AA president, similarly foresaw a time 'in the fairly near future, when full-time astrology courses will begin to appear in universities and at specialised schools. The serious would-be astrologer will expect to have to study and practise their science and art with as much dedication and discipline as a top-flight pianist or conductor.'

There are few signs of such noble visions becoming reality. Astrology remains not just shunned but actively loathed by scientific orthodoxy, and, as the preceding chapters on music and poetry illustrate, academia continues to struggle with the wayward ideas of the very artists it purports to champion. Astrology has flourished in recent decades principally because it offers an alternative to conventional thought, an escape from scientific certainty and academic rectitude into a universe charged with symbolic meaning and individual significance. For better or worse, it remains a renegade art. That is not to say that the craft's attempts to court respectability are entirely misplaced. Addey and Harvey, both of whom led by inspired example, successfully championed astrology's overlooked scholarly credentials and historical importance, while simultaneously renewing its organisations, extending its popular appeal, and refining its techniques.

Their ambitions to win mainstream respect may yet be realised. Twenty years ago the West's interest in Chinese geomancy – feng shui – was confined to passing mentions in books on ley lines and other 'earth mysteries'. Today feng shui is big business across Europe and America, a book-publishing phenomenon, a staple ingredient of interior-design magazines and a commonplace factor in corporate strategy. Calling in the feng shui consultant is more than respectable; it's chic. After all, who wants to miss out on anything that promises painlessly (fees aside) to enhance wealth, health, prestige and success?

The insights of star-lore do not, alas, blend easily with soft furnishings and paint finishes. On the contrary, modern astrology is blighted by a design quotient that usually inclines towards hippie kitsch. The zodiac's symbols come rendered as mock Gothic centaurs and water-bearers set amid Tolkienesque landscapes of spiky mountains and purple skies, or as gift-shop frivolities: grinning Piscean fish and droll Cancerian crabs. No recent painter or sculptor has been moved to produce the visual equivalent of Holst's 'Neptune the Mystic' or Björk's 'Pluto'.

Astrology's best chances of becoming socially acceptable voodoo remain in the contradictory realms of hard-nosed money-making and 'personal growth'. The successes of star-gazing for financial profit have already been documented here, and will doubtless continue to be minutely scrutinised by the fiscal powers that be. One suspects that psychological astrology will also prosper. At a time when psychotherapy has reached something of a crisis – *We've had a hundred years of psychotherapy and the world's getting worse*, as the title of James Hillman's 1993 best-seller succinctly put it – astrology offers a different dimension to 'the talking cure', one which, as well as probing the intricacies of the individual personality, might offer useful advice on the timing of decisions . . . and crises.

The acclaimed 1996 film, *Shine*, portrays a showcase scenario for psychological astrology, the story of the gifted but tortured Australian pianist David Helfgott, who was helped back to mental health by his astrologer wife Gillian (the two met when she was in Perth to open a new branch of the Federation of Australian Astrologers). *Shine* suggests that Gillian Helfgott's stellar therapy was instrumental in helping her husband. Helfgott's plight was extreme, but suggests that astrology can help individuals move towards greater self-awareness, a step in Jung's process of 'individuation'. An appointment with an astrologer may yet come to carry no more stigma than a visit to a therapist.

Yet astrology remains stymied by there being no rational reason why it should 'work', whether as psychology or prediction. As much is true of such practices as homoeopathy or Tarot reading, but astrology alone claims direct authority from planets and stars, from the solar system and the universe beyond. For even the findings claimed by Michel Gauquelin to be true requires a completely different model of astrophysics to the one that now pertains, astrology, in short, can never regain respectability until there is a scientifically acceptable model of the universe to sanction it.

For astrology's many followers, the approval of physics ultimately doesn't matter. For all the tremendous successes and insights of physics, biology and other branches of science, they remain unable to supply the answer to the questions that hang over numerous heads: 'What am I doing here? What is my life for?' Astrology is not a religion – as we have seen, attempts to turn it into one annoy even astrologers – but large parts of its practice assume that there is a spiritual dimension to human life, a mystical connection to the universe which it can help to clarify. This remains a major part of its appeal, and one which no amount of CSICOP scepticism can easily dispel. On the contrary, sections of the scientific community show alarming signs – alarming to the scientific establishment that is – of fusing their knowledge with spiritual teachings to develop a holistic culture in which modern technology, physics and biology are in harmony with the animist world of ancient and 'primitive' societies.

Ironically, science and the irrationalist doctrines of the ancient world increasingly seem to have swapped roles. A couple of centuries ago, physical determinism was seen as a liberating force, freeing humanity from superstition. Now genetics, and its offshoot, evolutionary psychology, have become the new fatalism, describing human destiny as the intractable result of inherited genes. In this paradigm, men can't iron because evolution didn't mean them to (or so a recent book title claims), and freewill is nothing more than a necessary illusion. By contrast, astrology and its kindred doctrines promise self-direction through self-knowledge and co-operation with the wider tides of the cosmos; an escape from nihilism and irrelevance and a return to psyche, to soul.

How true, then, are the stars above? My own attitude to astrology's efficacy is caught by the closing scenes of Arthur Penn's Western *Little Big Man*. Throughout the movie a sagacious, elderly Native American chief (Chief Dan George) has declared to his adopted white son (Dustin Hoffman) that 'Today is a good day to die.' He says it before every battle. Finally, he is convinced that his time has come and he climbs the sacred mountain, accompanied by Hoffman, to take his leave of life. He lies down on a rock in meditative silence. Then the raindrops start to fall, big round drops that splash on the chief's craggy features. He sighs and climbs up. Well, he declares, 'Sometimes the magic works, sometimes it doesn't.'

Sometimes the astrology works, sometimes it doesn't.

NOTES

1: Ancient Skies

1 Thomas Moore, *The Planets within: The Psychological Astrology of Marsilio Ficino* (Lindisfarne Press 1990).

2: Myth and Imagination

1 Maya Del Mar, 'Global Forecast', *Mountain Astrologer*, June 1996.
2 Denis Elwell, 'Age of Chiron', *Mountain Astrologer*, August 1996.
3 Michael Wolfstar, 'Newscope', *Mountain Astrologer*, April 1999.
4 Alexander Ruperti interviewed in *Mountain Astrologer*, December 1997.

3: Conjuring Gravity

1 Lilly wasn't the only astrologer who foresaw tragedy; one Richard Edlin had also predicted both plague and fire in 1664.
2 Diarist John Evelyn (quoted in Patrick Curry, *Prophecy and Power*).

4: Re-inventing Astrology

1 Chief among Leo's technical innovations was his use of 'secondary progressions' as a way of forecasting the future. This involves moving a chart's planets forward by a day's motion for every year of time elapsed. Much simpler than the previous method of 'primaries', it remains a widely used tool.
2 Jung's relationship with Nazism has been the subject of extensive investigation by his biographers and goes beyond the confines of this book. Like a great many others, Jung was undoubtedly seduced by aspects of Nazism during its rise, though as war loomed he shrank back from the phenomenon he had described in his essay *Wotan* as an eruption of a suppressed racial archetype. Having spent the war in his beloved Switzerland as a volunteer doctor in the home guard, Jung afterwards offered some psychological insights into Nazism's appeal, while distancing himself from his earlier

attitudes, which had included an anti-Semitic streak that seems to have been partly responsible for his feud with Freud. A rabbi friend of Jung claims the psychologist admitted to him, 'I slipped up.' Jung's politics, unlike those of many of his posthumous followers, remained strongly right wing throughout his life.

3 Astrologers keenly note that Freud's Sun, at 16 degrees Taurus, was conjunct Jung's Moon, at 15 degrees Taurus, indicating that the two men were more alike than they cared to acknowledge. In effect, theirs was a kind of professional marriage ... and divorce.

4 Another Sting album, *The Dream of the Blue Turtles*, stems from his interest in Jungian dream analysis.

5: Measuring the Universe

1 Dennis Rawlins, *Starbaby*, quoted in *Fate*, October 1981.

2 Hans Eysenck, letter to *The Psychologist*, December 1996.

3 Geoffrey Cornelius's *Moment of Astrology*, the major source of information on the astro-scientific experiments mentioned, gives a full and provocative account of them and others.

4 Marc McDonough, lecture to the Astrological Association, August 1999.

5 Science has some sympathy with the claims of Moonlore. A celebrated ten-year study by Professor F. Brown of North-western University Chicago, published in 1959, found that oysters kept in tanks far from the sea continued to open and shut according to lunar cycles, and that caged rats were twice as active when the Moon was above the horizon than below it. Other psychiatrists and biologists have correlated greater disturbance among mental patients, excessive bleeding during surgery and a higher than average incidence of births and menstruation with the lunar cycle. Anecdotal evidence from police and paramedics about full Moon mayhem has also been confirmed by detailed statistical studies such as the review of four thousand murders by psychologists Arnold Leiber and Carolyn Sherrin. Sceptical scientists such as physicist Roger Culver have launched withering attacks on such claims with counter-studies of their own.

6 David Thurman, 'Astrology and the New Physics', *Mountain Astrologer*, February 1996.

6: Headlines and Horoscopes

1 The basis of Naylor's prediction seems to have been the Sun opposing Uranus, planet of flight.

2 Adams evolved her own techniques to deal with her numerous clients, combining their natal planets with an Ascendant set not for their hour of birth but for the time of their arrival at her practice. Her fast turnaround, and a clientele which ranged from the super-rich to regular citizens, recalls William Lilly's corner-shop on the Strand two and a half centuries earlier.

3 One popular approach is to look where the planetary 'rulers' of the solar

chart fall. A Cancer solar chart, for instance, has an Aries tenth house (career). If Mars, ruler of Aries and hence the tenth house, is badly aspected, then the poor Crab is reckoned beset with professional worries.

4 Robert Bly, for one, reckons female intuition is as much physical fact as folk fancy, pointing out that the corpus colossum, the link between the two halves of the brain, is substantially larger in women. 'It's a wonder we men can string a sentence together,' is the poet's summation.

5 Interview in the *Mountain Astrologer*, December 1995. Hard science's view of the Gaia hypothesis is summed up in predictable style by Richard Dawkins in *Unweaving the Rainbow* as 'an overrated romantic fancy'.

6 Robert Schmidt, 'Transmission of Astrological Doctrine from Hellenistic to Medieval Times', *Project Hindsight* website.

7 In *The Roots of Coincidence* Koestler mused mightily about synchronicity. However, his history of astronomy, *The Sleepwalkers*, shows a marked hostility to astrology.

7: Love Will Steer The Stars

1 In conversation with psychologist Ean Begg, quoted in his 'Jung, Astrology and the Millennium', *Astrological Journal*, November 1999.

2 Tarnas, *Prometheus the Awakener*, chapter 2.

3 The birth chart for *Hair* itself shows no trace of Aquarius, being dominated by planets in Virgo and Scorpio, with a Gemini Ascendant. *Hair's* Sun in Scorpio is arguably appropriate for a show famous for its nude finale. Unlike its celebrated lyric, the *Hair* chart has the Moon in the Fourth rather than the Seventh House, though Jupiter is, indeed, in splendid alignment with Mars. The chart's dominant feature is the potent conjunction of Moon with Venus, Pluto and Uranus. The chart for the Broadway *Hair* has Sun in Taurus, Moon in Gemini and a Sagittarius Ascendant (sources: *Oxford Companion to Popular Music* and Lorrie Davis, *Letting Down My Hair* (1972)).

4 The show is periodically revived. In 1988 the Sydney Theatre Company had their remake, *Haircut*, filmed by Australian director Baz Luhrmann. Their winning, deep soul version of 'Aquarius/Let the Sun Shine In' can be found on Luhrmann's 1999 album, *Something for Everybody*.

5 The date adds up to 18, or 6 plus 6 plus 6, becoming 666, the number of the solar logos and of the Beast in the Book of Revelation.

6 Sagittarius is also reckoned to have strong links to aviation. The Wright Brothers' famous flight on 17 December 1903 has Aquarius Ascending and Uranus conjunct a Sagittarian Sun. The launch of Sputnik on 4 October 1957 has Aquarius on the Descendant and an Aquarian Moon. The manned Moon landing of 20 July 1969, cited by US astrologer Alan Oken as a start date for the Aquarian Age, is conspicuously bereft of Aquarian signifiers (source: Nicholas Campion, *The Book of World Horoscopes*).

9: Rhythms of History

1 'Born' on 7 November 1917, the USSR had its Sun at 14 degrees Scorpio, conjunct Mercury. Baigent noted that Saturn's passage across this point in 1925 and 1954 had coincided with major power struggles. In 1984 Saturn again returned to mid-Scorpio. In 1989 the conjunction of the three heavyweight planets of Saturn, Uranus and Neptune in the sign of Capricorn was a widely heralded omen for major planetary upheaval. Baigent noted that this rare conjunction fell opposite Pluto's position in the USSR chart, and made his prediction accordingly.

2 Greene made her predictions in a series of lectures in 1980. These are collected in *The Outer Planets and their Cycles* (CRCS 1996).

3 Sirius, the brightest star in the sky and the most revered star of the Egyptians, is connected to 'great deeds and assured success', according to Australian astrologer Bernadette Brady in *Brady's Book of Stars*.

4 Grant and Kraum, *National Council for Geocosmic Research Journal*, Spring 1994.

5 French astrologers have made a speciality of such global/historical graphs. Barbault himself was inspired to plot his index after reading the post-war work of Henri Gouchon, and he has been succeeded by Claude Ganeau and Pierre Julien, both of whom constructed similar indices.

6 Among the planetary configurations that troubled Elwell was the full Moon of mid-March, falling opposite Jupiter and squaring Neptune. *The Spirit of Free Enterprise* sank on 6 March 1987. The major aspect of the chart of the tragedy is a Mars–Pluto opposition, which is discussed by Sue Tompkins in *Aspects in Astrology*.

10: Pennies From Heaven

1 The observation is from Charles Harvey (*Astrological Journal*, September 1998), who also noted this date marked several helpful aspects to Gates's birth chart.

2 Quoted in the *Mountain Astrologer*, October 1997.

3 Personal communication to the author via his website.

11: Born to be With You

1 Tem Tarriktar, 'Clinton's Tangled Web', *Mountain Astrologer*, April 1998.

2 Bernadette Brady, 'Astrology of Groups and Families, *Mountain Astrologer*, December 1995.

3 Lois Rodden, 'The Roles We Play', *Mountain Astrologer*, April 1997.

12: Putting the Stars into the Stars and Stripes

1 Quoted in *Sunday Telegraph*, 1 September 1996.

13: Stars and Swastikas

1 Eugenics and 'racial hygiene' were popularised by Darwin's cousin, Francis Galton, in the 1860s. Many eugenicists came to advocate forced sterilisation of

the mentally retarded, syphilitics and others. In the 1930s the cover of the British eugenics journal, *Superman*, featured a swastika on its cover.

2 At the time of the failed putsch, the Sun, new Moon and Mercury in Scorpio all opposed Hitler's natal Mars and Venus in Taurus, and squared his Saturn in Leo.

3 The most commonly used birth chart for Hitler is for 6.30 p.m., 20 April 1889, Braunua, Austria. This gives a 27 Libra Ascendant, Moon in Capricorn and Sun in Taurus.

4 Frau Ebertin was killed in an Allied bombing raid in 1944. Her son, Reinhold Ebertin, claimed his mother knew of her danger, but stayed put since her neighbours felt 'as long as Frau Ebertin is here, we're safe'. Reinhold Ebertin became an internationally eminent astrologer after the war, despite some some malodorous connections with the Nazi era, and pioneered astrological research. Ebertin's 1930s magazine, *Mensch im All*, had flirted with Nazi ideas and, unlike most, survived until 1941, when he was flung in prison by the Gestapo 'for knowing too much'. Ebertin smuggled in an ephemeris in his sock, and claims to have correctly predicted when he would be set free.

5 Following Germany's defeat in 1945, the destitute Sebottendorff committed suicide by casting himself into the Bosphorus.

6 Williamson's account can be found in *Far Out: A History of New Age Britain* (Channel 4 Books 1999).

7 Albrecht Haushofer wrote about his father's relationship with Hitler: 'My father broke the seal. He did not feel the Devil's breath. He let the demon loose on the world.'

8 At the time of Hess's flight (5.45 p.m., 10 May 1941, Augsburg Munich), accident-prone Mars in Aquarius was square to six planets in Taurus. The full Moon in secretive Scorpio fell opposite the Taurus stellium. In 1998 British astrologer Tom Richards used the day's planetary set-up to argue the case for one of the conspiracy theories that cling to Hess: that the real Hess was shot down over the Channel by the Luftwaffe, and the man held by the Allies was a decoy.

9 Like Hitler and Hess, Himmler suffered from acute stomach pains. Like Hess, Hitler took homoeopathic remedies, which Hugh Trevor-Roper mistakenly reports as 'poisons' in *The Last Days of Hitler*.

10 Astrologers who should know better persist in peddling the myth of Hitler as astrologer: 'It's pretty common knowledge that Hitler had a stable full of astrologers to advise him, and when they began to advise him with warnings instead of promises of victory he began to shoot them.' *Nein!* (Liz Greene 1983).

15: Music of the Spheres

1 In a piece of astro-serendipity, Scriabin (born in Moscow on 6 January 1872) conceived his symphony as the Promethean planet Uranus crossed his natal

Saturn in 1907, and wrote it as Uranus crossed his natal Sun the following year. The work was first performed as Uranus exactly opposed his natal Uranus in 1912. The parallel with the creation of *The Planets* and Holst's horoscope is striking.

2 Claude Debussy, another composer intent on creating new musical forms, has also been described as a student of hermeticism, astrology and numerology. Debussy apparently made use of the 'Golden Section' of Pythagorean mathematics to punctuate the structure of his works. In their contentious best-seller, *The Holy Blood and the Holy Grail*, Michael Baigent and Richard Leigh allege Debussy was a Rosicrucian who became Grand Master of the Rosicrucian Prieuré de Sion. It is also alleged that Debussy's friend, the composer Erik Satie, was another Rosicrucian.

3 Holst later turned to the Tarot for inspiration for his opera *The Perfect Fool*, whose dramatis personae include the Tarot trumps The Fool and The Wizard (Magician).

4 Gustav Holst, born 21 September 1874 in Cheltenham. His birth chart is dominated by a Grand Trine between Sun in Virgo, Moon in Taurus and Pluto in Capricorn.

5 Sonny Blount, born 24 May 1914 in Birmingham, Alabama. Why he chose Saturn as his home is uncertain. His horoscope is dominated by five planets in Gemini, including a Sun–Mercury conjunction; very fitting for a man with two identities, obsessed with Mercurial wordplay and fanciful etymology.

6 John Coltrane, born 5 p.m. EST, 23 September 1926 in Raleigh, North Carolina. Coltrane's birth chart has a Sun–Mercury conjunction in Libra, though the most prominent planet in his horoscope is Uranus (rising, opposite Sun–Mercury). Coltrane's sacking by Davis and his subsequent reform coincided with his Saturn return.

7 Captain Beefheart similarly told British customs, in 1968, that he was 'from Venus'.

8 *The Urantia Book* claims to be a 'channelled' text, dictated by spiritual beings to an unnamed medium, and delivered to the world by a Chicago doctor, William Sandler. The book offers a complete history of Planet Earth ('Urantia') and the universe, or at least our portion of it, which is overseen by the archangel Michael with the help of a vast hierarchy of spiritual guides and overlords (Urantia's supernatural world sounds suspiciously like a cosmic civil service). The last third of the book is concerned with the life and teachings of Christ, humanity's exemplar and avatar. The book's Christian message, and the connections of Dr Sandler to the Kellogg family (of Wellville and Cornflakes fame), who are well-known Seventh Day Adventists, has led to suspicions that *The Urantia Book* is an Adventist, rather than cosmic, creation.

9 *British Entertainers*, by Frank Clifford, offers copious data and thumbnail sketches for most prominent British pop figures.

16: Pinned to Midheaven

1 For a detailed look at Hughes's and Plath's charts, see John Etherington, 'Written in Blood', *Apollon*, 2, April 1999. On the evidence of 'St Botolph's', Etherington gives Hughes a rectified birth time of 1.36 a.m. (BST), and an Ascendant of 6 degrees Cancer. He draws attention to the strength of his planetary placements (four planets in own signs, two in exaltation), and singles out Pluto as a signature of Hughes's profundity and obsession with primal forces. Olwyn Hughes, Ted's sister, has declared this birth time inaccurate.

2 Sylvia Plath born 14.10 EST, 27 October 1932. This gives an Ascendant of 29 degrees 22 minutes Aquarius. Plath's split with Hughes in 1962 came with her Saturn return. The pair were married on 16 June 1956. One wonders whether Hughes had not selected the day especially, so fittingly does that day's Moon in Libra sit on his Venus and her Moon.

3 Taken from 'Poetry and Magic' by Ann Skea, privately published paper. Further details can be found on her web site.

4 *Birthday Letters*, for example, was published in the USA on 26 February, the new Moon after its British publication. Its initial publication also marked the first day of Neptune's shift into Aquarius. The publication of Plath's unexpurgated *Journals* on 3 April 2000 also has some startling correlations with her birth chart, including Mercury, Venus and Moon in her first house, and Pluto exactly on her Midheaven.

5 Quoted in the programme for *The Astrology of William Shakespeare and His Times*, staged for the Faculty of Astrological Studies' fiftieth anniversary, 7 June 1998.

6 The opening was 7.26 p.m. BST, 12 June 1997 in Southwark. The Globe's horoscope gives it a Gemini Sun, Virgo Moon and Sagittarius Ascendant. Su Rose found many links between the charts of Wanamaker, the Globe, Rylance and that of the Faculty of Astrological Studies, with which she is associated.

7 See particularly Richard Ellman's *Yeats: The Man and the Masks* (1948), Virginia Moor's *The Unicorn* (1954), and Brenda Maddox's *George's Ghosts* (1999).

8 The birth time given for Yeats correlates with his own preferred 0 degree 4 minutes Aquarius Ascendant. For a full exposition of Yeats's birth chart see the researches of Elizabeth Heine, to whose articles the present author is indebted, especially 'Yeats and Astrology', *Culture and Cosmos*, 1, 2, Autumn 1997. Yeats's Grand Trine in air, made by Moon in Aquarius, a Sun–Uranus conjunction in Gemini and Saturn in Libra suggest an intellectual temperament. Yeats himself thought his Uranus–Sun conjunction accounted for his interest in astrology and esoterica. He may not have been so pleased with his Sun–Jupiter opposition (inflated ideas of his own importance, identification with God).

9 Quoted in *The Unicorn* by Virginia Moore. See also Charles Carter's blunt

summary in *Astrological Aspects* (1930): 'It does not favour happiness.' The difficulties of Venus–Mars aspects have been softened by psychological astrology. Compare Carter's outline with Sue Tompkins's in *Aspects in Astrology*. Curiously, Tompkins mentions that the aspect 'has a reputation for coarseness'. Although Yeats was sexually anxious, he had a lifelong love of dirty jokes.

10 Georgie Hyde-Lees, born 16 October 1892, had Sun in Libra and Moon in Virgo. Her Sun fell conjunct Yeats's Saturn, and her Mars conjunct his Moon. She and Yeats were married on 20 October 1917 in London. Georgie was the best friend of Dorothy Shakespear, daughter of Olivia Shakespear, one of Yeats's lovers. Dorothy was married to Ezra Pound, for whom Iseult Gonne later worked. Such was the incestuous nature of Yeats's literary–occult–personal relationships.

GLOSSARY

✳

Angles The two axes of a horoscope produce the four Angles. The Ascendant and its opposite point, the Descendant, are formed by the horizon. The Midheaven (MC) and its opposite point (IC) mark the highest and lowest points of the zodiac above the horizon. The Asc/Desc axis marks the cusps of the first and seventh houses. The MC/IC axis marks the cusps of the tenth and fourth houses. These are always significant points in a horoscope. See pages 61–63 for further explanation.

Ascendant The degree of the zodiac rising over the eastern horizon. A degree rises every four minutes, 360 degrees adding to 24 hours. An important factor in all charts, whether for a birth or some other event. See page 62

Aspects The angular distance between planets, measured in degrees, and considered favourable or difficult according to which angle they form. The main aspects are conjunction, opposition, trine, sextile and square.

Conjunction Two or more planets occupy the same point in the sky. A major aspect in a chart.

Cusp The starting point of a 'house' in a horoscope. For example, 'the fifth house cusp is 15 degrees Gemini.' Or 'Mars is on the cusp of the seventh house.' The Ascendant is the cusp of the first house. In popular parlance the term has come to mean something quite different: the division between one Sun sign and the next, as in 'I'm on the cusp between Scorpio and Sagittarius.' See page 34 for an explanation of this widespread fallacy.

Decan The division of a sign's 30-degree share of the zodiacal circle into three sub-sections of 10 degrees. Co-opted from Egytian astronomy.

Degrees The zodiacal circle is divided into 360 degrees, with 30 degrees allotted to each sign. Individual degree points within the circle – expressed as, for example, 8 degrees Gemini, or 12 degrees Capricorn – have sometimes been given specific meaning. Charubel's *Degrees of the Zodiac Symbolised* (1907) or Marc Edmund Jones's *Sabian Symbols* (1953) both give an image and explanation for each degree. For example, 20 degrees of Pisces is, for Charubel, 'An Angel Blowing A Trumpet', showing a message or a preacher.

Elements The four categories of natural phenomena according to ancient thought: Earth, Water, Fire and Air. The zodiac is divided up in this way. Sometimes known as the Triplicities.

Ephemeris (plural Ephemerides) A book or pamphlet listing daily tables of planetary positions, sidereal (star) time and other information necessary to draw up horoscopes. Nowadays inbuilt into computer software.

Glyphs Shorthand symbols for planets and signs.

Grand Trine A triangular aspect between three planets (or more) in 120-degree (trine) aspect, forming a triangle in a chart. Considered a potent and favourable aspect. A Grand Cross has four (or more) planets at 90-degree (square) aspect, forming a square in a chart, and is thought unfavourable or difficult.

Harmonics Mathematical system of astrology developed by twentieth-century astrologer John Addey.

Hermeticism Teachings derived from texts attributed to Hermes Trismestigus, 'Thrice Greatest Hermes', notably the doctrine of Correspondences, which links phenomena according to symbolism. The basis of much Western magical thought.

Horary Astrology Question-based astrology. A chart is cast for the time and place that an astrologer is asked a question. The chart's symbolism then supplies the answer, using rules somewhat different to natal astrology. Popular with traditionalists, though frowned upon by some as a fairground turn. Handy for retrieving lost property and pets, and for forecasting football scores.

Horoscope A map of the heavens as seen from a particular place at a particular time. Most usually taken to mean a birth chart, and the planetary patterns in play upon it at the time of enquiry. Derived from the Greek, *horos skopos*, hour pointer.

Houses The division of the horoscope into twelve segments, each corresponding to an area of human life. Their calculation and meaning are much contested, which has led some moderns to dispense with them altogether. Particularly important in horary astrology.

Lunar Nodes The points where the Moon's orbit intersects with the orbit of the Earth around the Sun, and therefore the points where solar and lunar eclipses fall. The North and South Lunar Nodes are always opposite each other, always retrograde, and are always marked on a horoscope. The importance granted them varies wildly. See page 40

Mundane Astrology The application of astrology to world events, nations and politics, rather than individuals. Forecasting weather, earthquakes and other natural phenomena are also part of mundane astrology.

Opposition 180-degree aspect between planets, so that they face each other across the zodiacal wheel.

Precession of the Equinoxes Slippage of the spring equinox point backwards through the zodiac, due to a spinning-top style wobble in the Earth's axis. The phenomenon has given rose to the idea of the 'Ages', as in the Age of Aquarius. Explained more fully in Chapter Seven.

Progressions Symbolically advancing the planets in a horoscope for predictive purposes. The most common method is 'a day for a year', meaning that if someone was 36 years old the planets would be placed where they fell 36 days after birth. The results are read off in the same way as Transits (see below). There are several other methods of progression, or 'Direction' – Primary, Solar Arc, Tertiary – all of which are employed to much the same predictive ends.

Rectification Deducing the time of birth – and therefore the Ascendant and Angles of a horoscope – from life events. Practised when no accurate birth time is available.

Retrograde The apparently backward motion of planets, an illusion caused by the relative speed of planetary orbits.

Square 90-degree aspect between planets, considered troublesome.

Synastry The comparison of two or more horoscopes, most often with a view to romantic compatibility, though the technique can also be applied to, say, a national horoscope and that of its monarch, prime minister or president.

Transits As the planets move around the zodiac they make significant aspects to the planets in an existing birth (or other) chart. These aspects are called transits. Jupiter passing over (conjuncting) a natal Sun, for example, is a favourable transit suggesting money and opportunity. By contrast, Saturn moving to 90 degrees of (i.e. squaring) a natal Venus suggests romantic difficulties. A major technique in astrological forecasting.

T-Square Triangular aspect between three or more planets in which one of the corners is a 90-degree angle. Considered troublesome.

Vedic Astrology Another term for Indian astrology, which is related to, but distinct from, its Western counterpart. By contrast, Chinese, Mayan and Tibetan astrology all employ an entirely different template to the Western and Vedic styles.

BIBLIOGRAPHY

✳

General Introductions & the Zodiac

Nicholas Campion, *The Practical Astrologer* (Cinnabar 1993)

Geoffrey Cornelius, Maggie Hyde & Chris Webster, *Introducing Astrology* (Icon 1995)

Linda Goodman, *Sun Signs* (Pan 1972)

Robert Hand, *Horoscope Symbols* (Whitford 1981)

Marc Edmund Jones, *How To Learn Astrology* (Doubleday 1971)

Felix Lyle & Bryan Aspland, *The Instant Astrologer* (book & PC program) (Piatkus 1998)

Alan Oken, *Pocket Guide To Astrology* (Crossing Press 1996)

Derek & Julia Parker, *Parkers' Astrology* (Dorling Kindersley 1991)

Debbi Kempton Smith, *Secrets From A Stargazer's Notebook* (Bantam 1982)

Paul Wright, *The Literary Zodiac* (Anodyne 1987)

Paul Wright, *Astrology In Action* (CRCS 1989)

Planets, Charts and Prediction

Stephen Arroyo, *Chart Interpretation Handbook* (CRCS 1989)

Eleanor Bach, *Ephemerides of the Asteroids* (Celestial Communications NY 1973)

Demetra George, *Asteroid Goddesses* (ACS Publications 1986)

Liz Greene, *The Astrological Neptune and the Quest for Redemption* (Samuel Weiser 1996)

Ariel Guttman & Kenneth Johnson, *Mythic Astrology* (Llewellyn 1996)

Ronald Harvey, *The Spindle of Meaning* (The Urania Trust 1996)

Alan Leo, *The Art of Synthesis* (Fowler 1968)

Melanie Reinhart, *Chiron & the Healing Journey* (Penguin Arkana 1989)

Marc Robertson, *Crisis Ages in Adult Life* (AFA 1973)

Martin Seymour-Smith, *The New Astrologer* (Sidgwick & Jackson 1981)

Richard Tarnas, *Prometheus the Awakener* (Spring Publications 1995)

The No Nonsense Guides to Astrology (Elements, Aspects, Transits etc.) (Wessex Astrologer 1998)

Astrological History

Geoffrey Cornelius, *The Moment of Astrology, Origins in Divination* (Arkana 1994)

Patrick Curry, *Prophecy and Power, Astrology in Early Modern England* (Polity Press 1989)

Patrick Curry, *A Confusion of Prophets, Victorian and Edwardian Astrology* (Collins & Brown 1992)

Robert Hand, *Chronology of Astrology* (pamphlet) (Arhat 1996)

Christopher Hill, *The World Turned Upside Down* (Peguin 1991)

Christopher Hill, *Milton & the English Revolution* (Faber & Faber 1977)

James Herschel Holden, *A History of Horoscopic Astrology* (American Federation of Astrologers 1995)

Louis MacNeice, *Astrology* (Aldus 1964)

Thomas Moore, *The Planets Within, The Astrological Psychology of Marsilio Ficino* (Lindisfarne Press 1990)

Derek Parker, *Familiar To All, William Lilley and Seventeenth-century Astrology* (Jonathan Cape/Ascella 1975)

Richard Tarnas, *The Passion of the Western Mind* (Pimlico 1991)

Theodore Zeldin, *An Intimate History of Humanity* (Minerva 1995)

Science, Astronomy & Physics

David Bohm, *Wholeness & The Implicate Order* (Routledge 1995)

Nicholas Campion, *The Great Year* (Penguin Arkana 1994)

Richard Dawkins, *Unweaving the Rainbow* (Allen Lane 1998)

David Ewing Duncan, *The Calendar* (Fourth Estate 1998)

Richard Grossinger, *The Night Sky* (Jeremy Tarcher 1988)

Nick Kollerstrom, *Astronomical Essays for Astrologers* (Ascella 1998)

F. David Pleat, *Infinite Potential, The Life and Times of David Bohm* (Addison Wesley 1997)

Percy Seymour, *Astrology: The Evidence of Science* (Lennard 1988)

Michael Talbot, *The Holographic Universe* (Harper-Collins 1996)

Michael White, *Isaac Newton, The Last Sorcerer* (Fourth Estate 1997)

Statistics

John Addey, *A New Study of Astrology* (Urania Trust 1996)

Suitbert Ertel & Kenneth Irving, *The Tenacious Mars Effect* (Urania Trust 1996)

Michel Gauquelin, *Cosmic Influences on Human Behaviour* (Aurora Press 1986)

The Magi Society, *Astrology Really Works!* (Astro Room 1995)

Gunther Sachs, *The Astrology File* (Orion 1998)

Carl Jung & Astrology

Maggie Hyde, *Jung and Astrology* (Aquarian 1992)

Maggie Hyde & Michael McGuinness, *Introducing Jung* (Icon 1996)

C.G. Jung, *Synchronicity* (Ark 1955)

C.G. Jung, *Jung on Synchronicity and the Paranormal* (ed. Roderick Main) (Routledge 1997)

Frank McLynn, *Carl Gustav Jung* (Bantam Press 1996)

Psychological Astrology

Charles Carter, *The Astrological Aspects* (Fowler 1972)

Liz Greene, *Saturn: A New Look at an Old Devil* (Samuel Weiser 1976)

Liz Greene, *Relating* (Coventure 1983)

Liz Greene, *The Outer Planets & Their Cycles* (CRCS 1983)

James Hillman, *A Blue Fire, The Essential James Hillman* (Routledge 1989)

Howard Sasportas, *The Gods of Change* (Arkana 1989)

Erin Sullivan, *Saturn In Transit* (Arkana 1991)

Sue Tompkins, *Aspects in Astrology* (Element 1989)

Prediction

Olivier Barclay, *Horary Astrology Rediscovered* (Whitford Press 1990)

Bernadette Brady, *Predictive Astrology* (Samuel Weiser 1999)

James Braha, *How To Predict Your Future, Secrets of Eastern & Western Astrology* (Hermetician 1995)

Robert Hand, *Planets in Transit* (Whitford Press 1976)

Lois M. Rodden, *Modern Transits* (AFA 1978)

Synastry & Other Facets of Astrology

Bernadette Brady, *Brady's Book of Fixed Stars* (Samuel Weiser 1998)

Robert Hand, *Planets in Composite* (Whitford 1975)

Ed. A.T. Mann, *The Future of Astrology* (Unwin Hyman 1987)

Marcia Starck, *Healing With Astrology* (Crossing Press 1997)

Komilla Sutton, *Vedic Astrology* (Wessex Astrologer 1999)

The Age of Aquarius

Nicholas Campion, 'The Age of Aquarius, A Modern Myth,' in *The Astrology of the Macrocosm*, ed. Joan McEvers (Llewellyn 1990)

Robert Hand, 'The Age and Constellation of Pisces' in *Essays on Astrology* (Whitford Press 1982)

Alice O. Howell, *Jungian Synchronicity in Astrological Signs and Ages* (Quest 1990)

C.G. Jung, *Aion* (Routledge 1991)

C.G. Jung, *Flying Saucers* (Routledge & Kegan Paul 1997)

Glastonbury & other Earth Zodiacs

Mary Caine, *The Glastonbury Zodiac* (Caine 1978)

Mary Caine, *The Kingston Zodiac* (Caine 1978)

Graham Hancock, *Heaven's Mirror* (Michael Joseph 1998)

Katherine Maltwood, *A Guide to Glastonbury's Temple of the Stars* (James Clarke 1929 rep 1982)

Katherine Maltwood, *The Enchantments of Britain* (James Clarke 1982)

John Michell, *A Little History of Astro-Archaeology* (Thames & Hudson 1977)

John Michell, *The New View Over Atlantis* (Thames & Hudson 1983)

John Michell, *New Light on the Ancient Mysteries of Glastonbury* (Gothic Image 1990)

John Michell, *Twelve Tribe Nations and the Science of Enchanting the Landscape* (Thames & Hudson 1991)

Ed. Anthony Roberts, *Glastonbury, Ancient Avalon, New Jerusalem* (Rider 1978)

Mundane & Political Astrology

M. Baigent, N. Campion & C. Harvey, *Mundane Astrology* (Thorsons 1995)

Nicholas Campion, *The Book of World Horoscopes* (Cinnabar 1992)

Charles Carter, *An Introduction to Political Astrology* (Fowler 1951)

Richard Deacon, *The Israeli Secret Service* (1977)

Ronald W. Howland, *A Chronology of American Charts* (Poz Publications 1998)

David Ovason, *The Secret Zodiacs of Washington DC* (Century 1999)

Noel Tyl, *Predictions For A New Millennium* (Llewellyn 1996)

Financial Astrology
Graham Bates & Jane Chrzanowska Bowles, *Money & The Markets* (Aquarian 1994)
Christeen Skinner, *Money Signs* (Headway 1998)
Henry Weingarten, *Investing by the Stars* (McGraw-Hill 1996)

Ronald & Nancy Reagan
Kitty Kelley, *Nancy Reagan* (Bantam 1991)
Joan Quigley, *What Does Joan Say?* (Birch Lane 1990)
Donald Regan, *For The Record* (1987)

Astrology & the Third Reich
Michael Baigent & Richard Leigh, *Secret Germany* (Jonathan Cape 1994)
Nicholas Goodrick-Clarke, *The Occult Roots of Nazism* (I.B. Tauris 1992)
Ellic Howe, *Urania's Children* (Reprinted as *Astrology in the Third Reich*) (William Kimber 1967)
Nigel Pennick, *Hitler's Secret Sciences* (Neville Spearman 1981)
Trevor Ravenscroft, *The Spear of Destiny* (Neville Spearman 1973)
Ron Rosenbaum, *Explaining Hitler* (Papermac 1999)
Hugh Trevor-Roper, *The Last Days of Hitler* (Macmillan 1947)
James Webb, *The Occult Establishment* (Richard Drew 1981)
Wilhelm Wulff, *Zodiac and Swastika* (Arthur Barker 1968)

Moon Queen, The Reign of Diana Spencer
Lady Colin Campbell, *Diana in Private* (St Martin's Press 1998)
Nicholas Campion, *Born To Reign* (Chapman's 1991)
Martin Freeman, *Forecasting By Astrology* (Aquarian 1982)
Kitty Kelley, *The Royals* (Warner Books 1997)
Andrew Morton, *Diana: Her True Story* (Michael O'Mara 1998)
Penny Thornton, *Synastry* (Aquarian 1982)
Penny Thornton, *Romancing the Stars* (Aquarian 1988)
Penny Thornton, *Divine Encounters* (Aquarian 1991)
Penny Thornton, *With Love From Diana* (Pocket Books 1995)

The Music of the Spheres
Michael Baigent & Richard Leigh, *The Holy Blood & the Holy Grail* (HDW 1982)
Frank Clifford, *British Entertainers: The Astrological Profiles* (Flare 1997)
Mya Tannenbaum, *Conversations with Stockhausen* (OUP 1987)

Ted Hughes & Other English Poets

John Addey, 'Shakespeare's Attitude to Astrology', from *Selected Writings* (American Federation of Astrologers 1992)

Richard Ellman, *Yeats, The Man and The Masks* (Macmillan 1949)

Ekbert Faas, *Ted Hughes: The Unaccommodated Universe* (Black Sparrow 1980)

R.F. Foster, *W.B. Yeats, A Life, Vol. I* (OUP 1997)

Elizabeth Heine, 'W.B. Yeats: Poet and Astrologer', in *Culture and Cosmos*, Vol. 1, No. 2, Winter 1997

Ted Hughes, *Birthday Letters* (Faber & Faber 1998)

Louis MacNeice, *The Strings Are False* (Faber & Faber 1996)

Maurice McCann, 'Shakespeare's Time To Be' in *Astrology Looks at History*, (ed. Noel Tyl) (Llewellyn 1995)

Brenda Maddox, *George's Ghosts* (Picador 1999)

Virginia Moore, *The Unicorn* (Macmillan 1954)

Sylvia Plath, *Letters Home* (Faber & Faber 1977)

Sylvia Plath, *The Journals of Sylvia Plath* 1950–62 (Faber & Faber 2000)

Anne Skea, *Poetry and Magic* (unpublished private paper, 2000)

Jon Stallworthy, *Louis MacNeice* (Faber & Faber 1996)

W.B. Yeats, *A Vision* (Papermac 1981)

Astrology's Future

A.T. Mann (ed.), *The Future of Astrology* (Unwin Hyman 1987)

Magazines

Appollon: Published three times a year by Liz Greene's Centre For Psychological Astrology. Scholarly, concentrating on birth chart analysis. BCM, Box 1815, London WC1N 3XX.

The Astrologer's Apprentice: Rigorous traditional methods, including horary, often applied to modern subjects, especially rock and football, with droll humour. Also re-examines classical and seventeenth-century ideas.

85 Steeds Road, London N10 1JB.

The Astrological Journal: Bi-monthly publication of the Astrological Association. Erudite and technical, but broad-based, with features on historical and current subjects. Includes beginner's section and lively letters page. Automatic subscription with AA membership.

AA, Lee Valley Technopark, London N17 9LN

Astrology Quarterly: Long-established journal of the Astrological Lodge of

London. Wide-ranging discussion of methods and birth charts with minimum of fuss.

50 Gloucester Place, London W1H 4EA.

Astrolore: Lively quarterly, includes Sun sign forecasts, pop culture, mythology, interviews and cartoons.

PO Box 3339, Poole BH12 4ZE.

The Mountain Astrologer: Prize-winning bi-monthly from California. In-depth articles on current planetary formations and conjunctions. Biographical profiles, articles on signs, planets and cycles, large forecast section. Lots of asteroids and modern methods.

Available in the UK via The Wessex Astrologer, PO Box 2751, Bournemouth BH6 3ZJ.

Traditional Astrology: Just what it says. Birth charts, horary methods and expositions of signs and planets in traditional terms. Also features herbalism, fixed stars and so on.

3 Avondale Bungalows, Sherwood Hall Road, Mansfield, Notts NG18 2NJ.

Societies and Organisations in the UK

Astrological Association, AA, Lee Valley Technopark, London N17 9LN
http://www.astrologer.com/aanet/index.html

Astrological Lodge of London, 50 Gloucester Place, London W1H 4EA.

Faculty of Astrological Studies, BM 7470, London WC1N 3XX
http://www.astrology.org.uk

INDEX

✳